REPRESENTING AMERICA

EXPERIENCES OF U.S. DIPLOMATS AT THE UN

REPRESENTING AMERICA

EXPERIENCES OF
U.S. DIPLOMATS
AT THE UN

Linda M. Fasulo

*With a foreword
by
Elliot L. Richardson*

Facts On File Publications
New York, New York ● Oxford, England

To my husband,
Mitchell Rubin,
for his encouragement,
support, and counsel

REPRESENTING AMERICA: Experiences of
U.S. Diplomats at the U.N.

Copyright © 1984 by Linda M. Fasulo
First published in paperback 1985
In cooperation with
Praeger Publishers,
New York, New York

Library of Congress Cataloging in Publication Data

Fasulo, Linda M.
  Representing America.
  Bibliography: p.
  Includes index.
  1. United Nations—United States. 2. Diplomats—United
States. I. Title
JX1977.2.U5F37 1984   341.23'73   84-3477
ISBN 0-8160-1304-7

British Library Cataloguing in Publication Data

Fasulo, Linda M.
  Representing America : the experiences of U.S.
  diplomats at the U.N.
  1. United Nations—United States 2. United
  States—Foreign relations—1945-
  I. Title
  341.23'73'0922   JX1977.2.U5
  ISBN 0-816013-04-7

Cover design: Eric Elias

Printed in the United States of America

Foreword
Elliot L. Richardson

As a forum for protecting and promoting U.S. interests in world affairs, the United Nations has been an important instrument in the conduct of American foreign policy for nearly forty years. Since the signing of the UN Charter in 1945, the United States has played a pivotal role in creating, refining, and supporting the United Nations and its system of specialized agencies and voluntary programs. This commitment to the notion of global interdependence and belief in the efficacy of collective security has constituted a major shift in U.S. foreign policy, for until 1945 most Americans believed that the United States must avoid "entangling" international involvements. The experience of the United States within the United Nations has been marked by this relatively recent recognition of the responsibilities that accompany global involvement, as well as accommodation to the burdens of exercising world leadership. Moreover, the United States has had to learn to function within a United Nations, that, due to the emergence and admittance of new African and Asian nations, has become markedly different in tone from the organization Americans had helped to create in 1945.

One of the most important realities that Americans had to face in coming to terms with the new U.S. role in foreign affairs was that the United Nations was an assemblage of individuals, as well as a community of government representatives. Delegates to the United Nations found that they would have to carry out their national policy decisions in a public, highly charged, often bellicose atmosphere among other delegates who would at times act out of pride, fear, anger, or insecurity. Because diplomacy is by nature unpredictable, the successful execution of foreign policy decisions is dependent upon the abilities of the delegates and representatives to respond to rapidly shifting world events, unexpected circumstances, and conflicting personalities.

This lively and engaging book, based on interviews with American representatives to the United Nations, examines the challenges these men and women have met in attempting to carry out U.S. policy decisions and uphold their mandate of protecting and advancing

American interests within this body of competing objectives, values, and personalities. Moreover, it provides an historical perspective on the differing attitudes of the last eight presidential administrations toward the U.S. role at the United Nations.

By observing the American role at the United Nations from the point of view of the representatives who undertook the day-to-day work, this valuable series of first-person accounts provides a unique and personal vantage point from which to examine and reassess the sources of U.S. conduct there.

Such an examination is particularly important at a time when many Americans seem to be growing increasingly frustrated and disillusioned with the effectiveness of the United Nations and the U.S. role in it. Critics complain about waste in the UN budget, and the endless debate in the General Assembly, not to mention the votes that go against the United States. They choose to forget that the UN has been largely responsible for eradicating smallpox in the world, that the long-winded debates are often surrogates for war, and that for most of the history of the UN it was the Soviets, not the Americans, who complained about the outcome of crucial votes, or the size of the UN budget. Until very recently, the United States has done well at the world body, better perhaps than any other nation. If the reader remembers nothing else from this book, except the discussions by American diplomats of how the U.S. managed so well at the UN in previous decades, it will have provided an important lesson.

Another lesson to be learned from the interviews is that the UN can work surprisingly well when it has full cooperation from member nations. In the Middle East, UN peacekeeping forces have, by consent of the nations involved, been able to perform their duties with great effectiveness at the Golan Heights. At the Sinai and in Lebanon they have worked when the parties involved have supported them, and failed when they did not. It is hard to imagine any other oucome. An even greater success story, but one that rarely makes the front page, is the UN's World Health Organization and its food and nutrition programs, which have saved and improved millions upon millions of lives, and which may help save more lives to come in the drought-stricken areas of Africa. Perhaps it is these successful programs that provide the truest indicator of what the UN could be if the nations of the world behaved with greater harmony and with less cynicism. American critics of the UN would better serve the nation by urging not only a stronger U.S. role, but a stronger UN in general, as a greater benefit both to American foreign policy and to world peace and prosperity. How to achieve these desirable goals will require serious thought and examination. If the United States is to continue to exercise effective leadership in a world whose problems are less and less manageable by any one country, Americans must come to terms with the challenges and responsibilities inherent in a multilateral response to global issues.

Considering the instrumental role of the United States in bringing the United Nations into existence and nurturing it through its early years, it is both gratifying and illuminating to have a book such as this. In its readable and often surprisingly candid interviews, *Representing America* provides a remarkable glimpse into the world body and American diplomacy, while at the same time revealing the complexity of past history and suggesting the challenges that lie ahead. It would be hard to imagine a more suitable gift to the reading public during this fortieth-anniversary year of the United Nations.

Preface

The idea for this book arose out of my firsthand experience with the world of the United Nations. For the past seven years, I have followed UN affairs, first as a graduate student participating in study and internship programs held at UN headquarters in New York and Geneva, later as an officer and administrator of a newly organized international organization and most recently as a board member of the New York chapter of the UN Association of the United States.
and most recently as a board member of the New York chapter of the UN Association of the United States.

My experience at the United Nations and my exposure to the political realities there triggered a strong interest in the important, and constantly changing, U.S. role at the world organization. When I looked for information about U.S.–UN relations, however, I found relatively little that was written from the point of view of the diplomats and representatives who were most intimately involved. It seemed to me that these people had a great deal to say about their experiences and impressions that would both contribute to an understanding of American foreign policy and diplomatic history and provide the broader public with a unique look into the world of American diplomacy.

For this book I interviewed more than 30 men and women who served (or are serving) on U.S. delegations to the United Nations. They represent the ambassadorial delegation, State Department assistant secretaries for international-organization affairs, and congressional and public delegates to the General Assembly.

Organized chronologically, beginning with the origins of the United Nations during World War II and coming up to the present time, the interviews present individual perspectives on a number of broad issues that have dominated both the United Nations and American foreign policy for the past several decades. How is international cooperation best achieved—through traditional diplomacy or through the newer channels of multilateral diplomacy as embodied in the United Nations and its agencies? What is the proper role of the United Nations in American foreign policy—should it be solely a "tool" to further national interests, or should it also have an altruistic component that sets world interests above national ones? And finally, however these questions are answered, how should the American delegations to the UN function—under close control from Washington or with greater latitude?

My own views on these issues are presented in the Afterword, but the real point of this book lies in the interviews, which I have tried to set in historical perspective through the use of short introductory overviews for each part of the book. A brief biography precedes each interview. I have edited each interview for the sake of clarity, brevity, and coherence, as well as readability, but I believe that each person's unique character comes through. I have not tried to smooth or soften strong opinions or the occasional harsh comments directed at nations or individuals, but I have given each person the chance to read and slightly revise his or her interview. I hope in this way to avoid some of the problems inherent in the interview format—short and selective memories, and ambiguous statements open to misinterpretation.

Acknowledgments

This book would not have been possible without the advice, encouragement, and great amounts of time I have received from many people. To all the persons whom I interviewed, I would like to express my thanks for their cooperation and good humor during the long process of transforming oral conversation into the written word. In the early stages of the project, I received invaluable advice and support from William E. Schaufele, whose reflections deserve the book I hope he will write someday. Additional help and advice came from Marietta Tree, William vanden Heuvel, Franklin H. Williams, and Ernest Gross, all of whose remarks deserve more space than could be provided in a single book. Elliot Richardson, the chairperson of the UN Association (UNA–USA) of the United States, took a special interest in the project.

Special thanks are due Dorothy Thomas for the initial encouragement she gave me in pursuing this project, to Jim Thomashower for helping shape the early manuscripts, and to Don Young for his editorial work. Among the many people who either read portions of the manuscripts and made useful suggestions, or helped me to obtain introductions, are Marie-France Dougherty, Page and Thomas Wilson, Frank Taylor, Tom Wallace, Barbara Abrash, and Katy Brooks.

Researching the history of American involvement in the United Nations was facilitated by the following publications and policy studies which were especially helpful: UNA–USA, the press office of the U.S. Mission to the United Nations, the UN library, the nongovernmental organizations accredited to the United Nations, and the nongovernmental office (NGO) by Sally Swing Shelley.

From William Zeisel, director of *Editors & Scholars*, I received help in preparing the manuscript for submission; the typing and (seemingly endless) retyping were done by Barbara Evans, Marion Eines, Becky Miller, and my mother Mary Fasulo.

I received moral support from many friends and colleagues and from the members of The Institute for Research in History. I would also like to thank my editor at Facts On File, Kate Kelly, for her enthusiasm in preparing this edition.

Contents

PART IV: THE CARTER YEARS, 1977–80

List of
Photographs

Introduction

THE FOUNDING AND ORGANIZATION
OF THE UNITED NATIONS

The origins of the United Nations lie in the 1930s, when the rise of aggressive totalitarian states in Europe and Asia destroyed the precarious world peace that had been nurtured by the League of Nations. For over 20 years the League, headquartered in Geneva, had tried to function as a center of international cooperation; a noble experiment in international relations, the League tried to complement traditional bilateral diplomacy with multilateral diplomacy.

The League had itself come into existence as a result of war. The death and suffering of World War I, usually regarded as the first "total war," shook the Western world deeply and gave an impetus to efforts at creating some instrument that might forestall another such devastating conflict. While Europe was recovering from the social, economic, and political chaos of the years immediately following the war, the first steps were taken to establish the League of Nations.

The new organization was not a world government—as many had advocated—but an association of sovereign nations. Its powers were sharply limited by the unwillingness of many nations, among them Germany, Italy, and Japan, to entrust their national interest to the uncertain care of an international body. Another handicap was the absence from the League of its potentially most important member, the United States. The Senate had refused to ratify U.S. entrance to the League, and a powerful isolationist sentiment in this country supported that decision. The League's difficulties were also exacerbated by the inexperience of its staff and leaders in running an international organization. It is therefore not surprising that the League never grappled successfully with major international conflicts and never replaced national governments in the exercise of power politics (*realpolitik*). Its greatest contributions were, rather, in such areas as international law (the World Court), and labor relations (the International Labor Organization).

The League's fragility became evident from 1931 onward, as a succession of nations began following aggressive foreign policies that ran contrary to all the League stood for. The Japanese invasion of Manchuria (1931) and Italy's invasion of Ethiopia (1934) drew no effective sanctions from the League, despite strenuous efforts by some parties to obtain them. With Hitler's rise to power in Germany in 1933, that country started on the road to rearmament and war.

From the mid–1930s the international political situation rapidly deteriorated. The major powers, trying not to be caught unawares or unprotected, began constructing various defenses. Sometimes, as in the case of Russia's invasion of Finland, to one side a move seemed necessary to strengthen border defenses, but seemed grossly aggressive and self-aggrandizing to the other. Sometimes, as in the case of the infamous Munich Agreement, attempts to reassure a nation by making concessions only increased the desire for more concessions. The League had by then become irrelevant to most nations. It mattered little that Japan had voluntarily left it in 1933, angered by League criticism of its adventures in Manchuria and China, or that Germany had left at about the same time.

The onset of World War II came, in a sense, from the failure of the League of Nations. Yet the idea that an international body should exist did not die. Instead, attention turned to how such a body might be made more effective in the future. This remarkable faith in the importance of a league of nations, whatever it might be called, arose perhaps out of the realization that, however flawed, the League functioned no worse than the traditional forms of international relations, and might at least provide a forum for nations. Behind the apparent failure of the League lay an awareness that traditional diplomacy, too, had failed, and that something else, in addition, was needed if there was not to be yet a Third World War. At first, this argument seemed a monopoly of the pacifists—amid the death and destruction of the new war, it seemed pointless to talk about ideals of world peace—but as the war years advanced, and as the defeat of the Axis powers approached, government leaders on all sides of the Grand Alliance began to ponder the future way of running international relations.

As early as 1941, before the United States had entered the conflict, an Inter-Allied Declaration called for cooperative efforts to halt international aggression. Soon thereafter, President Roosevelt and British Prime Minister Winston Churchill issued the Atlantic

Charter, in which, among other things, they alluded to the future of world peace:

> Since no future peace can be maintained if . . . armaments continue to be employed by nations which threaten, or may threaten, aggression outside of their frontiers, they [Roosevelt and Churchill] believe, pending the establishment of a wider and permanent system of general security, that the disarmament of such nations is essential.

On January 1, 1942, three weeks after the United States had entered the war, 26 nations who were fighting the Axis powers signed a Declaration of United Nations (the words "United Nations" having been coined by FDR), in which they committed themselves to establishing world peace through joint action.

In light of the fact that the United States had never joined the League of Nations and had thereby contributed to its ineffectiveness, the extent of America's commitment to a new organization was a matter of great speculation. Isolationist sentiment in the United States remained strong, but in 1943 a young member of the U.S. House of Representatives, J. William Fulbright of Arkansas, introduced a resolution advocating U.S. participation in an international organization to establish and maintain peace.

In a conversation with the author of this book, Fulbright explained why he acted when he did: "The League of Nations wasn't considered until after the [First] World War was over. People no longer focused on the tragedy of war, but began thinking about other things. . . . I wanted it considered in the middle of the war so that the House members would vote upon it while they were conscious of how terrible the war was and how destructive."

The strategy worked, and the House overwhelmingly approved the resolution. A Senate resolution, introduced by Tom Connally of Texas, was adopted soon after. From then on, there was no serious doubt about U.S. involvement and leadership. As Fulbright noted, "We had done very well, not having entanglements. The trouble was, the world changed, and communications, airlines, and all that projected us into foreign affairs, whether we liked it or not. It wasn't a question of having any choice any longer. The question became what to do about it, because we were involved."

Concurrently, at the Moscow Conference in October 1943, the governments of the United Kingdom, China, the United States, and the Soviet Union, represented by, respectively, Anthony Eden, Foo Ping-Sheung, Cordell Hull, and V. M. Molotov, recognized "the necessity of establishing . . . a general international organization, based on the principle of the sovereign equality of all peace-loving states, . . . for the maintenance of international peace and security." Later that year, at the Teheran Conference, Churchill, Roosevelt, and Stalin reiterated the need for peace.

The next step occurred in 1944 at Dumbarton Oaks, an estate in Washington, D.C. A series of conferences involving American, British, Chinese, and Russian representatives produced concrete proposals for UN principles and objectives, as well as for the structure to be used to reach those objectives. The principal body, the Security Council, would include the four Dumbarton Oaks participants and France as permanent members. The major question left undecided concerned the voting procedure in the proposed body.

The last preparatory step in the founding of the United Nations took place at the Yalta Conference in February of 1945. Churchill, Roosevelt, and Stalin, meeting together for the last time, resolved the major procedural questions. The veto system would be used in the Security Council by permanent members; and the Soviet Union, which had claimed 16 voting units (the 16 Soviet republics), would get three votes in the General Assembly—those of the USSR, Byelorussia, and Ukraine. In addition, they agreed to convene a founding conference in San Francisco on April 25, 1945.

At the San Francisco conference, delegates from 50 nations met to review various proposals for the United Nations and to draw up the charter. The U.S. delegation of seven members included four members of Congress: the chair of the Senate Foreign Relations Committee, Tom Connally of Texas, and its senior Republican member, Arthur Vandenberg of Michigan; and the ranking Republican on the House Foreign Affairs Committee, Charles Eaton of New Jersey, and the committee chairman, Sol Bloom of New York. Secretary of State Edward R. Stettinius Jr. headed the U.S. delegation.

The presence of members of Congress on the delegation was an important factor in the eventual U.S. decision to become a member of the United Nations. It helped avoid the unfortunate situation that occurred with the founding of the League of Nations, when the Senate refused to allow American membership in the new organization, despite the efforts of President Wilson and his supporters in the administration. The fact that in 1945 the Democrats controlled both houses of Congress, as well as the White House, also eased the way. Finally, it was clear that most Americans favored the creation of some kind of world body. A Gallup poll in July 1944 reported that 72 percent of Americans favored joining such an organization, with 15 percent being undecided and 13 percent being against. When the UN Charter was finally submitted to the Senate for ratification, on July 28, 1945, it passed handily by a vote of 89 to two.

On June 25, 1945 the assembled delegates in San Francisco unanimously adopted the charter. It then went to the various member countries for ratification, and took effect formally on October 26, 1945—a date later proclaimed UN Day.

The charter states the broad aims of the United Nations, which may be summed up under four headings: first, to maintain international peace and security; second, to develop friendly relations among nations, based on respect for the principle of equal rights and the right of peoples to self-determination; third, to achieve international cooperation in solving economic, social, cultural, or humanitarian problems; and fourth, to act as a harmonizing center for the community of nations, as they seek the three ends described above.

The United States invited the United Nations to establish its headquarters in this country. Until permanent facilities were completed, the United Nations operated out of temporary quarters, first at a campus of Hunter College in the Bronx, New York, and then at Lake Success on Long Island. It moved into its present site, at First Avenue between Forty-second and Forth-eighth streets, in 1950. The UN building was constructed with an $8.5 million gift from John D. Rockefeller, Jr. on land donated by New York City.

From its inception, the United Nations was envisaged as a body that would represent all the world's nations, but for the first two decades the actual admission policy was rather selective. The original 51 members included 20 Latin American countries, eight European, six from the British Commonwealth, and the Philippines and Taiwan. Through 1954 only nine additional nations were admitted, which meant that the American "automatic majority" was protected.

After 1954, however, the number of new members admitted to the United Nations began to increase rapidly. This occurred for two reasons. The first was the wave of decolonization that was sweeping all the old empires of the British, French, Dutch, Portuguese, and Belgians. As the former colonies reached nationhood, they applied for UN membership. The second reason was the rehabilitation of the

Axis powers and other nations that had fallen under a cloud as a result of the war—Italy, Japan, Spain, and many Eastern European countries. In 1955 alone, 16 new nations were admitted; by 1983 the total membership had grown to 158.

STRUCTURE

The charter stipulates that the main UN bodies are the Security Council, the General Assembly, the Economic and Social Council (ECOSOC), the Trusteeship Council, the International Court of Justice, and the permanent Secretariat. The charter also mandates the establishment of several subordinate agencies.

The Security Council, which can function in continuous session if necessary, is the highest UN body. It has the primary responsibility for maintaining international peace and security. Five permanent members—the United Kingdom, China, France, the USSR and the United States—and (since 1966) ten nonpermanent members selected for two-year terms by the General Assembly, make up the council. In 1971 the People's Republic of China (Communist China) replaced the Republic of China (Taiwan) as the occupant of China's seat on the council. The Security Council can recommend peaceful settlements of disputes and has binding power in cases where aggression has taken place. It can also establish observer and peacekeeping forces. Security Council resolutions are passed by majority vote but may be vetoed by any of the five permanent members.

The General Assembly operates on a two-thirds majority basis on important questions. It is the only major UN body in which every member nation is represented. The assembly meets annually in a three-month session commencing on the third Tuesday of September, and it can also hold resumed, special, and emergency sessions at other times. The General Assembly can make only nonbinding recommendations concerning any appropriate dispute or question not being discussed by the Security Council (unless it is asked to do otherwise by the Security Council). The assembly transacts much of its business in standing committees: the First (Political and Security) Committee; the Special Political Committee; the Second (Economic and Financial) Committee; the Third (Social, Humanitarian, and Cultural) Committee; the Fourth (Trusteeship and Non-Self-Governing Territories) Committee; the Fifth (Administrative and Budgetary)

Committee; and Sixth (Legal) Committee. There are also various special committees.

The Economic and Social Council is responsible for coordinating all UN activities and programs relating to economic and social development and cooperation. Composed of delegates from 54 nations, with its headquarters in Geneva, and acting under the oversight of the General Assembly, ECOSOC consists of six functional commissions, including those on Human Rights, Status of Women, and Social Development. Five regional commissions assist and implement development projects.

The specialized agencies are autonomous intergovernmental organizations which work with the UN and report annually to the Economic and Social Council. They include the International Labor Organization (ILO), the World Health Organization (WHO), the International Monetary Fund (IMF), the International Bank for Reconstruction and Development (World Bank), and the Food and Agriculture Organization (FAO). Some of these antedate the United Nations itself; many are based in Geneva, the former home of the League of Nations.

The Trusteeship Council oversees those territories that are administered under a UN trusteeship. Today only the Trust Territory of the Pacific Islands remains. The council members include delegates from the nations that do the administering (at this time only the United States) and the four other permanent members of the Security Council. During the early years of the United Nations, eleven territories were administered under trusteeship, and the council was relatively more important than it is today.

The International Court of Justice (the World Court) is a tribunal for legal disputes involving nations, not individuals. Composed of 15 members elected for nine-year terms by the Security Council and the General Assembly, the court is headquartered at The Hague.

The United Nations finances its budget by contributions from its members. The assessments are revised every three years by the Committee on Contributions to the General Assembly. In 1957 the assembly agreed, in principle, that no single member nation should contribute more than 30 percent of the regular UN budget. The assessment of the United States, which until that time had been about 40 percent of the UN budget, was reduced to the lower level. In 1972 the U.S. assessment was further reduced to a maximum of 25 percent of the UN budget. The regular budget for 1981 was nearly $670 million, of which the United States paid about $167 million. In the most recent assessment (1983–85), seven Western countries and the United States provide nearly 62 percent of the regular budget; the Soviet Union provides slightly over 10 percent.

In addition to the regular budget, special accounts are established to finance peacekeeping operations. Assistance programs such as the UN Development Program (UNDP) and the UN Children's Fund (UNICEF) are funded through voluntary contributions.

THE U.S. MISSION TO THE UNITED NATIONS (USUN)

The United States is represented at the world body by its mission, headed by the U.S. permanent representative (permanent rep.), who has cabinet status (since 1953) and ambassadorial rank. In addition, four deputies have, since 1961, also carried the rank of ambassador: the deputy permanent representative to the United Nations, the deputy representative on the Security Council, the representative of the Economic and Social Council, and the alternate representative for special political affairs (formerly known as the representative on the Trusteeship Council). The main purpose of the mission is to carry out U.S. policies in UN sessions and negotiations, in coordination with the State Department, and to fulfill American responsibilities as the host government for the United Nations.

Technically, the head of the mission in New York, despite cabinet status, reports to the assistant secretary of state for international-organization affairs, whose bureau is often referred to as the IO. As the contents of this book reveal, permanent representatives have developed a variety of relationships with the president, the secretary of state, and the IO, and have done so with varying degrees of effectiveness depending on their political and diplomatic acumen, base of political power in the country, and other factors.

There are other slots to be filled annually on the U.S. General Assembly delegation of ten, and presidents have named prominent figures from the worlds of science, academe, and the arts. Finally, each year two members of Congress are included in the delegation. In years when all the members of the U.S. House are up for reelection, two U.S. senators who are not up for reelection are appointed; in the alternate years, two members of the House serve. Normally, in each two-person congressional delegation, there is one Republican and one Democrat.

In addition to the mission in New York City, missions represent the United States in other UN bodies. The U.S. Mission to the European Office of the United Nations, in Geneva, headed by a representative with the rank of ambassador, oversees American interests at the various Geneva-based agencies, such as the WHO, ILO, and UN Conference on Trade and Development (UNCTAD). U.S. missions represent American interests in the Food and Agriculture Organization in Rome; in the UN Educational, Scientific, and Cultural Organization (UNESCO) in Paris; and in Vienna, the International Atomic Energy Agency (IAEA) and the UN Industrial Development Organization (UNIDO) in Vienna.

SOURCES

Everyone's U.N. (New York: UN Office of Public Information, 1979); John Stoessinger, *The United Nations and the Superpowers* (New York: Random House, 1965, 1970); *U.S. Participation in the U.N.* (Washington, D.C.: Department of State, 1946–81).

PART I:
THE TRUMAN–EISENHOWER YEARS,
1945–60

OVERVIEW

The United States dominated the United Nations in its early years. America had provided the military leadership in the defeat of the Axis powers; until 1949 it held a monopoly on nuclear weapons. It paid substantially more for the support of the United Nations than any other country and was, in fact, the home of the UN headquarters. It launched major programs of economic assistance for other countries. And the United States, relatively free of the taint of colonialism among the major powers, exerted a strong moral and inspirational force in international affairs because of its democratic institutions and its environment of personal freedom. Nonetheless, the influence of the United States would decline in the United Nations over the decades, and at a rate faster than its slippage in international influence outside the United Nations.

The early years brought promise that the goals of the preamble to the UN Charter would be fulfilled. In 1948, for example, the General Assembly adopted the Universal Declaration of Human Rights, under which the international community, for the first time, assumed responsibility for the protection and pursuit of human rights as a permanent obligation. Eleanor Roosevelt, the U.S. delegate to the Human Rights Commission, was the driving force in securing adoption of the declaration.

From the outset it was apparent that the success of the United Nations depended upon cooperation between the great powers, especially the United States and the Soviet Union, if only because of the veto that either nation could exercise. But postwar tensions accelerated rapidly with the growth of the Soviet Union's hegemony over its neighbors in Eastern Europe. After the war, Winston Churchill, speaking in Geneva, warned against Soviet expansionism and called for a union of democracies in Europe. This event came to be known as the "Iron Curtain" speech. Speaking later in Fulton, Missouri, the British leader advocated an Anglo-American union against the Russians.

In 1947, the Truman Doctrine, calling for U.S. efforts to "contain" communism, was proposed; the Communists seized power in Czechoslovakia in 1948. Soon thereafter, the United States introduced the Marshall Plan as a means to help rebuild the European economies. About the same time, the Communist Information Bureau (Cominform) was founded as a means for strengthening ties between the Soviets and the various European Communist Parties. (Cominform was disbanded in 1956.)

Before long, acrimonious exchanges between the Western states and the Soviet Union became the norm in the Security Council and General Assembly. The Berlin blockade, imposed by the Soviets in 1948 and thwarted by an American airlift, and the fall of China to Communist forces in 1949, added to the thunder of debate in the United Nations. That year, the Western nations formed the North Atlantic Treaty Organization (NATO) to provide a military counterweight to the perceived threat from the East. In 1953, East Berliners revolted against the Communist regime, and their action was quelled only with troops and tanks. Two years later, the Soviet Union and its allies formed the East European Mutual Defense (Warsaw) Pact.

The next year saw another East-West crisis develop when a revolt broke out in Hungary against the Communist regime. The Russians, under Nikita Khrushchev, countered this threat to their control by dispatching the Red Army to crush the revolt—an action which the General Assembly condemned in a resolution. After a Soviet veto of a Security Council call for a pullout from Hungary, a special emergency session of the General Assembly convened under the "Uniting-for-Peace" procedure (which allowed the assembly to recommend collective action if the Security Council was unable to act because of a veto by one of its members). The assembly condemned the invasion as a violation of the UN Charter that deprived Hungary of its "liberty and independence, and the Hungarian people of the exercise of their fundamental rights."

Peacekeeping Activities

In 1950, the Chinese Communist regime that had taken power the previous year attempted unsuccessfully to gain representation in the United Nations. The Soviet delegate announced that his country would not recognize the legality of or participate in UN activities until the Nationalist Chinese delegate was removed and replaced with the Communist regime's delegate. The USSR withdrew from the Security Council and about 40 other UN bodies that January. When the Soviet representative was scheduled to become president of the Security Council in August 1950, the Soviets resumed participation.

However, much had taken place in the interim. In June 1950, Communist North Korea invaded South Korea. With the USSR absent, the Security Council was able to adopt, without risk of a veto, a resolution calling the attack a breach of the peace by the Communists and urging an immediate cease-fire and North Korean withdrawal. Soon thereafter, the United States successfully obtained resolutions calling for UN intervention on behalf of South Korea and creating a UN unified command under American leadership. General Douglas MacArthur was placed in command. After being held to a small foothold near Pusan, the UN troops—representing 16 nations, but mainly consisting of Americans and South Koreans—pushed the invaders back across the thirty-eighth parallel and well into North Korea. These actions represented the first use of combat troops under the UN flag.

In late July, the Soviets announced that they intended to return to the United Nations. With the Soviets back on the Security Council, further action by that body concerning the Korean question was likely to be vetoed. The General Assembly then passed the Uniting-for-Peace Resolution. The assembly thus became the political overseer of the UN actions in Korea. This took place despite Soviet protests that only the Security Council—where they had a veto—had the right to engage in peacekeeping activities. U.S. Secretary of State Dean Acheson pointed out that the UN Charter also gave the General Assembly "authority and responsibility for matters affecting international peace."

Late in 1950, the General Assembly established the UN Commission for the Unification and Rehabilitation of Korea (UNCURK). The Soviets proposed a number of unsuccessful resolutions calling for the pull-out of all foreign troops. In October 1950, the Chinese

Communists intervened to aid North Korea, forcing a UN retreat back toward the 38th parallel. Various armistice agreements were soon proposed. Their success in 1953 led to the withdrawal of the UN troops and reestablishment of the conditions that obtained before the North Korean invasion.

The crisis that would cast the longest and darkest shadow over the United Nations approached a flash point in 1947, when Britain announced that it would terminate its League of Nations mandate over Palestine, which was divided between bitterly hostile Arab and Jewish populations. Faced with increased violence, Britain called for UN intervention. In 1947, the UN Special Committee on Palestine (UNSCOP) was established by the General Assembly. Later that year, the UNSCOP majority opinion recommended a partition of Palestine into Arab and Jewish sectors, while the city of Jerusalem was to be an international area. Despite Arab opposition to any division of Palestine, the General Assembly approved the recommendation.

Increasing turmoil in the Middle East during 1948 prompted the Security Council to appeal to the affected parties to avoid hostilities. On May 14, the Palestine mandate expired and Israel was proclaimed an independent nation. The next day, the new Jewish state was attacked by the Arab nations. The United Nations named Count Folke Bernadotte, president of the Swedish Red Cross, as mediator in the dispute. Bernadotte was assassinated a few months later in an Israeli-held part of Jerusalem.

In 1949, Ralph Bunche, Bernadotte's successor, negotiated a cease-fire among the belligerents, which included Egypt, Lebanon, Jordan, Syria, and Israel. A special group of observers—the UN Truce Supervision Organization (UNTSO)—and the newly created UN Relief and Works Agency for Palestinian Refugees were dispatched to the area to report on developments to the United Nations and to provide aid for Palestinians who had fled from Israel during the fighting.

The armistice lines, determined by territory occupied, gave Israel more land than the original partition proposal had included. Partly because of this, the armistice brought no true peace, and Arab states refused to acknowledge Israel's right to exist. The tides of Palestinian refugees away from Israeli-occupied areas created a problem that seemed to defy solution. Their care was largely provided for through the UN Relief and Works Agency.

During the early 1950s, Israel complained that Egypt was blocking the Suez Canal. In 1954, the Soviet Union vetoed a Security

Council resolution calling for Egypt to comply with a 1951 Security Council resolution regarding restrictions on international shipping. As tensions between Egypt and Israel continued to mount, Dag Hammarskjöld, the UN secretary general, went to the region in 1955 in the hope of obtaining a lasting peace. After Egypt's President Nasser nationalized the strategically crucial canal, Israel finally invaded the Sinai in October 1956. The British and the French called for a cease-fire between the two nations and for the placement of Anglo-French troops as a buffer and to secure the Suez Canal for shipping. Shortly thereafter, the two European powers invaded Egypt at Port Said. The United States introduced a resolution calling for a cease-fire and pressuring its allies to comply. By this time, Israel had taken control of the Sinai. Meanwhile, England and France argued that theirs was a "police action." Canada's Ambassador Lester Pearson called for the creation of an international force to "secure and supervise the cessation of hostilities," and Britain and France expressed a willingness to withdraw if such a force were brought in. But when Britain, France, and Israel—without American knowledge or consultation—extended their occupation to the Suez area, President Eisenhower decided he had no choice but to side with those who were condemning the action and asking for a withdrawal of the troops. Under heavy pressure from the United States, the two European powers withdrew, in December 1956, when the UN Emergency Force (UNEF) arrived. Israel withdrew in March 1957, after it was agreed that the canal would be open to all international shipping and that the UNEF would take positions in the Gaza Strip. After the UN secretary general had mobilized a fleet of over 40 salvage vessels to clear the canal, Egypt announced its reopening in April 1957. The UNEF remained in the Sinai until 1967.

The United Nations got another taste of peacekeeping in the Congo. The year 1960 saw the climax of the rush toward independence by African colonies. After two centuries of rule by foreigners, the peoples of the former Belgian Congo found themselves ill-equipped to cope with self-determination and fell into a bloody power struggle. Although the conflict was internal, Belgian forces had intervened and the USSR and other nations showed a similar interest, so the United Nations stepped in essentially as a colonial administrator. Architect of the UN involvement was Secretary General Dag Hammarskjöld, who had succeeded Trygve Lie, the first secretary general, in 1953. With Security Council approval, he created a 20,000-man peacekeeping force—primarily from other African states—which maintained a semblance of peace and order.

Hammarskjöld's refusal to use force to control the breakaway province of Katanga, which was anti-Communist in orientation, incited the anger of the Soviet Union. The Soviet premier, Nikita Krushchev, attended a meeting of the General Assembly in 1960 and demanded that Hammarskjöld be replaced by a three-man directorate, or troika, whose members would represent the interests of the Communist bloc, the West, and the nonaligned states. The Russian proposal was rejected and Hammarskjöld continued his difficult task until he died in a plane crash in the Congo in 1961.

Arms Control

The control and possible elimination of nuclear (and conventional) weapons have been major concerns of the United Nations since its inception. The development of the atomic bomb by the United States in 1945 and by the Soviet Union in 1949 lent a sense of urgency to such efforts. Nevertheless, no international accords of substance were established during the 1940s.

The UN Charter (in Articles 11 and 26) provides that the General Assembly and the Security Council can both take up arms-control proposals. In 1946, the General Assembly established the UN Atomic Energy Commission (AEC) for the purpose of limiting atomic energy to peaceful uses. Later that year, the USSR—which was not a nuclear power at the time—proposed a ban on the production and use of atomic weapons. While praising the Soviet initiative, the United States pointed out that reliable verification and inspection procedures must be part of an effective disarmament agreement. With the two nations still differing on the issue, the AEC suspended its activities in 1949. The Commission for Conventional Armaments, which was founded in 1947, also failed to produce a compromise on non-nuclear-force reductions. The General Assembly did approve a resolution calling for the regulation and verification of conventional forces, but the proposal failed to pass the Security Council because of a Soviet veto.

In 1952, the General Assembly established the Disarmament Committee to supersede the Atomic Energy Commission and the Commission for Conventional Armaments. Like its predecessor bodies, the Disarmament Committee was plagued by major disagreements between the West and the Soviet Union. One year later, the USSR announced the explosion of its first hydrogen bomb. Also in 1953, the United States proposed the creation of the International Atomic Energy Agency (IAEA), to cover the peaceful uses of atomic energy—it was approved by the General Assembly in 1955. The IAEA's first conference, in Vienna in 1955, drew scientists from 75 nations. In addition, the General Assembly approved proposals for mutual aerial inspection of military installations for the United States and the USSR. Two years later, the General Assembly endorsed a series of Western proposals for arms control, such as a halt on production of nuclear materials for weapons and on nuclear testing; reductions in conventional forces; and studies of the peaceful uses of outer space. The USSR rejected these proposals and presented its own, which were rejected by the General Assembly.

The United States and the General Assembly continued to emphasize that a system of verification, inspection, and control was needed if disarmament was to be effective. A group of American, British, and Soviet experts met in Geneva and agreed that detection of nuclear testing was feasible. As a result, negotiations began on the banning of nuclear-weapons testing. A General Assembly resolution endorsed technical verification of disarmament and praised "a balanced and effectively controlled worldwide system of disarmament." In addition, a Disarmament Commission with universal membership was approved in 1959. Also in that year, 65 nations spoke at the Fourteenth General Assembly session on the question of disarmament. Resolutions expressing a hope for general and complete disarmament and for the elimination of nuclear testing were passed. The General Assembly established the UN Committee on the Peaceful Uses of Outer Space.

The U.S. Mission

Edward R. Stettinius, Jr., who, as secretary of state, had signed the UN Charter for the United States, became the first U.S. permanent representative to the United Nations. When he resigned after a short time, President Truman named Senator Warren R. Austin of Vermont, a Republican of internationalist views, as permanent representative. Austin, a gentleman of the old school and a good negotiator, served from 1947 to 1953 and established the U.S. Mission to the United Nations as an effective entity in U.S. foreign policy. Austin faithfully carried out the policies made in Washington. Though restrained in his responses to the Russians, he firmly opposed their objectives. During his bouts of ill health, his deputies, Philip Jessup and Ernest Gross, gave him strong support.

The next permanent representative was Henry Cabot Lodge (1953–60), whose grandfather and namesake had led the fight against U.S. participation in the League of Nations. The younger Lodge, who had already served in the Senate, was a close adviser to President Eisenhower, whose campaign for the White House Lodge had managed in 1952. Lodge felt secure in his position vis-à-vis the State Department, though he showed due respect for John Foster Dulles, another forceful personality, who was secretary of state during most of Lodge's tenure. Unlike Austin, Lodge took a publicly combative stance against the Soviets and checked them at every turn, both in the propaganda war and in the majorities run up by the United States in the voting. Lodge's effectiveness helped bring about an increase in U.S. public support for the United Nations, and it earned him the nomination for vice president on the Republican ticket in 1960. When Lodge resigned to campaign, he was succeeded briefly by James J. Wadsworth, his deputy.

With the admission of 17 new states in 1960, all but one of them African, the United Nations had doubled in size to 99 members. The unpredictable voting habits of the newcomers signaled the end of domination of the proceedings by the United States and its allies.

During the Truman years, the American representatives to the United Nations included Eleanor Roosevelt, Adlai Stevenson, John Foster Dulles, Dean Rusk (assistant secretary of state for UN affairs from 1946 to 1953), Anna Lord Strauss, and Benjamin Cohen. The congressional delegates to the General Assembly included Senators Tom Connally, Arthur Vandenberg, John Sparkman, and Henry Cabot Lodge; and Representatives Mike Mansfield and Helen Gahagan Douglas.

During the Eisenhower years the congressional delegates included Senators J. William Fulbright and Hubert Humphrey, and Representatives Brooks Hays, Walter Judd, John Pastore, and Clement Zablocki. Other delegates included Henry Ford II, Mary Pillsbury Lord, Roger W. Straus, Jacob Blaustein, Paul Hoffman, Ellsworth Bunker, George Meany, Irene Dunne, and Marian Anderson.

SOURCES

On the Cold War, see John Stoessinger, *The United Nations and the Superpowers* (New York: Random House, 1965, 1970). For the Congo, see Roger Hilsman, *To Move a Nation* (New York: Dell, 1964). General information about the United Nations and the U.S. Mission during this period may be found in *Everyman's United Nations* (New York: UN Office of Public Information, 1968); Thomas Hovet, *A Chronology and Fact Book of the United Nations, 1941-1979* (Dobbs Ferry, N.Y.: Oceania, 1979); Richard Hiscocks, *The Security Council* (New York: Free Press, 1973); *U.S. Participation in the UN* (Washington, D.C.: Department of State, 1946-81); and Seymour Maxwell Finger, *Your Man at the UN* (New York: New York University Press, 1980).

W. AVERELL HARRIMAN: Adviser to President Roosevelt at Yalta, 1944; Delegate to the UN Special Session on Disarmament, 1978.

I wanted the UN to play an important role in preventing war and in organizing itself so that it would be taken seriously. I was very hopeful that the United Nations would be a body that could review difficulties and find some way to settle them. It didn't take quite that position. That may have been expecting too much.

William Averell Harriman was vice president of the Union Pacific Railroad (1915-17) and then head of the Merchant Shipping Corporation (1917-25), before founding W. A. Harriman and Company, a private bank that later merged with Brown Brothers (1931). He rejoined Union Pacific in 1932 as chairman of the board and carried out a successful expansion during the depths of the Great Depression.

Originally a Republican, Harriman switched to the Democratic Party and later became an administrator of the National Recovery Administration (NRA). In 1941, he was the president's personal representative in London, coordinating America's lend-lease program with England and Russia.

President Roosevelt appointed Harriman ambassador to Russia in 1943. The ambassador became convinced that in the post-war era, the Soviet Union would seek not only the security of its borders but also to spread its ideology abroad. He advised the ailing president to take a firmer stance regarding the Soviet occupation of Eastern Europe. After Roosevelt's death, President Truman accepted Harriman's views and toughened his position toward the Russians. In his memoirs, Harriman argues that Roosevelt had already decided that U.S.-Soviet conflict was inevitable.

After a brief stint as ambassador to Great Britain, in 1946 Harriman returned to the United States to become secretary of commerce. Harriman's continuing interest in foreign affairs was manifested in his support and aid in implementing Secretary of State George Marshall's European recovery program. He argued that the economic stability of Europe—and particularly Germany—was essential in containing Soviet expansion on that continent. Harriman resigned his Commerce post in 1948 to oversee the distribution of aid in Europe.

Harriman became a special assistant to Truman in 1950, and was involved in the decisions that led to U.S. involvement in the Korean war. As director of the Mutual Security Agency (1951-53), the financier and diplomat took charge of distribution of foreign aid.

Harriman made unsuccessful bids for the Democratic presidential nomination in 1952 and 1956, but did serve as governor of New York from 1954 to 1958. Returning to the world of foreign affairs, Harriman became assistant secretary of state for Far Eastern affairs (1961-63) and negotiated the Laotian neutrality treaty of 1962. As undersecretary of state for political affairs (1963-65), he negotiated the U.S.-Soviet nuclear-test-ban treaty of 1963. Before his retirement from government in 1969, he was President Johnson's ambassador at large and head of the U.S. delegation to the Paris peace talks on Vietnam (1968). Harriman has remained active in Democratic politics.

I was, of course, the adviser to President Roosevelt at the Yalta Conference. I was with him all the time. He wasn't feeling too well, but he was well enough to carry on discussions thoroughly. He knew exactly what he was talking about. All these stories that he was confused just aren't true at all.

One of Roosevelt's principal objectives was to get Stalin to agree to have the United Nations and to join it. He had not agreed up to that time, but Roosevelt got that agreement. When Roosevelt, Stalin, and Churchill got together, not only did they agree to have the United Nations, but they agreed it would be organized in April in San Francisco.

The UN voting procedure was also discussed at Yalta. The East European states hadn't yet been organized; they didn't have representation and they didn't have influence with Communist countries abroad. Stalin was very much in the minority, and he was troubled by that. He wanted all of the Soviet states, the republics, to have a representation. He wanted them to have 16 votes. There was an argument about that at Yalta and they got it down to three: Byelorussia, the Ukraine, and the Soviet Union. So they got three votes.

The United States was offered three votes in the United Nations but of course it was America's policy to have one country, one vote. We didn't deviate from that, despite the fact that Roosevelt knew it would cause some difficulty in Congress to give the Russians three votes and only have one for ourselves. But I don't think we had too much trouble with the Congress about it.

Roosevelt felt that once he got to know Stalin better, he would be able to influence him. He was a little bit over-optimistic about it.

Some people said he was naive. I don't call it naive at all, because he could have had an influence on Stalin and he did.

At the Teheran Conference in 1943, the first conference in which Roosevelt, Stalin, and Churchill got together, I noticed that whenever Roosevelt spoke, Stalin leaned forward and paid special attention to him. With Roosevelt he had, I'm sure, a feeling of very great respect not only because the United States was the strongest nation in the world, but because of his respect for Roosevelt's leadership in the world. He wanted to make certain that he understood him, which was very interesting, I thought. I don't know that anyone has every fully recorded that.

Churchill played a great morally-supporting role and a very active role, as I recall it, between Stalin and Roosevelt in the important talks. He was always very cooperative and he was in sympathy with all of those objectives, although it was primarily Roosevelt who took the lead. I can tell you this, that Stalin had a feeling of camaraderie for Churchill. At the Kremlin once, there was a dinner party for Churchill, and Stalin made a toast. He said, "My comrade in arms in this war. . . ." The way he talked about it, I got the feeling that Stalin realized that after 'this war,' Churchill would go on to support British imperialism, whereas Stalin would go on to achieve [the] Soviet objective, which [was] of course the expansion of Soviet influence.

When Stalin was around, [Foreign Minister] Molotov was very much a second. When Molotov was in charge of things, he was a very strong, negative influence. I used to say that Molotov only knew one word: *nyet*. But Stalin didn't pay attention to him.

I remember a discussion in Moscow between Stalin and me about the Soviet representation at San Francisco. It happened in April when I went to see Stalin the day after Roosevelt's death. Stalin was very serious. I had never seen him so moved by anything. He said this would be a very great disaster for the whole world. I said, "Well, you can help stabilize things." Stalin said, "How?" I said, "By taking a greater interest in the United Nations and sending Molotov."

I understood that they had arranged to send [to the U.N.] Vishinsky, who was a deputy in the Foreign Office with Molotov. I told Stalin that I thought that would indicate he didn't have as much interest in the conference as the other important nations which were sending their foreign ministers. It was very important for Molotov to go.

He said, "All right, Molotov will go." Molotov then whispered in his ear, which I couldn't fully hear, but said something to the effect of, "Oh, I can't go, I have other engagements." Stalin said, "Molotov will go," and brushed him aside. That's how Molotov got to the United Nations.

I had sought to carry out Roosevelt's policy objectives. I thought, of course, in carrying out those objectives, that it was very important for the Russians to be there and to have their first team. I didn't think Mr. Molotov was the most cooperative man in the world, and in some ways, I believed much more could have been accomplished with Vishinsky, who was very clever. But as far as the objectives of the United Nations were concerned at that time, I was very much in support of them.

Truman was also very anxious to carry out Roosevelt's ideas. I saw him when I came back from Moscow. He said, "I want to know everything that Roosevelt felt on the issues that are coming up in the United Nations." He said, "It was Roosevelt that was elected president. I wasn't, so I must find out what the Roosevelt ideas are and carry them out." Of course, when he got reelected, he was very much himself and Truman put a stamp on the American political scene in his own right. But in his earliest days, he was very anxious to fully carry out Roosevelt's programs. Of course, he continued to carry them out, . . . the New Deal and that sort of thing, because he believed in them. But in the early days, it was in order to make sure he carried out what was in Roosevelt's mind. There was a certain unity of purpose between Roosevelt and Truman. I think the time [periods] that the two men served as president will be joined together as one period in our history.

It's a great tragedy that the American people haven't been brought to respect the UN more closely. It is very important to have men and women of stature representing the United States at the United Nations. They carry weight with the public as well as with the UN delegates from other countries. I'm not against the bureaucrats in the United Nations, but some important personalities contribute especially effectively. I think George Bush, for example, is one of the very important personalities in the American political scene today. I knew his father intimately; he was my partner. Anything George Bush did I was very respectful of. I hope someday he will be president when we have to have a Republican.

Andrew Young was in charge of the U.S. Mission when I was leading the American delegation in the Special Session on Disarmament. He was so busy doing other things, I don't think he paid very much attention to this subcommittee work. He was in charge of everything that went on in the United Nations with regard to our representatives. I recognized that and tried to keep him in touch. I was very fond of him and welcomed any participation he would take. But I don't remember his participating that much. He may deny that. I hope he finally did because I would have welcomed it.

I have always been a strong believer in the United Nations and I feel we ought to give it our full support. If we do, I think it will continue to have an influential effect, and I am one of those who is using every opportunity that I have to strengthen our position in the United Nations and encourage others to do so as well. I think we have to recognize that there's been no world war since the UN was started. That has probably been its greatest achievement.

PHILIP C. JESSUP: Deputy Representative to the United Nations, 1947–49.

I think the UN is not going to secure or obtain or be given any more authority than it has now. In the early days, we kept thinking it was just the Soviets who resisted giving authority to the UN. But actually the veto provisions were just as important to the United States Senate as they were to Moscow.

Philip C. Jessup had a distinguished career as a lawyer and law professor before being named assistant secretary general of the UN Relief and Rehabilitation Administration (UNRRA). He later became assistant secretary general of the UN Monetary and Finance Conference at Bretton Woods, New Hampshire.

Jessup's activities in international law extended beyond the classroom. In 1945, he was an assistant for judicial organization with the American delegation to the San Francisco Conference on International Law. He was also a proponent of a new international organization that would replace the League of Nations. "I had been teaching international law and had great interest in all of the League's affairs, particularly in the development of the international court," he notes. "I was already committed to the idea of an international organization. I felt very strongly about it. Indeed, this went back all the way to my experience as a private in the American Army in France and Belgium [during World War I]. The reaction I had after that was a desire to work for international peace."

Jessup became active in the newly formed United Nations, where, in 1948, he presented a series of proposals for voting rules in the Security Council. One of the major problems he saw during the early days of the United Nations "was misrepresentation of the official views that the United Nations was going to solve all the world's problems and create peace. This notion," he continues, "was spread around in the public's mind to a certain extent, but certainly not in the official mind."

As deputy to the U.S. representative (1948), with the rank of ambassador, Jessup participated in a series of discussions on the Palestine issue. He announced that an Arab refusal to prolong the truce in the Middle East was tantamount to a threat to world peace (as defined in Chapter VII of the UN Charter). The Arabs soon capitulated and continued the truce. Later that year, he presented an American proposal for Israeli membership in the United Nations. He was involved in U.S. protests over Russia's blockade of Berlin.

Jessup was named Hamilton Fish Professor of International Law at Columbia University in 1948. During the 1950s, he continued his teaching duties and served as a delegate in the General Assembly over several sessions. He was U.S. ambassador-at-large from 1949 to 1953.

After 36 years at Columbia, Jessup left his teaching post in 1961 to become a judge on the International Court of Justice, where he served until 1970.

The Berlin blockade came in 1948 while we were at the General Assembly meeting in Paris. There was a good deal of discussion, after the Russians imposed the blockade, whether we should take it to the United Nations or whether, as General Clay at one time advocated, we should try to break the blockade by pushing through an armed force. The decision eventually was to take it to the UN. I had some part in the discussions as to whether it should go to the General Assembly, the Security Council, or the International Court. We decided to go to the Security Council even though we knew that the Soviets would veto any measure agreed upon there.

I think our stand at that time was very important in terms of our general relations with other members of the UN and in terms of the functioning of the UN itself. We were very firm in our position vis-à-vis the Russians, but not bellicose. The Russians came out badly in their public image among the rest of the members of the United Nations. Then there was a great deal of activity on the part of individuals who thought they could find a settlement. Secretary-General Trygve Lie and the president of the General Assembly got out an appeal to the Big Four to settle the Berlin blockade, but they put their appeal in such a way that, we felt at the time, they had hindered things more than helped them.

Finally, in 1949 I had my talks with Ambassador Jacob Malik, which led to an agreement on the lifting of the blockade toward May. General Marshall, who was then secretary of state, assigned me the job of arguing the case in Paris at the Security Council. Later, when it came to the negotiations here, Dean Acheson and I were assigned to work it out at the United Nations very quietly without publicity. I've always thought that was a very good example of the importance of privacy in negotiations of this kind.

Soviet Diplomacy

I will always remember an episode during the first assembly, of 1948, at one of the committee meetings, involving a Soviet delegate, Arutiunian. The alphabetical seating arrangement had him sitting next to the United Kingdom's delegate. I was sitting next to the U.K. [delegate] also, and Arutiunian delivered one of the typical Russian speeches denouncing the United Kingdom for its role in Palestine. When he was finished, he grinned and turned to his U.K. neighbor, started to jab him in the ribs and said, "I gave you a good one that time, didn't I?" And the Englishman said, "Wait till I get back at you!" This was the sort of gamesmanship, you see, not expressive of basic hostilities, and that was generally characteristic.

On the more political level, when you got to the General Assembly and had the higher Soviet officials, then you began to get the regular pattern of bad language, bad talk, particularly with Vishinsky representing the Soviet Union.

On the American side, I can remember discussions in the State Department on the question: Is it helpful to respond to Soviet attacks, slanders, and vituperation with the same kind of language, or does that pass over the heads of the delegates? Should we be more reasonable? The answer varied from time to time among various people. But in later stages, for instance when Cabot Lodge was our ambassador, he always felt that you had to reply to the Soviets in kind, with the kind of bad language that they used in attacking us. This was a constant problem, which we see brought out very clearly in the Reagan administration today, but again that varied with individuals with the times. I didn't feel there was any use in denouncing the Russians, certainly not in the UN, because other delegations were very well aware of the Soviet method. They rather expected the United States to take a calm or matter-of-fact point of view. But in the general public-relations role of someone in the State Department, when you were going around making speeches, you had to take a firm line about the Soviet Union, particularly a few years later in the 1950s. I think most of the speeches I gave, in line with the State Department policy, attacked the Soviets rather strongly.

I don't think the Soviets were more effective in using the UN to further their goals than we were. At that period they didn't have a substantial following. In the case of the Berlin blockade, it's true that many people were seriously afraid of war breaking out between the Soviet Union and the United States, and they were doing their best to find a way to appease the Russians, to bring them together with the United States. But, in general, I think the Russians did not get alone very well with the other countries. I'll give you an example.

In the second assembly session, . . . in Paris, one of the items on the agenda was disarmament. We worked hard on that. Dean Acheson, who headed the delegation, made the principal speech introducing our disarmament proposals, which had been worked out with the British and the French. Acheson made a very effective speech, which was very persuasive to most of the delegations. Vishinsky, replying for the Russians, said that when he heard Acheson's suggestions, he laughed all night long—a ridiculous thing, this proposal! Naturally, this response got around. Everybody heard it because it was a speech in the assembly, and it turned almost everybody against Vishinsky.

Acheson didn't participate in the detailed committee debates. I was in charge of that. Every proposal Vishinsky just shot down or voted down until finally somebody suggested that the Big Four should have a separate meeting under the chairmanship of the president of the assembly. The president was then Padia Nerva of Mexico, who was one of my colleagues later on the International Court. We did meet. It was a small subcommittee: [It had] French, British, Russians, and Americans. Jules Moch was the French representative. He was quite a specialist on disarmament matters, a very interesting and very able man. He originally represented the same French point of view which I suggested; i.e., the thing to do to conciliate the Russians was to meet them half-way—then everything would be likely to work out all right.

You would think that Vishinsky would be aware of this and would therefore be nice to him and try to work with him. Instead, almost from our first meeting, Vishinsky began denouncing France and denouncing Moch personally. Moch turned to me (I was sitting next to him at the table) and said, "My God, that man is not even a gentleman." We got nowhere with the committee, but it was illustrative of the failure of the Russians in the Vishinsky period to accommodate themselves to circumstances and to try to get a compromise position.

Ambassador Malik was not at all difficult to deal with in comparison with Vishinsky, who was always very violent and disagreeable. When Malik arrived as the Soviet representative to the UN, he took the place of Gromyko, who is now such a prominent figure, but then was a minor official. Gromyko had always been very stolid and unsmiling, and while not violent like Vishinsky, very uncompromising and hard. Malik came trying a different tack. He was all smiles and jokes most of the time, and, on an individual basis, was very easy to get along with. My relations with him were very easy and cordial, and the negotiations we had at the Soviet mission up here at Sixty-eighth

Street and Park [Avenue] were on a very friendly basis. We just took it slowly and let the thing unwind. I had no trouble at all dealing with him.

I came back to negotiating with Gromyko, a year and a half later I guess, when we had the meetings at the Palais Rose in Paris. Gromyko was very stiff and uncompromising then and seemed to have no latitude in his instructions. The problem in that negotiation was merely to establish the agenda for another meeting of the Council of Foreign Ministers. Gromyko began by saying, "The first item on the agenda must be the aggressive imperialistic policy of the NATO powers." We said, "Don't be silly, we're obviously not going to put that on the agenda. If you want to discuss the Warsaw Pact and the NATO Pact, we can compare those, but obviously we can't take your statement." He just kept on day after day, the same thing. I was working with the British and French. This was a tripartite effort on our side, and at that time we felt that the French were rather too eager to be accommodating to the Soviets. They assumed that the Soviets wanted to reach an agreement and were therefore giving a little bit and were saying, "Oh well, if this is what you like, let's do it this way"; not hard bargaining. The British were more or less going along with the French. In the course of the negotiations, it was as much a matter of persuading our allies as it was a matter of trying to get an agreement with Gromyko.

After, I guess, nearly a month and a half, I proposed that we suggest to Gromyko that they give up the idea of a detailed agenda and just leave it to the five magistrates when they met. The French and British thought that was fair enough, so we put it up to Gromyko. He said no, the first item on the agenda must be the aggressive imperialist policies of the NATO alliance. That was enough to convince the British and French that there was no use going on. We just terminated the discussions and they had no agenda.

Working Procedures

Dean Rusk was assistant secretary in charge of UN affairs—international-organization affairs—and we became great friends as we went along. It's very important to note that the delegation in New York was always acting under instructions from the State Department. We could make suggestions, and we did from time to time, but the basic lines of policy and sometimes even the detailed phrasing of the resolutions were matters for the State Department in Washington.

One thing which Washington didn't always take into account, and it came up from time to time, was the fact that there were sometimes last-minute changes in the wording of a resolution. Say you had a particular resolution and were authorized to support it. In the course of the debate in the Security Council or the committee of the assembly, wherever it was, somebody would suddenly suggest an amendment. You had to act quickly in a parliamentary sense. You couldn't always get the time to consult with the State Department, so you would have to use your own judgment.

When the UN was at Lake Success, we had a little booth with a telephone, a direct line to the State Department. Sometimes we could keep the talk going, in committee, for instance, or ask for a recess. Then a member of the delegation would get on the line and talk to Dean Rusk or somebody else in the State Department and say, "Here's the situation now. Should we go ahead and support this change or introduce this amendment?," and so on. Some of the delegates from other countries had authority to make decisions for themselves without consulting their government at home. A number of the Latin American delegates I knew were on their own.

One of the typical aspects of the operation at the United Nations was the rounding up of opinion so that you could tell in advance what was going to carry. That was done by various members of the delegation circulating around and sounding out various other delegates. Some of them became extremely expert at this, particularly Jack Ross, who was one of the most active and valuable members of the permanent staff in New York. He was very close to Senator Austin [the permanent rep] and worked very well with him. Charles Noyes had a phenomenal memory; he could talk to six or seven delegates and then come back and reconstruct the conversations. He would make a memorandum showing how the delegations were going to vote, so that we could frequently size up in advance what the chances were of getting the resolution adopted. It was also a standing procedure that the United States should not try to go too far out in front but should try to get one of the other delegations associated with us to make a joint submission of a resolution.

It was not unusual to have a lunch party with the principal delegates from a region, such as Latin America, and get a discussion around the table as to what stand to take on a particular measure. It was more common to negotiate over cocktails in those days because we were, relatively speaking, so small. Today it would be impossible to recognize and deal very personally with 150 delegates.

UN Accomplishments

There was a very notable success in ending the colonial conflict between Holland and Indonesia. I was in charge of those negotiations and was particularly pleased that we finally brought it about, although the Dutch for a time dealt with it as a police action. Eventually it led to the Round Table Conference at The Hague and the establishment of Indonesia as an independent republic in 1949. This was one part of my effort to ensure that the United States support the nationalist groups in what is now called the Third World.

Among the people who were working in the U.S. government on UN affairs, I can't remember any who thought the UN was about to save the world from all future conflict. On the other hand, there was really a dedicated feeling on the part of most of the people. They were intent upon trying to make it work, make it succeed as far as possible.

The Uniting-for-Peace Resolution of November 1950, in the Korean affair, was a big step forward in enhancing the powers of the UN. It amended the rules of procedure of the General Assembly so that special emergency sessions of the General Assembly could be convened when the Security Council was deadlocked. I see little prospect of that kind of trend continuing now, but it's perfectly possible that as far as the United States is concerned, in a Democratic administration you might get an entirely different plan. In the same way, you would have had a very different situation if Adlai Stevenson had been elected president. If you had somebody else with a comparable vision and attitude, coming in four, eight, or ten years from now, you might get a new initiative from the United States. I doubt very much the Soviets will change in that time. Therefore, I don't think there's going to be any radical change in the political aspect. In terms of the actual administration of the world, the UN plays a much more important part than many people realize. People are beginning to see, I think, that the United Nations is not only a peacekeeping organization, but it is this whole international organization containing specialized agencies like the International Monetary Fund, UNESCO, and the World Health Organization.

We have to bear in mind that not all of the world's political problems are just those between the United States and the Soviet Union. We see other conflicts all around the world. I think this is where personalities count a good deal. It may well be that the UN will carry more influence if you have another secretary general like Dag Hammarskjöld and if he has the backing, say, of a new U.S. administration. You might find such a person playing a more effective role in the circle of secondary conflicts between states other than the superpowers.

ERNEST A. GROSS: Deputy Representative to the United Nations, 1949-53.

The Soviets have been fighting a defensive, rearguard action at the UN from the very beginning. In fact, I can't think of any respect in which, from their point of view, their membership in the UN has been helpful to them. I cannot recall any resolutions of consequence which they introduced which they felt were important, and which were adopted against the wishes of the West. They must often wonder about the UN and what it has really meant to them. I think they have never been clear in their own minds about membership in the UN, except perhaps for two factors: In its early years they undoubtedly regarded the UN as a safeguard against recurrences of German aggression. I think that was a primary motivating factor in their adherence to the charter—that and their fear of being isolated from potential supporters in the Third World.

Ernest Arnold Gross was trained as a lawyer and worked in government and industry before joining the State Department in 1946. He served as deputy assistant secretary of state for occupied areas (1946-47), State Department legal adviser (1947), and assistant secretary of state for congressional relations (1948).

In 1949, Gross became deputy representative, with the rank of ambassador, to the United Nations. He had "the four qualities that United States diplomacy at the United Nations has often lacked: clarity, brevity, humor and a good notion of when to hold his tongue," observed James Reston. As acting head of the U.S. delegation in Warren Austin's absence, Gross played a significant role in UN deliberations during 1950. He called for the appointment of a mediator to settle the Indo-Pakistani dispute over Kashmir and maintained U.S. opposition to the admission of the Communist Chinese to UN membership.

During the aftermath of North Korea's invasion of South Korea in June 1950, Gross sponsored a successful Security Council resolution denouncing the invasion, calling for North Korea's withdrawal, and urging "all members to render every assistance to the United Nations in the execution of this resolution." The resolution passed, since the Soviet Union was boycotting the Security Council in a protest over the China-representation question. When the Russian delegation returned in August 1950 (it was the Soviet delegate's turn to serve as president of the Security Council), Gross helped shift the matters concerning Korea to the General Assembly, where the USSR could not veto UN actions and where the United States still had a workable majority of the votes. He later continued to serve as a U.S. delegate in UN attempts to arrange a Korean cease-fire and in the UN Peace Observation Commission.

Gross left the United Nations at the end of Truman's presidency in January 1953. He remained involved in foreign affairs at a U.S. delegate to the Far Eastern Commission, to the UN Peace Committee, and to the General Assembly. Among his publications is *The United Nations—Structure for Peace* (1964).

The UN Charter

The United Nations Charter represents a choice among several alternatives that were suggested by individuals both within the U.S. government and abroad. Churchill was in favor of a "supreme council" of the principal powers dividing up the responsibility for world peace, and he was not inclined toward a universal organization of the sort that emerged. Stalin favored continuing the military type of alliance after the war. Their principal objective was to keep down the Axis, the enemies during the war, so Stalin favored continuing the wartime alliance into the peace. It was really [U.S. Secretary of State] Cordell Hull who favored an organization on a universal, democratic basis, more or less in the American tradition. His views prevailed and the charter reflected a U.S. goal: the principle of universality in treating economic and social problems as a general condition that warranted universal, not selective, attention.

Stalin's whole concern was directed against a recurrence of German aggression. It appeared at once, very early, that he was not interested in the sort of peace that the United States and the Western Allies were, and I think the best evidence of his attitude is shown in the very direct and dramatic statements that President Truman particularly included in his memoirs about his reaction to Stalin's whole approach, which Truman had encountered at the Potsdam Conference. It was there that he came to conclude that the Russians were bent on world domination, as he put it.

A lot of people think that the UN Charter, which Truman supported very strongly, was based upon his misconceptions, misunderstandings, and even, some say, his illusions regarding Soviet intentions; and that Truman and other U.S. leaders were somehow fooled or tricked into accepting the UN Charter on the theory that the Russians would cooperate fully and carry it out. Just the opposite was true. My own impression, although I have not seen the fact referred to very often, is that Truman and other leaders, including Vandenberg, really felt that the UN was all the more important because they lacked confidence in the Soviet Union. I myself wrote, in a memorandum to the State Department in January 1950 [at which time the Soviets had temporarily withdrawn from UN affairs as a way of pressing for the admission of Communist China and for the expulsion of the delegation from Taiwan]:

> The [U.S.] Mission assumes that it remains basic UN policy to seek to preserve world peace through universal collective action in the United Nations. With regard to the Soviet Union, it is assumed that the United States believes that the Soviets can best be held accountable for their actions through membership in the United Nations and that the UN is the only available instrument for potentially bridging the gap between the Soviet world and the free world. It follows, then, that it is to the interest of the United States that the Soviets resume participation as early as possible; not only [so] that pursuit of these long-range U.S. objectives may be begun again within the UN, but also to avoid the prospect that other developments might result in permanent withdrawal.

So the myth—put forth by the historical revisionists—that the UN was built upon a false assumption, upon an illusion, that the Soviets would cooperate in the postwar period, is simply not historically correct. I think the revisionist view reflects a confusion over two things. It confuses the abortive provision in the UN Charter that was based upon the unanimity of views of the permanent members of the council—in other words, the veto power—with actual Western views about the Soviet Union. Obviously, the veto system could only work if, in important matters, the United States and the Soviet Union exercised restraint and saw themselves as having common interests or a common point of view. To that extent, Chapter VII of the charter, which relates to the maintenance of international peace and security, depended upon cooperation between the United States and the Soviet Union. The fact that there was obviously not that sort of cooperation, and that Chapter VII of the charter was doomed from the beginning, has sometimes confused historians or scholars into assuming that the U.S. leaders, at that time, assumed or took it for granted that the Soviets would cooperate. But the record shows that apart from that, the more the Soviets obstructed orderly development, the more important it was for others to come together in the UN. In Senate speeches by Vandenberg during the charter debates and in a lot of documents, you'll find, if you look, that it's absolute nonsense to say that because the Soviets misbehaved—and they were obviously misbehaving when the charter was being drafted—the concept of the United Nations is therefore invalid. Quite the contrary.

The great problem the charter has always presented to the Soviet Union is that basically it is incompatible with the Soviet political concept. After all, the democratic form of voting in the General Assembly, for example, is contrary to the political concept of the Soviet system, where there is no such thing as a free ballot or vote—the ideological perspective determines the whole thing. The clearest example of that was the Soviet attack on Dag Hammarskjöld, which basically reflected their dilemma with the United Nations Charter. It was natural for them to oppose an independent-minded secretary general because that wasn't their conception of what the international organization was supposed to do—that was not a quality they associated with the UN, to have more or less an independent executive with an independent international civil service. They were very frank at times and if you talked with them, they would just take it for granted that a Secretariat official would be, first and foremost, loyal to and responsive to his own national government. The concept of the international civil servant was absolutely baffling to them. I used to talk with Ambassador Malik about this very often.

The idea of having the Security Council charged with actual power to enforce the peace, with the use of military means if necessary, meant that the Security Council had to have military forces available to it. The only basis by which the United States consented to that scheme was conditioned by Article 43, which required a separate and independent agreement to be approved by the U.S. Congress, pursuant to which we would make forces available to the Security Council. The Security Council then could, by appropriate decision, really assume command and direction over those forces. But it proved to be impossible to carry out Article 43.

One problem was that we could not agree with the Russians, and indeed the Western Allies could not agree with each other, about the basis upon which these forces should be composed and made available. The French and British, for example, had different views from the United States as to whether each major, national contingent should be completely balanced within itself or whether forces should be made available from different countries according to what they could effectively contribute.

From the beginning there was a basic disagreement not only between the Allies, but also between the United States and the

Russians. The Russians were very anxious not to be caught short; in other words, they did not want the United States to contribute more of any particular unit to the Security Council than they themselves would. They wanted equal, balanced national forces. It was not geographical representation; it was more of a strategic concept. They didn't want any one country, least of all the United States, to have a stronger position strategically and take charge by having a stronger air force, etc. After all, we had an atomic monopoly in 1946 and for several years thereafter. Therefore, there was no basis upon which we were able to come together, and it became clear that the discussions had broken down.

It [Article 43] was really an overambitious experiment anyway, because I don't think in peacetime nations had ever been willing to assign forces to a central allied command. I have always doubted that, even if we and the Russians and our Allies had agreed on the nature of the forces to be made available, the U.S. Congress would have approved making U.S. forces available to a centralized command. The whole concept of the Article 43 forces, which were to be made available to the Security Council, and the idea of giving the Security Council actual military power to use force against an aggressor, fell to the ground, very early, around 1948, and so for the past 35 years, the Security Council really has lacked actual military power to enforce the peace.

Sino-Soviet Relations

There was an assumption, I suppose, during the Cold War, that the Soviet and Chinese Communist regimes were working quite closely together, but we never knew how much suspicion was growing between them.

There were well-informed people who foresaw that Communist China and the Soviet Union would fall back upon their ancient suspicions and end their friendly relations. But at that time, particularly up to and including the Korean War period, there was little reason to doubt that there was a monolithic Communist conspiracy between China and the Soviet Union, working together against the United States. I never had the slightest doubt about it in my own mind.

While that attitude continued, it was considered by most of us to be unwise to make a change of Chinese representation in the UN. We came very close to it in the Security Council. Only one vote made the difference, and that was the French. Had the French voted with the British and some other members of the Security Council at that time [1950], the Chinese Communists would have been seated. The French finally decided not to vote in favor because of Vietnam—because of their position in Indochina, where the Chinese were bearing down on them. The United States had opposed seating Communist China but we weren't going around lobbying against it. In fact, my instructions were to make it clear that we were going to vote against it, but that we were not going to lobby or press; we were going to maintain a neutral position. It fell on the French to make the decision during those years. With the Korean War, of course, admission of Red China to the UN was out of the question.

On January 13, 1950, Soviet UN Ambassador Jakob Malik walked out of the Security Council in an effort to expel the representative of Nationalist China and seat the representative of the Chinese Peoples Republic, the Communists. Not having any instruction, because we didn't anticipate that move, somebody had to say the obvious thing, which was: to ask for the floor as soon as Malik was out of the room; and to say that according to the charter, the Security Council should be always available to be called into session; and that no member had the right under the charter willfully to obstruct the work of the council by a deliberate absence from the council. That bit of wisdom prevailed and we proceeded with the next item, which was a disarmament item.

We went scurrying around, as I imagine the State Department also had instructed other missions and embassies in foreign posts, to get whatever wisdom there was and explanations or conjectures about the reason for the walkout. The long-term significance of it, the reason expressed, which we took at face value, was that the Chinese and the Soviets were in cahoots, and that for whatever reason, the Russians at that point saw fit to support the Chinese-representative cause even at the expense of not participating in the events of the Security Council from that point until their return, if ever.

The general consensus was reflected in a telegram I sent to the [State] Department on January 31. I reported to the secretary of state: "It is our view that the Soviet walkout is probably designed to embarrass the United States in its relations with Communist China and with those countries that have not recognized the new regime." And that was certainly one of the reasons for it. But then I went on to say that "consideration should be given to the possibility that the Chinese move is designed to arrange the Soviet absence from the Security Council to avoid embarrassment over any projected direct or indirect aggressive action." In other words, we thought of the possibility that it might be part of a cover plan, although this was four or five months before the Korean invasion.

We didn't think particularly of Korea as distinguished, say, from Indochina, or Taiwan, but one of the reasons for our suspicions (and I think that it was true, not only of the U.S. mission people but other embassies as well) was that the Chinese and Soviet leaders had been in secret conversations in Moscow for an unusually long period; I think it was from December 1949 to February 1950. And it seemed, therefore, that they were planning something. Then we had information about troop movement in Korea. Indeed, soon there were border incidents across the North Korean-South Korean border, and obvious troop redeployments. The Soviets began to ship large quantities of ammunition, tanks and so forth, into North Korea, which they controlled—the Soviets, not the Chinese. The UN Commission on Korea was in the Republic of Korea (i.e., the South), and they were monitoring the border. So the actual invasion did not catch us entirely by surprise. Four or five months before, we had alerted the department that this might be a cover plan for that. My own feeling later was that it *was* part of a cover plan. And it went beyond the mere interest of the Soviets in pressing for Chinese Communist representation.

That was our view. When I say our view, I mean the view of the mission, and that was our collective view, based on our political advisers' [efforts at] fanning out and talking with other delegations and with the nongovernmental organizations and with foreign missions and so forth. I was then acting head of the mission, as I was from time to time because Senator Austin—a wonderful guy—had been ill. So that was part of my duties, to take over in his absence.

The Soviet representative, Malik, announced that he was going to return to the council on August 1, when it was the Soviet [rep's] turn to be president under the rotation system—the presidency of the council was a monthly rotation. We, I mean the State Department and the U.S. Mission people, had the idea that prior to the Soviet return, the Security Council might act to put itself in a better position to deal with threats to world peace, the threat of aggression, or actual aggression. One of the ideas that we floated was getting support from our friends, including the British and French; [the idea was] for the council to adopt a resolution, which the council would have done in the Soviet absence, establishing a kind of a peace-observation commission, under the Security Council aegis, that would be authorized to act, to go into areas of threat and tension. We thought that it would be highly desirable for the Security Council to establish a peace-observation group reporting to it. We were pretty certain that the Russians would veto it, once they got back. So we considered seriously, and actually consulted with other delegations, as to how they would feel about supporting a resolution setting up a Security Council peace-observation commission. Well, they were absolutely against it. They thought that it would be regarded generally by neutrals as an underhanded trick, to act in that way, knowing the Soviets were going to come back to the Security Council. They also thought that it might induce the Russians to walk out again, to disrupt the work of the UN, maybe this time for good.

We dropped it until the Uniting-for-Peace Resolution [November 1950], later that same year in the General Assembly, when we transferred the Korean question to the General Assembly after the Russians had fouled up the Security Council process. The main purpose of the Uniting-for-Peace Resolution was to amend the rules and procedures of the General Assembly so that special emergency sessions could be called, because the original rules threw that into doubt. It wasn't any constitutional change, or charter change; the Russians insisted it was, but it really wasn't. It was basically, apart from the peace-observation-commission idea, an amendment of the rules of procedure, to simplify and expedite the work of the General Assembly so that it could be convened in a quicker time and move ahead when the Security Council, and only when the Security Council, was obstructed from performing its functions. We were all for it; the president was for it, the secretary of state was for it, because it was a very common-sense thing to do, given the experience with the obstruction of the Security Council by the Soviets.

When we received word on June 25 of the Korean invasion, we called the other members of the Security Council, and told them that we had asked for a meeting of the Security Council, and that they should get instructions between my call, say two or three in the morning early Sunday, and the time of the afternoon meeting—we were scheduled to meet at two o'clock in the afternoon. But one of the perfectly clear indications of the unanimity of concern about the

North Korean aggression was precisely in the fact that several delegations did the unusual thing of voting for this resolution without consulting with their governments and calling upon the UN members to assist in repelling the attack. They didn't want to use the word "aggression"; but they said "armed attack" against the Republic of Korea, and they felt all the more willing to do that without instructions—several of the delegations—because of the fact that there was in existence the UN Commission on Korea. That was one of the reasons why we saw such great value in the UN having eyes and ears in areas of tension or of threat.

Would the UN have been able to act without the Soviet absence from the Security Council in that period? The answer to that is yes. We didn't know, of course, whether the Soviet representative would come back for the meeting on June 25th, the Sunday meeting. In the morning, I went by the office of Secretary General Trygve Lie on the way to the Security Council, and talked with him and his general counsel, the late Abe Feller. We discussed what would happen if the Soviet representative were to come back into the council that afternoon. We decided, because it was obvious that if he did, it would be for the purpose of vetoing any resolution that was calling for action; so we decided that in that event the secretary general would convene the General Assembly and that the permanent missions in New York would attend. According to the rules at that time, which were later changed in the Uniting-for-Peace Resolution, the idea of a special emergency meeting was not foreseen, was not in the charter or in the rules of procedure of the General Assembly. But the assembly is always master of its own rules. They can always waive notice, just like any board of directors which can convene a meeting of the board without the kind of notice that the bylaws require.

We would have convened within 24 or 48 hours at the outside, I'm quite sure. The permanent representatives would have made up the majority, certainly a quorum of the General Assembly. And then we would have proceeded to do exactly what we would have done in the Security Council, exactly the same type of resolution. So that's really what we had planned, as a contingency, a fallback plan. There again, scholars don't consider that possibility. They say, by the circumstance that the Russians were absent, the UN was able to do so-and-so. But as I have said, although the Security Council was able to act only because of the Soviet boycott—since the Soviets would have vetoed the resolution—nonetheless, we were prepared to proceed in the General Assembly on short notice.

It's a question for speculation as to whether Truman would have gone into action in Korea without UN support, but certainly it would have involved an entirely different set of relationships with the Congress. Obviously, it would have involved the warmaking power—whereas the UN Charter, as ratified by the United States, allowed the president to take action pursuant to resolutions [passed by] the Security Council under the charter. From a constitutional point of view, it was quite a difference, set in motion quite a different chain of events within the workings of our system.

We didn't know, nobody knew, what the implications were with respect to the possible expansion of hostilities. NATO—the North Atlantic Treaty Organization—had been created the previous year; the Soviets had their army poised in Eastern Europe. There was considerable turmoil and unrest, and still the ravages of the war in Western Europe were not entirely healed, by any means. Therefore, to have united action was very important because of the implications with respect to the global responsibilities of the United States. That's why it was important also to have a group of nations who met regularly in Washington with the Assistant Secretary of State, Dean Rusk, later Secretary of State. They were briefed about what was going on, really were consulted about everything except perhaps the most important single thing, which was MacArthur's dash up to the Yalu River, that disastrous MacArthur operation. But apart from that, during the early part of the war, as well as in planning the defense of NATO, a lot of questions could have been confused, maybe even undermined, in terms of Allied policy if we had acted unilaterally. After all, there were also the side effects of Korea. That was the moment at which the administration gave much greater support to the French in Indochina; that was the beginning of our really serious involvement with Indochina, with all its historic consequences.

Also, there was some suspicion that the Soviet-Chinese conversations in Moscow [mentioned earlier] might well have produced a coordinated plan including not only Korea but also a Chinese Communist attack on Taiwan. Which is really why President Truman ordered the Seventh Fleet into the Formosa Straits. So to act unilaterally would have been completely out of character, and very much contrary to our broader global interests.

The UN action in Korea accomplished its purpose, which was really, in the beginning, to restore the situation that was upset by the attack. Of course, we would have preferred to see Korea unified—which the series of UN resolutions contemplated—but that was blocked early on by the Soviets, who established a strong sphere of influence in North Korea. I'm not sure the Chinese really liked that. It's purely speculation, but I think the Russians were afraid the Chinese might move into Korea, and they were a step ahead of them. Curiously enough, when MacArthur made that disastrous move and got clobbered by the Chinese [at the Yalu River], and we finally recovered our poise and moved back again, it was the Russians, not the Chinese (who were fighting there), who said it was time for negotiations for an armistice.

I think the Russians and the Chinese were terribly suspicious of each other. The Chinese Communists were obviously feeling very heady about the results of having driven Chiang Kai-shek off the mainland, and I imagine that they made it clear to the Russians—some of the information we got pointed that way—in those famous consultations in Moscow, that they were going to move onto Taiwan and maybe into Korea, that there'd no longer be a Western flag there. Japan was part now of the American sphere. So it seemed logical. There was a very curious lack of explanation on the part of the Soviet representative when he returned to the Security Council on August 1st. Several of us asked him, privately, why he had walked out and had now returned. He explained it to me in dialectical terms. He said that when it was clear to the Soviets that we were obstructing the seating of the "legitimate" representative of China, the Soviet government could no longer participate in the "illegal" Security Council. He had said that in his parting speech in January, but he repeated that when we talked. However, he said, the situation was changed because of the American "aggression" in Korea, as he called it with a straight face; it came time for the Soviets to assume the presidency of the council, to come back and restore peace.

Well, of course, it was pure baloney, but nonetheless, about as good a reason as he could give under the circumstances.

I think that there has been a toll taken by the Cold War and the U.S.-Soviet tension confrontation. There hasn't been the requisite leadership so that members of the UN bodies really feel that there is a sense of common interest and common purpose. And until you have another Truman, that probably will not work that way. You must have somebody at the top who has a conception of the potential values of international cooperation—not only that it is valuable, but that there is no substitute for it, no alternative but chaos. But there is a phenomenon which is very, very damaging to the UN and to our foreign policy generally: Each time a new administration comes in, or almost every time a new UN representative is appointed, there doesn't seem to be a sense of history or continuity. Each time, we start from square one, without knowing that whatever has gone before has been a disaster, or has been ineffectual, and so forth. It is very sad that there has been such a complete lack of perspective, of continuity, and a sense of history. That's what I find the most damaging aspect of the puny U.S. efforts to use the UN facilities and the cooperative processes—which are just a reflection of the fact that we don't really consult with anybody, that we still operate in a way which makes consultations with others difficult.

I think the last secretary of state who really had a strong feeling and background in the UN was Dean Rusk, and he was one of the few. Of course, Dean Acheson himself never had a very high interest in or regard for the UN. This is reflected in his memoirs, so I won't go into that. That was really too bad, but nonetheless, he gave it support, although when I told him that I'd like to come up to the UN, he rather thought that I was a little bit silly.

FRANCIS O. WILCOX: Adviser to Congress at the San Francisco Conference, 1945; Assistant Secretary of State for International-Organization Affairs, 1955–61.

> *I don't see any great harm in getting voted down from time to time. We don't have to win every vote in the United Nations if we stand up for what is right. . . . Of course, some people have felt that if we get voted down too much, maybe we ought to reexamine some of our policies.*

Francis Orlando Wilcox began his professional life in the fields of education and government, before becoming active in foreign affairs during the mid-1940s. He was a delegate to the San Francisco Conference of 1945, as well as to the First General Assembly (London, 1946), the Third (Paris, 1948), and the Fifteenth (New York, 1960). Between 1947 and 1955, he served as chief of staff of the U.S. Senate Foreign Relations Committee; and from 1955 to 1961, he was assistant secretary of state for international-organization affairs. A delegate to the World Health Assembly in 1956 and 1958, and to the ILO in 1957 and 1958, Wilcox has been a member of the President's Commission on the United Nations since 1971.

In addition to UN-related posts, Wilcox has been active in academic affairs, serving as dean of the Johns Hopkins School of Advanced International Studies from 1961 to 1973. He has been director general of the Atlantic Council of the United States since 1975.

The Bureau of International Organization Affairs [IO], my bureau, is the part of the State Department responsible for the transmission of instructions to the UN Mission and for collaborating, both with the other bureaus in the State Department and with the other departments in the government, to develop our policies. Labor, Agriculture, Commerce, and other departments are concerned in international affairs insofar as they are handled in the United Nations. Some 55 government agencies are interested in international affairs, not all of them involving UN relations. Also, the bureau is responsible for coordinating the relations with 15 specialized agencies, like the World Health Organization, the ILO, UNESCO, and the FAO.

If the UN Mission by itself attempted to formulate policy, without relating it to the totality of American policy, you'd have absolute chaos. And if the State Department attempted to formulate policy without consulting the UN Mission, that would be a mistake, too. So there must be close cooperation between the two. IO does that by pulling together all of the information that we get, including that from the mission in New York. We're in constant touch with the other agencies here in the government. Then, we also take the lead in the State Department in securing from the other bureaus the kind of support we need for resolutions and actions in the UN. If we're involved in a serious issue in the UN and we need votes, we send telegrams and messages, and we rely a bit on arm-twisting by our ambassadors and others in foreign countries, who win the support we need to achieve our objectives in the United Nations.

That is the role of the bureau. Now the mission chief, of course, is a member of the cabinet and does have access to the president, and so has a kind of special role. The assistant secretary of state ought to be on very close, friendly terms with the chief of the mission and the others in the UN, our representatives in New York. Our bureau members, the professional-staff members, have constant working relationships with those people. When I went to the State Department in 1955, I was told that Ambassador Lodge was rather a difficult person to work with because he was close to President Eisenhower and was a member of the cabinet. He therefore felt that he had complete access to the president, and it was assumed that I might have some difficulty with him. I didn't find that the case. He had been a member of the Senate Foreign Relations Committee, and I had worked closely with him there and was a good friend of his. He was cooperative. Lodge told me once he had a "pan-of-popcorn" mind: He said he wanted people around him who could put him on the right track if he tried to jump to the quick conclusion that wasn't too sound. He spoke well. He had a commanding presence. He had a remarkably good personality. He had a little bit of the reserve of a New Englander—just a little of that, but not enough to hurt him. He handled his relations very well with other delegates. Of course, he freely and vigorously asserted his point of view, which we wanted. But I never had any difficulty with Ambassador Lodge. He told me on one occasion, "I'm a good soldier. All you have to do is tell me what to do and I'll do it." He was very cooperative.

A typical day at the State Department in my bureau, the International Organization Bureau, during the time that the Assembly was in session [three months out of the year] or when the Security Council was meeting on important issues, would normally begin with a staff meeting at 8:30, to go over the cables that had come in from New York and from various posts around the world about United Nations affairs. When Mr. Dulles was secretary, I would go to [the office of] the secretary of staff meetings, where the assistant secretary and the under secretary met each morning at nine o'clock, to report on any important development of interest to the other members. We would take a look at all the cables that came in from the mission, get in touch with them by telephone, and be constantly in touch with the mission in New York by telephone as they reported on what was happening to different resolutions relating to the budget or to arms control or whatever; we would suggest to them ways of winning support. We would meet with each other in the State Department and would bring in people from HEW and Labor and other parts of the government.

It was perfectly clear to me that the mission in New York was not in a position to make decisions about our foreign policy. In New York there is a tendency for people to become a little, shall I say, inclined to go along with the crowd. They want to be cooperative, they don't want to be looked upon as obstacles to progress toward successful resolutions. They tend to respond to pressures up there, and it is in the interest of our government that we give them the kind of instructions that would be in the national interest of the United States and not necessarily in the interest of the mission in New York.

The State Department is set up in such a way that IO sends instructions to the mission and the mission follows instructions. You can't have it any other way, and if there is a rebuttal or rejoinder, or a comment or an addition, or an amendment, it is up to the mission to come back and say, "Look, we think this speech is not toned properly to the situation here and we would like to put in a few paragraphs on Soviet relations," or whatever.

Ambassador Kirkpatrick, I know, has complained that the relationship between the mission and the IO is clumsy, structured for disaster. Well, she has said things up there that I think are rather disastrous, too. As a matter of fact, I don't think an ambassador ought to go to a post and then downgrade it by talking it down. Jeane Kirkpatrick is very bright, but I think some of the things she has said have not been in good taste for the ambassador of the United States. It may be that she feels she has close relations with Ronald Reagan and should report to him and so on, but you can't have the mission running off on its own, or you get into real trouble.

Maybe the department is a little conservative on some things, but that's where the nerve center is, and if it isn't reflected in New York, the government will speak with more than one voice, which it so often does. That doesn't mean she should demean herself, take orders from the mission, from the State Department. I think the assistant secretary should be the kind of person that she can work with, and if they don't get along, maybe a change should be made there or here. The way to achieve harmony is to invite people from the mission down to the State Department, from time to time, for briefings and exchanges of views, so that they know what the department's position is and give their views, too.

My own job as assistant secretary of state was to administer the bureau concerned with organizing and sending instructions to conferences. I think it's 800 or 900 conferences now that we have taken part in, and our job was to make sure that the delegations were properly equipped and organized. We had to make sure that their instructions were adequate and proper and that we had on board enough experts in different fields, either by meetings or telephone conversations or whatever, to formulate the policy decisions for our missions attached to any international conference where we were participating. Our most important cables would be signed by the secretary of state; sometimes we would even consult with the president. At certain times, therefore, we were very busy, with conferences going on all the time—either getting ready for, say, the General Assembly, or following up on the results of the General Assembly, or taking care of other conferences in which we were participating at a given moment, such as [those of] the ILO or the World Health Organization. I went on a mission of three weeks to Africa as the first fairly high-level representative in the Eisenhower administration to make a trip to Africa, to explore the evolving situation there, because so many states were getting their independence in 1960, and we wanted to analyze the impact of this movement on our foreign policy.

The Suez Crisis (1956)

The Suez Conflict was a major crisis. Our allies were involved, and we did not want to let them down, but when Israel and then Britain and France, without our knowledge or consultation, invaded the Suez area, President Eisenhower felt that he had only one thing to do, and that was to side with those who were condemning the action and asking for the withdrawal of the troops. Of course, he's been criticized for that by some, but I think in the long run that history will suggest he was right. I remember the day we took the final decision. Our bureau was considering it, and also the Bureau of Middle Eastern Affairs, [under] William Roundtree, was considering it. I started down to see the secretary of state about it and I met Roundtree at the secretary's door. He and I had the same answer, the same point of view, which was shared by others in the department. The Bureau of European Affairs had some reservations because of their ties with the British and the French. But I think, in general, it was agreed in the State Department that this was the proper course of action.

I remember, too, someone said to President Eisenhower [that] we should be very careful because this was right around election time, and he would not want to offend those in this country who might object to our criticizing the British and French and especially the Israelis. But Mr. Eisenhower said that he was going to do what he thought was right, and that the election would take second place in his thinking—which I thought was a courageous thing to do.

It was, of course, an important issue. I remember when Mr. Dulles went to New York [to address the UN]. On the plane we drafted the resolution [calling for a cease-fire] in consultation with Herman Pflagar, who was then legal adviser. Mr. Dulles made a speech that night in which he said his heart was very heavy because our closest allies were involved. He hesitated to do what we were about to do, but he felt that it was in the interest of the UN and world peace and the fundamental principles of international law to take this stand.

The Suez crisis and later the Lebanese (1958) and the Congolese (1960) crises were the first times we had gotten closely involved in the creation of a multilateral force. We had to do a good deal of work with Dag Hammarskjöld and with the UN staff, developing a concept of a United Nations force: determining what countries ought to be participating in it; how big it should be; where it should be located; what proportion of troops should come from one rather than the other country; how they should be equipped; who would take care of the transportation; other logistics; who would provide the equipment that they needed and the air transport; and so forth.

These are the kinds of things that we got into in our bureau, through the Defense Department and with the mission in New York, and with the other interested parties in the State Department and the government.

Between 1955 and 1961, when Hammarskjöld died in an airplane crash, there was a good deal of feeling in the department that we had a staunch individual up there who would stand for what was right, and to whom we could turn to get out of difficult situations. So there was a greater tendency to have confidence in the United Nations. Nothing succeeds like success, you know.

The Soviets, however, were against him, and Khrushchev made his speech proposing a trilateral arrangement, a triumvirate for the top post. Eventually, the Soviets crossed Hammarskjöld off their list. They didn't invite him to their receptions and things of that sort. That was in the late fifties. He had probably outlived his usefulness in the UN by that time. I think the secretary general really must command the confidence, up to a point anyway, of the superpowers, and if he doesn't, it's obviously going to be very difficult for him. Now, given the distance between the United States and the Soviet Union, this is not easy, and the secretary general has to be very diplomatic, certainly, so that he can't be accused by one or the other of failing to discharge his duties. The Soviet Union felt he was going beyond his constitutional responsibilities. We did not think so, but I doubt if another secretary general can go as far as he did in interpreting his role and powers under the UN Charter. Dag Hammarskjöld's successors have been curbed in their enthusiasm somewhat because of the realization that they have to, if not please both powers, at least not displease them too much.

Multilateral Diplomacy

In bilateral diplomacy you're negotiating only with one person, but when you have 158 people to convince, or at least a majority of them to try to convince, it's a much, much more difficult job. You've got to think of the blocs of states in the UN, the leaders— whom can you turn to? Who are the individuals in the assembly that carry influence and weight, that you can count on to help you when the chips are down? I remember Hans Angen from Norway, who was their representative in the United Nations. He had a good deal of influence because of his ability and because of the fact that, being from a small country, he had to analyze the voting situation there in each case—which countries would take leadership in delivering what kind of votes to which party—and this meant a pretty careful analysis of the voting situation and the personalities there, and how they might be influenced to do the right thing at the right time. One of the problems we found was that many of the delegates had been appointed as a political favor. Maybe there was a son-in-law of the president of the country from which he came, or a cousin of the prime minister, or something—[a person] not necessarily with any real capacity to conceive of legislative maneuvering or action. It makes an awful lot of difference whether a person is good at this. Some were quite good; so what you had to do was to find out where the leadership lay and then tap it if you could, and get the Brazilians to help you, or the Norwegians to help you, or the Indians or whoever. This was one of the problems that we had in the field of multilateral diplomacy in convincing the [State] Department that the leadership up there was good, strong, sound, and dependable. And then we had to make the proper effort to get the support we needed.

Choosing the Best Delegates

I don't think we've sent our strongest delegations to the UN. The Soviet Union brings ambassadors from France, Germany, Britain, and other countries, or people high in the Foreign Office, to the United Nations as members of their delegation. These people are experienced in foreign policy. They have a very good grasp of the issues that are involved from the Soviet point of view. We haven't done that. We have determined, rather, that we would like to have leading citizens like Mrs. Roosevelt or Henry Ford or Marian Anderson go to the UN General Assembly and take part in it, profit from the experience, and then go back home and be helpful.

I remember when Mrs. Roosevelt went to London to attend the first meeting of the assembly in 1946. Senator Vandenberg, who was not particularly enthusiastic about Democrats anyway, had reservations about Mrs. Roosevelt because he thought she shouldn't go to the UN just because she had been President Roosevelt's wife. When she got there she demonstrated an ability to get along with people and to establish good working relations. One day at a meeting of the delegation in the morning, Mr. Dulles, then secretary of state, said, "Ladies and Gentlemen, if you don't mind I am going to wait just a few minutes; Mrs. Roosevelt is going to be about five minutes late and I want her here when we start the meeting." So we waited. Vandenberg spoke up and said, "Mr. Chairman, I would like to say something about Mrs. Roosevelt: She is a remarkable delegate, she's done an excellent job, she has gotten on good terms with so many delegates here from so many countries, and she has just handled her role so beautifully—I want to say that I take back everything I ever said about that lady, and, believe you me, it has been plenty." He was honest about it and generous enough to admit in public he was wrong.

I worked with Mrs. Roosevelt. I remember she invited me to tea in her stateroom, on the way over on the *Queen Elizabeth*, and we had a good talk about the assembly and about the problems that we faced there. She was a remarkable person. I have tremendous admiration for her.

Some delegates didn't take their responsibilities very seriously and didn't participate actively in the work of the delegation. Some, like Irene Dunne, the actress, were effective. Whenever she spoke, the other delegates listened with great attention even though she spoke on the trusteeship problem, which she didn't know very much about. They sat on the edge of their chairs, you know. So there's some advantage in having people like that, at least well-known personalities; but I don't favor giving the assignment to people just for political reasons. We ought to have a stronger delegation and it ought to be primarily a professional delegation.

Lodge complained that he had to brief the nonprofessionals and bring them all up to date on what was happening, what the UN system was like, and what they needed to do. Each year he would have to take a new group and give them a kind of indoctrination and briefing, which they needed to be effective. This need not be done if you have well-qualified people—professionals—top people who have had experience in the field of diplomacy.

The permanent representative should be someone of considerable personal stature. It's still an important assignment, and I think when you have people like Adlai Stevenson and Henry Cabot Lodge representing us there, we can do a better job, we will be more respected; we can be more effective than if we have someone who isn't known, or who is not a national figure; and certainly you don't want someone who is hypercritical of the United Nations system. I think the person who handles the job ought to be reasonably convinced that the job is worth doing, and that he or she can play an effective role on behalf of the United States. The morale in the mission is important; the leadership there can be detrimental or helpful in carrying out the mission's goal or objectives. Therefore I like to think of a fairly strong individual with good ties to the president, the secretary of state, and the State Department, preferably someone who's had some experience in the field of diplomacy.

One of the things that I'm constantly intrigued by is how the issues persist over time. When I meet a colleague from the State Department—a younger member—I'll say, "What are you working on now?" "Well, I'm working on this problem." And I would say to myself, and to him, "My golly, you mean you're still working on that problem? We worked on that 30 years ago. You haven't made any progress?" But we shouldn't expect too much in the way of change in the world situation: Don't expect to deal with the problem satisfactorily and constructively every time; don't expect to settle these problems, because they're like the health problem in the United States, or the housing problem, or the education problem— they're with us for a long time. You work on them and ameliorate the situation, and you help move things along maybe a little bit. In the assembly in the United Nations, we had what we called the hardy perennials; they were on the agenda every single year.

When Dean Rusk was made secretary of state, I went into his office one day after I had left the department. He was sitting there with a big yellow pad and was writing. I asked him what he was doing and he said, "Well I am just fixing up a list of problems, problem areas, bilateral disputes, for the most part, where we have no direct interest, but in which we are involved because one of the parties or the other or both want us to get on their side." And he said, "You can just look at the list and you can see the differences between Greece and Turkey [over Cyprus] or Italy and Austria [over South Tyrol], or whatever. We have no particular interests there, but it's the penalty we pay as a great power—they want our support." As assistant [secretary], one of the toughest problems I had to face, looking at all of these issues, was trying to determine what we could do to resolve them or to help move them along toward a solution. And that's true of the United Nations: They all want our support and they're disappointed if we aren't willing to help. It's the penalty we pay for being a great power. We can't duck our responsibility, we can't withdraw from the world; we have to live in it.

PHILIP KLUTZNICK: Representative on the Economic and Social Council, 1961–62; and Delegate to the General Assembly, 1957.

Diplomacy is something that isn't self-executing. It's like prayer. You can pray all you damn please, but unless you go and do something about it, it's not going to get you anywhere. Diplomacy is that way.

A lawyer by training, Philip M. Klutznick was appointed by President Eisenhower as a member of the U.S. delegation to the General Assembly in 1957. From 1961 to 1963, he was U.S. representative, with the rank of ambassador, to the Economic and Social Council. Over the next two decades, Klutznick remained active in Jewish and international affairs. He has been president (now emeritus) of the World Jewish Congress since 1977, and served in the Carter administration as secretary of commerce (1980-81).

I have a conviction that every state does what it thinks is best for itself. It's the old rule that Gladstone recognized: Nations don't have permanent friends or permanent enemies, they have only permanent interests. So there is no nation, large or small, and particularly the small, that has anything to gain by the destruction of the United Nations. What pains me is that they do so much to make it less useful. I don't think anybody wants to kill it except people that have never been inside of it.

In 1957, my first year at the UN, it was a smaller place than it is today. It was not only smaller, but there were unwritten rules that seemed to prevail that I think were better. For example, we managed to maintain a Western majority in those days. I'm amused when people tell me today, "Well, look at the Third World; it's riding roughshod over everybody." We did pretty well in those days when we had an issue and we wanted it handled. We exercised a measure of restraint in using the majority of that day. There was a deep interest in preserving the institution as much as there was in winning the vote. At times, I think we almost deliberately permitted ourselves to lose rather than to press the issue too far. That was a period when we prided ourselves on not using the veto.

There was a sense that we were going somewhere and we were going together. Everybody was trying to make the United Nations live up to what it never could live up to, which was the dream that everybody had. I guess we were idealistic enough to think that in a diverse world we could make an instrument like this work when, after all, it had limited power.

There were those who felt—I guess I was one of them and still am to a degree—that having experienced the horrors of World War II, it was not too big a price to pay to have a little modesty in what we sought to make this organization do. It was a more compatible atmosphere in many ways than emerged later on.

Personalities

Ambassador Lodge, the permanent rep during my first period at the UN [1957], had great rapport with Washington, which was important. He was enough of a pro so that you were never quite sure whether he agreed with some of the things he was compelled to handle. You always had a feeling that he loved what he was doing and was doing it because he loved it. In that sense, for the outsider coming in, he was a good person. You didn't lose confidence in what you were doing. Lodge was a good host. He worked very hard at his job but if he was going to work in the evening, he would take a little time off. I guess the permanent representative is entitled to do it because it is a seven-day-a-week job with no hours. I had worked with him on the outside when he and I used to have a few differences, but on the inside he was very reasonable.

During my second period at the UN [1961–62], our permanent rep was, of course, Adlai Stevenson. One April session, I had a niece and nephew who sat in the audience at the UN while on vacation. They wanted to meet the governor. (Everybody wanted to meet Stevenson.) I said, "Adlai, before you leave, I want you to say hello to my niece and nephew. They had dinner with me tonight and they sat here all the way through this." So he asked me, "Where are they going to stay?" I said, "They're staying at our apartment. Where do you think they'll stay?" He said, "They are not going to stay at your apartment. You've only got one extra bedroom. They're going to stay at the embassy." And he took them to his place. He was a very warm person. Aloof to some that he didn't trust, but if he was a friend, he was your friend.

For example, he had his problems with the president. I'll never forget the first delegation that was selected. The president invited them all to Washington. That included the five ambassadors from outside, too. We walked into the president's office. Adlai was there; Dean Rusk was there. You would have thought that the president was working for Adlai. He took over right away. As far as Dean Rusk was concerned, he didn't get a chance to say a word. They had a certain strain between them, maybe because that was the post that Adlai had always wanted. He wanted to be the secretary of state—it was his great ambition.

After we were sworn in (this was the first delegation), we had problems in Latin America. We weren't getting along as we should. Stevenson had gone to Latin America before with Bill Benton and made a lot of friends there. So the president wanted him to go there. He [Stevenson] was reluctant. He said, "They messed this thing up in the State Department; I'm not going to go down there and help them pick up their pants—that's their business."

I got a call and I went down. I came back and I said, "You know, I think you should go. After all, they haven't got anybody else." They didn't have anybody that had the prestige that he had. Well, he went. When they heard that he was going, I could have made a fortune just selling tickets for him. Really. The Latin Americans got reports of his trip and they wanted to have a special affair for him. Everybody wanted an appointment with him. They lionized him and they idolized him.

He was a great draftsman. We started a custom that year that they followed ever since; that the permanent representative, instead of the representative of the Economic and Social Council, would make the economic speech for the United States. I pleaded with him to do it. I said, "Look, you're always making speeches on political issues. It's time to show that the United States is interested in this." He said, "You make it." I said, "I don't want to make it. I'll have many opportunities to make speeches there. You've got to come over and do this to show that the administration cares that much about economic and social matters." So when he came in I had one of the best fellows working on that speech, and I said, "Adlai, it's not your style." He said, "What's my schedule?" I said, "We don't need you until tomorrow." He said, "Give it to me. I'll go home and work on it." He went to the hotel and he worked on it. The next day he came back and he said, "What do you think of this?" It sang. It was the same but it sang. He was a big hit. He had the capacity to make words say what he wanted them to say in a way that people like to hear, which is a talent, of course. We used it where we could.

Adlai never had any problem, when he had a difference with Dean Rusk, of taking it to Jack Kennedy or to Lyndon Johnson. He didn't try to hide his feelings. I remember when he said to me, before he went to London (where he died), that he couldn't stand the Vietnam War anymore and he was going to quit. I said, "I don't think you are." He said, "Why not? You quit." I said, "Because if you quit you've got to go out to the people. That's your job and you won't do that. You're a former candidate for president. I agree with you that the Vietnamese policy was wrong. I could quit because I didn't run for president. I'm not a party leader. But you can't quit on that ground without running a campaign against the president. And you're not going to do that because you're not cut out that way." And he never did.

Adlai was a man of international stature, primarily because he had run for president twice. But he was a gifted man in many ways. There's nothing worse than having a man of stature who has no gifts to back it up. It's easy enough to get stature. His strength became greater as he went along. This was the period of the great opening up of the African continent. These people loved to be with him. And he would spend time with them.

Decade of Development

In the 1960s we did a lot in the Third World issues. After all, it was Kennedy [who] in 1961, in 25 words, I think it was, announced our support of the United Nations Development Decade, the first one. It took me an hour and ten minutes to explain it to the Second Committee.

First, President Kennedy had the kind of grace that people accepted what he said as being honorable. Then they started thinking about it. By this time, in 1961, we had over 100 countries. They were thinking, What is he really going to do? And it became quite an extended negotiation and debate. In this connection, I argued that the big problem with the United Nations Development Decade was that it was too specific in concept and too general in commitment.

At that time, we had food surpluses and George McGovern was our Food-for-Peace administrator. I had several talks with him. I also argued with the White House that the thing to do was to commit $1 billion worth of food to the developing world. Make it $1 billion. It is very dramatic. Well, McBundy and everybody else said that's too specific. So we came up with a formula based upon a commitment to reach a goal of 1 percent of our gross national product. No one has really reached it since.

Fiscal Problems

The UN in those days had never—and it has not to this day— matured to the point where it handled its fiscal matters properly. How can it, really? When you've got a board of directors of 158 people and the variety that you've got there, you're lucky that they even come to the meeting, let alone discuss anything where they get something resolved.

The UN is also a place where sometimes things get done in a hurry, and people don't know why they did them. When the Congo civil war started, the United States and the Western powers felt that there ought to be a special fund set up to help save the Congo from the ravages of inflation. When we came in, that fund, which was to have $100 million, had all of $19 million in it. I think at that time we had put in about $11 [million] or $12 million of the $19 million. So when I had to go to Geneva for ECOSOC, I said, "I'd better go over and take a look and see what's going on over there." I went to the Congo and spent about a week there trying to understand what was happening. There just wasn't any inflation. I said in my report that the reason was very simple: The Africans had gone back to the bush to stay with their relatives. When things were rough they didn't inflate, they went back to the bush and ate with their family. As a result, the whole $100 million fund was forgotten; it really wasn't needed.

That's one of the problems you have when you have 156 or 158 nations trying to know what things are like. Operating in New York is better than operating in Washington, because at least you get a microcosm of what is the world. In Washington the officials talk mostly to each other. In New York you begin to understand part of their problems at least—which is the great importance of the UN. You may not like what you understand but you get to understand it.

When it was clear that we could never get another resolution passed [to fund peacekeeping in the Congo], U Thant had by that time become the secretary general. I went to see him about how he viewed this. What were we going to do now? We had been playing around with the idea that the United Nations, since it couldn't get cash contributions, should sell bonds to its members to help finance [our] action [in the Congo]. There was an argument in Washington over it and the governor [Stevenson] and I went down. We met with the secretary of the treasury and we met with the secretary of state. We finally got the O.K. of the president and the Bureau of the Budget to suggest the idea of a bond issue. The governor and I discussed it with U Thant. So he said, "Well, if there's no other way to do it, why not? Have you talked to Gene Black about it?" (He was then the president of the World Bank.) I said, "Yes; he thinks it's perfectly valid, too." "When are you going to present it?" I said, "When the governor comes back, tomorrow. I've discussed it with him and he wanted to present it to you personally, but since we're fighting a tough time schedule, let me give you the message he's going to give you: that is that we are not going to present it. You are going to present it." He said, "You don't want me to do that." I said, "Yes, that's the only way it'll pass. We don't have that much credibility and you're on your honeymoon. It's a logical moment." "Well," he said, "let me talk it over with my advisers." We had a struggle with the Congress afterward to buy the bonds. We had to put in a provision that the United States could not buy more than one-half of the bonds. It would be $150 million. After that I went around the world selling them. I went to Tokyo for the ECAFE [Economic Commission for Asia and the Far East] meeting and then all the way around into one office after another, selling these bonds. It was tough. I met Nehru at that time and I got very little from him. They were so tight, they didn't have it. I did a little better with the Shah of Iran because we had a good ambassador there. But everywhere I went, it was difficult. Tokyo was tough. But I was a salesman for about four to five weeks. We sold enough so that we kept the [UN] door open. This was in '62.

The U.S. Role

We have a movement in this country that keeps talking now about how maybe we ought to withdraw our support of the UN. Well, part of it is a kind of an inferiority complex, because we're losing too many votes. Maybe if we would change our policies, we'd gain a few more votes. I think we are shooting ourselves in our own foot in the whole East-West, North-South contest. If you look about you, there is no way in the world that there can be economic strength in the big countries, the superpowers, if the rest of the world lives below a decent standard.

The UN has done a great deal in its specialized agencies and in its affiliated programs. What would we do without the World Bank today? Or the International Monetary Fund? The only way we can save Poland today is if it finally gets into the International Monetary Fund. These are instruments that tend to bolster the weaknesses of the world. Attacking the instrument because the world is lousy is not the way to do it. You've got to recognize what the realities of the world are and use the instrument to, in some way, solve or ameliorate the situation. I have very little sympathy for those who say we're always right and everybody else is always wrong.

SEYMOUR MAXWELL FINGER: Senior Adviser on Economic and Social Affairs, 1956–64; Ambassador and Senior Adviser to the Permanent Representative, 1967–71.

A great deal of subtlety is required in dealing with governments around the spectrum. We should be willing to accept pluralism in the world, and have constructive relations with governments of various economic and social systems, including socialist. In the long run, we have all the aces in dealing with the new countries, because what they need for development are technology, capital, and markets. And it's the West, and especially the United States, that has all those things. The Soviets have relatively little to offer in these critical areas. Consequently, I believe that, with a little patience, we'll come out all right.

Seymour Maxwell Finger was appointed ambassador and senior adviser to the permanent U.S. representative to the United Nations, by President Johnson, on January 27, 1967. Finger had joined the Foreign Service of the United States in 1946. His first appointment, as vice consul in Stuttgart, was followed by assignments in Paris and Budapest. The State Department detailed him to Harvard University for graduate study in economics in 1953-54. Subsequently, he served in Rome and in Vientiane, Laos.

Finger was appointed senior adviser on economic and social affairs in September 1956 and has been a member of the U.S. delegation to the eleventh through the twenty-fifth General Assemblies. He was one of the initiators of the UN Special Fund (now the UN Development Program) and of the UN Institute for Training and Research. In 1966 he was appointed counsellor, with the rank of minister. From 1967 to 1971, he served as ambassador and as the Senior adviser to the permanent representative. Now professor of political science in the City University of New York and director of its Bunche Institute on the United Nations, he is the author of numerous books and articles, including *Your Man at the UN: People, Politics and Bureaucracy in the Making of American Foreign Policy* (New York: NYU Press, 1980).

I spent my first seven and a half years in the UN on economic and social issues, and probably those were the most rewarding, because I could look back on concrete achievements. I developed plans for the UN Special Fund and the World Food Program, and I got the UN Development Decade proposal through the General Assembly unanimously. These were concrete things (often on political issues you spend your time making the obnoxious into the meaningless—you water down resolutions). But then when I became minister-counselor and later ambassador, I had a much wider mandate and dealt for the last seven years or so mainly with political issues, although I still oversaw the economic operation and was involved in budgetary and administrative issues. [In periods] between ECOSOC representatives, I pinch-hit and served as our ECOSOC representative.

There is a big difference between the U.S. Mission then and now. By around 1965, Dick Pedersen had had about 16 years of experience, Al Bender 17. Dick was running political and security operations; Al, financial, budget, and administration. I by that time had about ten years' experience and wound up with 15 years, and I was running economic and social issues. The three of us, as senior advisers, really knew everything that was happening at the UN. This kind of experience is gone now. At the upper level, you just don't have that continuity. Andy Young did some of the damage, and Jeane Kirkpatrick has done the rest. There just is not much continuity. The mitigating factor for Andy Young was that at the top level, he did have experienced people.

My attitude toward the UN has changed somewhat as the UN and its political complexion have changed. In the late 1950s, and in fact all the way through the mid-1960s, I thought the General Assembly was a very useful vehicle for American foreign policy, and it was used as such. Sometimes we used our ability to control the majority to score Cold War points against the Soviets, just as I think the Third World countries are now abusing their majority to hit specific targets like South Africa, Israel, Chile. No one can prevent a majority from acting foolishly if they want to.

So I believe that discussion and exchanges of views in the assembly can be very productive. And often the most productive ones don't even end in a resolution but result in changes of attitude. They're carried on in the committee, usually. In fact, the most significant discussions are carried on informally in back rooms, in lunches, and things like that. I've rarely seen a speech that changed votes. Votes are changed usually on a one-to-one basis, [by] talking over issues in the lounge, in places like that. That's why I think it's important for our delegation to have a lot of contact with other people and use what Dean Rusk called "the persuasive ear"—to do a lot of listening. We're not doing that very well now. Jeane Kirkpatrick is a very busy woman, and she spends a lot of time in Washington, so there is a tendency on her part to make a statement and then leave

Charles Lichtenstein in the Security Council, and somebody else in the assembly, to listen. This does not go over well with other delegations. They feel their opinions are of some importance. And I think the United States, since it's not part of any geographic bloc, has to make a special effort to have people floating around the delegates' lounge and the assembly, just listening to what other people have to say, as well as selling whatever U.S. line is to be sold at the time.

I also feel that we ought to be talking to the Soviets at all times, through good times and bad, because communications are important and we are the only two countries who could blow up the whole world. I used to have lunch once a month with my Soviet counterpart, year in, year out, no matter what was happening, because even in the worst of times we had areas of mutual agreement. The easiest one was to keep the [UN] budget down. But there were other areas. The Soviets are somewhat paranoid in their view of outside countries, and they are no more anxious to have the General Assembly make decisions on matters important to the Soviet Union than Mr. Reagan is with respect to the United States. When it looks like a Third World majority might be overstepping the bounds on certain issues, there are places we can cooperate. I remember once in Geneva, in the early 1960s, my Soviet counterpart rushing over because there was a resolution asking that 10 percent of all military budgets be devoted to economic aid. The Soviets didn't like that, of course, and he wanted to know how we could work together. So I think it's important to keep communications open.

I had an interview with Jeane Kirkpatrick in April [1983] and we talked about the deterioration of the Security Council and [about] Secretary General Perez de Cuellar's efforts to get the members together in order to work out ways to have it function more effectively. She said consultations were going on, and [that] she had talked to the British about it. And I asked, "Have you talked to the Soviets?" And obviously this had never occurred to her. I said: "The Soviets also have an interest in making the Security Council work. They may be on opposite sides from us on most issues that come before the council, but they don't want it to become so ineffective that the whole issue of security is taken over by the assembly, because they don't really trust the assembly, either." But the thing that struck me was that she apparently had not talked to [Soviet Ambassador] Troyanovsky. When you say the Russians will lie, they'll cheat, they'll do anything, this sets an ideological tone which does not encourage other people in the administration to have contact with the Soviets. You don't have to love them, you don't even have to trust them to have contact, but contact is important.

Kirkpatrick does not defend the United Nations, and she's constantly critical of it. This, I think, does great damage to the image of the UN. Of course, she doesn't deserve all the credit for that. The GA majority, when it acts foolishly, feeds that same thing. Kirkpatrick is one of a number of people who have taken the position that the UN is more of an obstruction to peace than a help, and that it tends to exacerbate conflicts, instead of helping to resolve them. Kirkpatrick makes three main points in this regard. Her first is that UN debates and resolutions are intensely ideological, leaving little room for compromise and negotiation. There is a lot of truth to this, I think, but [it is] not the whole truth. UN resolutions are only a small part, and usually the least important part, of what happens at the UN. Often, behind the resolution, behind the debate, negotiations take place which help to resolve conflict. Sometimes, too, fiery statements at the UN by Third World countries are a substitute for redeeming their pride by going to war when they know going to war would be disastrous. So I don't think the fact that these debates are rhetorical and ideological is necessarily an obstacle to peace, because there's so much that happens around them that can be helpful.

The second point Kirkpatrick makes is that participation in disputes is globalized, bringing nations with no real interest in the problem to involvement through the voting and debating process. This allegedly complicates the process of negotiating settlements to disputes. I think that, again, there's a great deal of truth in it. More countries do make statements and vote on resolutions than would do so if the matter were not brought to the assembly. But I don't think this complicates the process of negotiating settlements if the parties to the dispute are ready to negotiate. None of the discussion at the UN stopped Camp David, because the parties wanted to get into negotiation. One might then say the UN is irrelevant. That brings up another point. It would be a mistake to feel that everything must be done at the UN. But I think it's equally wrong to think that nothing should be done at the UN. And some of the best action takes place because of both. I remember that when Henry Kissinger negotiated the disengagement agreement between Egypt and Israel, people said, "Well, doesn't that make the UN irrelevant?" Of course it didn't. There was a certain complementarity. Without UNEF II [UN Emergency Force II, put into the Middle East after the 1973 Yom Kippur War], Henry Kissinger would not have been able to negotiate the disengagement agreement; and without the disengagement agreement, Camp David and peace between Israel and Egypt would have been impossible.

We in the United States have to have a pluralistic approach to problems. You can't just dump a problem in the UN and think, okay, let the UN come up with the answer. But there are times when discussion in the UN is useful. There are times when it's better to work outside the UN, and there are times, as in the Cyprus case, for example, where you want to use both.

Kirkpatrick's third point is that bringing an issue to the United Nations is likely to be regarded as a hostile act. I suppose that is true, if there are two parties to a dispute and one of them brings the case to the UN Security Council. Obviously, the other feels that it's hostile, but this does not necessarily mean that a peaceful solution is excluded, as in the case of the *Pueblo* in Korea, where we didn't bring the issue to the Security Council to please North Korea. And still a peaceful solution eventually emerged.

Leroy Bennett, in his book *International Organizations*, does a rundown on the disputes that have been brought to the United Nations and how many of them remain unresolved. He calculates that out of 150 major disputes brought to the UN, all but a dozen have been resolved, not all of them by UN processes. The charter does provide for negotiation between the parties. That's what I meant: that you don't expect all of it to happen at the UN.

I'm convinced that on balance, the UN is a useful instrument for peace. I'm also convinced that it loses credibility and effectiveness if it adopts too many one-sided resolutions, say, against Israel, as it has tended to do. Its main impact is not the coercive provisions of Article 42 of the charter, which have not been used, but rather its impact on the thinking of governments. That will rise or fall to the extent that the maturity, objectivity, and good sense of the members are demonstrated. I'm not a dreamer, but I still think that governments will many times act sensibly.

I don't like confrontational approaches from either side. I don't like the United States to take a confrontational approach, and I don't think the Third World countries should, either. But they have moderated. If you look at the results of the last nonaligned meeting in New Delhi, if you look at the results of the last UNCTAD meeting, which I think was in Belgrade, they have stopped emphasizing the grandiose goals of the new international economic order and they have zeroed in on practical, urgent, immediate problems, such as the huge, overhanging debts, the threat of protectionism in the industrialized countries. And that's where I think we ought to meet them. I don't mean that we ought to give in to the will of the majority anytime the assembly passes a resolution, but I think we owe them a good hearing on these issues.

PART II:
THE KENNEDY–JOHNSON YEARS, 1961–68

OVERVIEW

The election of John F. Kennedy to the White House promised to open a new era in both American politics and international relations. Impatient with what he considered the lack of energy and vision exhibited by his predecessor, Dwight D. Eisenhower, Kennedy moved quickly on a wide range of issues, from corruption in the Teamsters Union to the threat of armed subversion in South Vietnam. He showed a special concern for the U.S. position in the United Nations by appointing Adlai Stevenson, one of America's most eminent political figures, as permanent representative to the mission. Kennedy also originated the concept of the UN Development Decade, and was widely admired for his youthful vigor and idealism by diplomats and the people around the world. Whether or not he would have been able to continue the momentum in international relations that he had generated during his tragically brief presidency is impossible to say; what can be said is that his successor, Lyndon Johnson, although a man of enormous skill and force of character, could not prevent the growing American involvement in the Vietnam War from affecting the atmosphere in the United Nations and vastly complicating American diplomacy in general.

The Caribbean

After Fidel Castro took power in Cuba (1959) and made an alliance with the Soviet Union, Cuban diplomatic relations with the United States deteriorated and were eventually severed. On three separate occasions between 1960 and 1962, Cuba complained to the Security Council that the United States was planning an act of aggression against the Castro regime. In April 1961 the Cuban fears gained credence when a group of anti-Castro Cubans landed in Cuba's Bay of Pigs, with the hope of overthrowing the government. The Cubans immediately spoke of U.S. complicity, a charge denied at the United Nations by Adlai Stevenson, who had not been informed that, in fact, the United States was supporting the invaders. But Stevenson's prestige and credibility were so great in the world community that his reputation and effectiveness at the United Nations were not diminished when the truth about the Bay of Pigs was finally admitted by the U.S. government. All this occurred while the assembly was meeting. Cuba brought the issue before it and denounced the United States; the invaders were quickly repelled; and there proved to be no need to request a Security Council meeting.

Cuban Missile Crisis

Little more than a year later, Cuba was again the focus of world attention. This time the United Nations proved to be a valuable forum in resolving a superpower confrontation during the Cuban missile crisis. In October 1962 Kennedy revealed that the Soviets were installing missile bases in Cuba and ordered a blockade of the island. At the United Nations, Stevenson graphically refuted Soviet Premier Khrushchev's denial of having missiles in Cuba by displaying incriminating photographs at an emergency meeting of the Security Council. Secretary General U Thant persuaded Khrushchev to divert Soviet ships from their course of collision with the U.S. Navy. Ultimately, the Soviet leader backed down and agreed to remove the missiles, ending a two-week period when a nuclear exchange seemed possible.

Elsewhere in the Caribbean, in April 1965 Johnson landed the marines in the Dominican Republic, ostensibly, at first, to protect American lives but in fact to prop up a shaky anti-Communist junta. Johnson said the troops would prevent "another Cuba." The Organization of American States gave its endorsement; the United Nations sent observers; and Stevenson, without enthusiasm, defended the intervention of the Security Council. In 1966 an election established a stable anti-Communist government.

Peacekeeping Efforts

The largest UN peacekeeping effort was its operation in the Congo (ONUC), begun in 1960 when the Katanga Province seceded from the former Belgian colony. Under UN auspices, negotiations succeeded in reuniting Katanga with the rest of the Congo, and ONUC was terminated in 1964. Although ONUC had achieved its goals, the operation strained UN finances and produced a fiscal crisis. Opposed to the UN Congo operation, France and the Soviet Union refused to pay their share of the ONUC budget. As a result, the United Nations was forced to float a bond issue to cover part of the deficit. Nevertheless, the problem of nonpayment remained unresolved, thus leading to the Article 19 crisis of 1964 and 1965. (Article 19 of the UN Charter states that a UN member shall have no vote in the assembly if it is intentionally more than two years behind in its financial contributions.) The Soviet Union had also refused to pay for the UNEF emergency force in the Sinai. It argued that the countries directly involved in such operations—in the Suez crisis, for example, Britain, France, and Israel; and in the Congo situation, the Belgian "colonizers"—should have the main financial burden, and that contributions from other countries should be voluntary.

The USSR threatened to withdraw from the United Nations if stripped of its assembly vote. The United States did not press wholeheartedly for enforcement of Article 19 because it appeared to lack sufficient support for this position in the General Assembly and because of American concern that someday a particular UN operation might not be in its own interest. The 1964 session of the assembly was postponed as negotiations continued on the Soviet-arrears situation. When it did convene, in December, normal operations remained nearly at a standstill. Repeated efforts to find a settlement failed, and the situation demonstrated the assembly's ineffectiveness, particularly its inability to enforce UN assessments. The concept of collective responsibility for peacekeeping operations was thus undermined. It appeared that future UN efforts would have to be more modest in scale and acceptable to the superpowers. In 1965 the assembly met as usual, tacitly agreeing that Article 19 would not be applied. The deficit was to be made up by "voluntary" donations. As a result, the United States assumed a relatively larger share of the UNEF and ONUC budgets.

During the mid–1960s, continuing tensions between Israel and the Arab states preoccupied the United Nations. Violence escalated as Arab terrorist attacks were followed by Israeli reprisals. Egyptian President Nasser—acting on Soviet allegations that Israel planned to attack Syria—placed his forces on alert and in May 1967 demanded the removal of the UNEF troops stationed between his nation and Israel. Despite the fact that Israel had withdrawn from the Sinai in 1957 on condition that the forces remain in the area, Secretary General U Thant decided to promptly remove the UNEF; critics contend that U Thant could have played for time. Egypt blockaded the Gulf of Aqaba. Israel then struck, initiating the Six-Day War in which it crushed Egypt, Jordan, and Syria and occupied the West Bank of the Jordan River, the Gaza Strip, and much of the Sinai Peninsula.

In November 1967 the Security Council unanimously adopted Resolution 242, which called for an Israeli withdrawal from the occupied areas and the "acknowledgement of the sovereignty, territorial integrity and political independence of every State in the area and their right to live in peace within secure and recognized boundaries. . . . " The secretary general appointed Gunnar Jarring as the UN special representative in the Middle East. An unsteady cease-fire was soon established. The negotiations were a great achievement for Arthur Goldberg, who had been named U.S. permanent representative after Adlai Stevenson died in 1965.

Although the ONUC and UNEF were the major peacekeeping activities of the United Nations in the early 1960s, several smaller operations were also conducted. The arrival of a UN mediator in West New Guinea (West Irian) helped avoid a conflict there in 1962. In 1965 the United Nations was active in Cyprus (where it helped avert a confrontation between Greece and Turkey), in the Indo-Pakistani War, in Korea, and in Israel; and an observation team was sent to the Dominican Republic. By 1966 the Indo-Pakistani War had ended with the Tashkent Declaration, resulting in a withdrawal to prewar military positions.

The United Nations proved to be ineffective, however, in coping with the long struggle in Vietnam. During the Kennedy administration, the number of U.S. military advisers in South Vietnam rose from 2,000 to 15,000 in the face of expanding pressure from Communist North Vietnam and its southern ally, the National Liberation Front (or Viet Cong). In 1964, North Vietnamese naval vessels attacked U.S. ships in the international waters of the Gulf of Tonkin. President Johnson ordered retaliatory strikes against Hanoi and won approval of the Gulf of Tonkin Resolution, by which the U.S. Congress authorized him to take whatever steps were necessary to defend American military forces. Throughout the 1960s, as American troop strength in Southeast Asia rose to 500,000, Secretary General U Thant offered his services as a mediator between the United States and Hanoi. However, his habit of publicly criticizing U.S. policy, especially the bombing of North Vietnam (which began in 1965), damaged his effectiveness with President Johnson. Ambassador Stevenson, until his death, publicly supported the need for the United States to show a firm resolve to stop Communist expansion in the region, though he also believed that the bombings would harden Hanoi's resistance.

Stevenson's successor, Arthur Goldberg, who had been a Supreme Court justice before coming to the United Nations, hoped that in his new position he would be able to influence U.S. policy in Vietnam, about which he had serious reservations. He did succeed in getting the Security Council to take up the issue, but few positive results ensued. The failure of the United Nations to produce an escape from the impasse in Southeast Asia tarnished its reputation in the eyes of the Johnson administration.

In 1968, the Viet Cong launched its "Tet offensive," whose success helped fan domestic opposition to the war in the United States. President Johnson soon halted the bombings of North Vietnam; later that year, peace talks began, involving the United States, Saigon, and Hanoi, as well as the Viet Cong. The inability of the United Nations to intervene in the face of determined action by a superpower became evident again in August 1968, when troops from Warsaw Pact armies entered Czechoslovakia to put an end to the liberal trend there—the "Prague Spring." The issue was debated passionately in the Security Council, however, and the Soviet Union's position was discredited even as its veto prevented the council from condemning its aggression.

Third World and Development

The first wave of decolonization was well under way by the 1960s, as, one after the other, European colonies around the world began achieving independence, most times peacefully, sometimes through force of arms. By 1961 the new nations had nearly doubled the size of the United Nations from 51 charter members to nearly 100 members.

The United States was quick to take the initiative in supporting the new nations. With President Kennedy's recommendation and American urging, the 1960s were declared the UN Development Decade, and a goal of at least 5 percent annual growth was set for the developing countries. During the boom years of the 1960s, when the world was enjoying one of its greatest periods of prosperity, this goal seemed quite attainable. In the less prosperous 1970s, however, most developing countries saw their economic aspirations disappointed—which was surely one factor in the resentment they increasingly showed toward the developed nations. The United States, as the world's richest nation, soon came in for its share of the criticism. By the late 1960s, as the less-developed countries (LDCs) pressed in the United Nations for more help in economic development, their speeches and demands seemed to some Americans as attacks on the United States itself. American defensiveness was increased by the fact that the LDCs were also beginning to influence voting patterns in the United Nations, simply through their growing numbers.

One aim of the LDCs was to create international organizations that could help coordinate economic development. They were instrumental in creating the UN Conference on Trade and Development as a subsidiary organ of the General Assembly. Although UNCTAD never achieved its goals, it gave birth to a new political organization, the Group of 77 (the 77 developing nations then members of the United Nations). Membership in this group soon expanded to beyond 100 and included almost all countries in Asia, Africa, the Middle East, and Latin America. The group began to articulate the interests and demands of the Third World in the successive UNCTADs and in other UN bodies.

The UN Development Program (UNDP) resulted from the merger of the Expanded Program for Technical Assistance and the Special Fund; established in 1965, it was a major effort to aid developing countries. Supported by voluntary contributions, it became involved in thousands of projects in agriculture, industry, power production, transportation, health, housing, and education. The UNDP conducted surveys and developed farmlands, forests, and mineral deposits; stimulated capital investment; provided professional training; adapted and applied modern technologies; and engaged in economic and social planning. The World Bank and its affiliates distributed over $1 billion in loans and credits to LDCs. The World Health Organization sought to prevent the spread of malaria and smallpox; the World Meteorological Organization attempted to improve weather forecasting through international cooperation (the World Weather Watch); and the Food and Agriculture Organization sent agronomists to various developing countries. In addition, the United States contributed $200 million to the new Asian Development Bank, also a UN agency.

Arms Control

The United Nations and the atomic age were born in the same year, and arms control has been a popular topic for UN debate from the start. The words "general and complete disarmament" appeared regularly on the assembly's agenda from 1959, and in the 1960s some movement was made in restricting the use of weapons, if not in reducing their total. The parties to the partial nuclear-test-ban treaty in 1963, including the United States, the USSR, and Britain, pledged not to test nuclear weapons in the atmosphere, in outer space, or underwater. (China, a nonsignatory, exploded its first nuclear device in 1964.) Another treaty, in 1966, affirmed that outer space was to be used only for peaceful purposes. The Nuclear Nonproliferation Treaty of 1968 sought to halt the distribution of materials and technology useful in producing nuclear weapons.

The U.S. Mission

Adlai Stevenson, twice a Democratic nominee for the presidency, had hoped to become Kennedy's secretary of state. He accepted the UN position with grace, but, privately, found it often a frustrating position to hold because usually it carried little real power over the course of events. Though often quite effective in his UN post, and admired throughout the world for his commitment to peace and his deep sense of justice and internationalism, Stevenson seems never to have won the full confidence of either Kennedy or Johnson.

Arthur Goldberg, a former labor lawyer, was a highly skilled negotiator and a good administrator. In his three years (1965–68) as permanent representative, he helped resolve the Article 19 crisis: helped end fighting between Pakistan and India; advanced efforts to resolve the white-black deadlock in southern Africa; was instrumental in bringing the outer-space and nonproliferation treaties to reality; negotiated the 1967 cease-fire in the Middle East; and helped gain the release of 82 navy men from the U.S.S. *Pueblo*, which had been captured by North Korea.

Goldberg resigned in 1968 and was followed briefly, during the last months of the Johnson administration, by George Ball, a veteran of the State Department, and by Charles Russell Wiggins, editor of the *Washington Post.*

In 1961 the U.S. delegation to the United Nations was expanded to include four deputies with the rank of ambassador: Francis Plimpton, a close friend of Adlai Stevenson, was appointed deputy representative (the number-two spot); Charles Yost, a career diplomat, served as deputy representative on the Security Council (the number-three spot); and Phillip Klutznick became the representative on the Economic and Social Council (the number-four spot). Jonathan Bingham, later a congressman, was the representative on the Trusteeship Council, the number-five spot.

Franklin H. Williams was the first black appointed representative on the ECOSOC, in 1964; Marietta Tree became the first woman to enjoy ambassadorial rank, as representative on the Trusteeship Council. When Goldberg became permanent representative in 1965, a new group of ambassadors was appointed. Goldberg favored career diplomats in the number-two spot, as reflected in the appointment of James Nabrit and, later, William Buffum to that post. James Roosevelt, son of Eleanor Roosevelt, served as representative on the ECOSOC during 1965–66.

During his presence at the 1963 General Assembly, Secretary of State Dean Rusk served as head of the U.S. delegation. Among the congressional delegates during these years were Senators Albert Gore, Clifford Case, Frank Church, Stuart Symington, and John Sherman Cooper, and Representatives Marguerite Stitt Church and Peter

Frelinghuysen. The delegation to the General Assembly included Eleanor Roosevelt, Carl Rowan, Marietta Tree, Jane Warner Dick, Sidney Yates, Deputy Assistant Secretary of State (for International Organization Affairs) Richard Gardner, William P. Rogers (later secretary of state under Richard Nixon), Patricia Roberts Harris, Harding Bancroft, Robert Benjamin (of Orion Pictures) and Jean Picker of the UN Association of the United States.

SOURCES

On the Cold War, see John Stoessinger, *The United Nations and the Superpowers* (New York: Random House, 1965, 1970). For the Congo, see Roger Hilsman, *To Move a Nation* (New York: Dell, 1964). General information about the United Nations and the U.S. Mission during this period may be found in *Everyman's United Nations* (New York: UN Office of Public Information, 1968); Thomas Hovet, *A Chronology and Fact Book of the United Nations, 1941-1979* (Dobbs Ferry, N.Y.: Oceania, 1979); Richard Hiscocks, *The Security Council* (New York: Free Press, 1973); *U.S. Participation in the U.N.* (Washington, D.C.: Department of State, 1946-68); and Seymour Maxwell Finger, *Your Man at the UN* (New York: New York University Press, 1980).

FRANCIS T. P. PLIMPTON: Deputy Representative to the United Nations, 1961–65.

There's no doubt about the fact that Soviet Ambassador Fedorenko's speeches against the United States were much more savage than any speeches that we ever made against the Russians. I always wanted to blame the Russians for having started World War II, which, of course, they did because of the agreement between Molotov and Von Ribbentrop for the partition of Poland. The Russians are really responsible for the whole damn thing. But Adlai would never let me say that.

A longtime friend and roommate of Adlai Stevenson at Harvard Law School, Francis Taylor Pearsons Plimpton was appointed Stevenson's deputy at the United Nations in 1961. "Adlai lassoed me for the UN and got Kennedy to appoint me," Plimpton recalls. Plimpton was known for his skillful and urbane arguments in favor of U.S. positions. Politically, like Stevenson, he was a moderate liberal.

After the death of Stevenson in 1965, Plimpton left his UN post and rejoined the Park Avenue law firm that he had helped found in 1933. "Of course, my chief claim to fame is being the father of George," Plimpton once noted. He died in 1984.

I had roomed with Adlai Stevenson in our second year at Harvard Law School and kept in touch with him frequently during the succeeding years. When he was appointed ambassador to the UN, we bumped into one another in New York; I don't remember just where or why. He asked me to be his number-two man—which, due to a peculiarity of the statute, entitled me to be ambassador extraordinary and plenipotentiary. I am not sure what those words mean, but in any event, I was vastly extraordinary and his deputy for every purpose.

When he asked me to come on board, I hesitated a little bit, although I had always been interested in foreign affairs. I had been, for example, director of the Foreign Policy Association from somewhere around 1933 till somewhere around 1945—later than that I guess. I was also involved in the International Far East Affair, which was accused of being pro-Communist. I don't know how I ever cleared the FBI with that. I was also active in Mrs. Roosevelt's "Open Road," which was accused of being somewhat pro-Communist. In any event, Stevenson had made a condition of his acceptance of the job: that Kennedy would appoint anyone whom he suggested. So I slid in that way.

There was not very much formal training. I remember vividly the training we did receive as to the presence of Communist bugs and how they listened in on someone else's conversation. We were told that the Communists listened through the use of reflectors. It was a vivid explanation of the various methods of deception that the Communists used.

Adlai was a good head of the mission. He didn't pay very much attention to it. He let us all do what we wanted to do and we did what we were supposed to do. The most important thing during the General Assemblies was the work of the various committees. The First Committee dealt with disarmament, and the Special Political Committee dealt with the Palestine question, which I had to handle, and apartheid and other difficult problems. Stevenson was interested in these matters. He didn't have to pay very much attention to them, but he knew something about everything that was happening.

Many people thought it was symbolic of the high esteem President Kennedy had toward the UN when he appointed Adlai Stevenson. Obviously, to appoint someone of Adlai's international reputation to the UN meant something. Ideally, you should have somebody who knows quite a lot about international affairs. Adlai was superb in that respect, he knew everything. You [could] mention some forgotten town in Africa, [and] Adlai had been there and knew the mayor or something. He was fantastic because he knew so much about all the rest of the world, and that's a great advantage that he had.

Stevenson kept a little bit of an office in Washington and he occasionally went to cabinet meetings there. The contrast between his behavior and Arthur Goldberg's was fantastic. Goldberg insisted on having his own secretary and an elaborate suite of offices. He went down to Washington and never missed a cabinet meeting, and was much more glorifying of Washington than Adlai was. Goldberg undoubtedly was a good negotiator; so was Adlai. Adlai was really a very good lawyer, and I would rate him, on the whole, very much higher than Goldberg, because Goldberg was a Zionist, and I'm afraid that he let that color his thinking on the Palestine question in general.

We had good relations within the delegation; we were a fairly strong team. I was number two. Charlie Yost, who afterward became the actual ambassador in 1969, had very good judgment and was a very experienced diplomat. Then we had Phil Klutznick, who was secretary of commerce in the Carter administration. He's a very bright, forceful Jewish gentleman. I do remember that he apparently stepped on some toes in his attempt to get Congress to subscribe to the $150 million UN bond issue that financed the Congo operation. Stevenson finally called me in and told me that I had to take the job over from Klutznick, but Stevenson never made it clear to Klutznick. The first that Klutznick knew about it was when he read a few cables that said that I was going to take over for him. But Klutznick was a good man.

I didn't get along very well with the Russians. I certainly never got to like [Ambassador] Fedorenko, who was very unpleasant to me, and I never could figure out quite why. He had a sort of nasty quality to him which was very unpleasant. I remember he once insinuated that I must have been involved in unsavory activities on behalf of the United States. He was sort of sly, but he didn't do it publicly. (Oddly enough, he had a very attractive daughter, a lovely girl. I once succeeded in getting him to dinner at 1165 Fifth [Avenue], where we lived, and also [succeeded in] getting him out to our country home in Cold Spring Harbor once. The daughter seemed to me more or less in love with my son, George, which is not an unusual affair. But she eventually married a Russian and disappeared.) Fedorenko disappeared from the public eye, certainly. I think there was a feeling at the UN that he'd been disciplined for misbehavior.

Dag Hammarskjöld was a really good international official. He didn't play any favorites at all between nation and nation. He was absolutely impartial and he was very consistent. I remember going to see him once about the Indian who was in charge of the UN force in the Congo. He was disliked by the Congolese because he looked down on them—which in general you have to look out for in the Third World—and I wanted to have him removed. I made the mistake of pointing out that the United States was by far the largest contributor to the expenses of the Congo and, therefore, our viewpoint ought to be governing in areas where there was disagreement. But Hammarskjöld just set me right back on my heels. He did not pay any attention to the United States any more than to anybody else. He had steel-blue eyes that just bore right into you, and I retreated very hastily.

U Thant was very different from Dag Hammarskjöld. I thought of him as having a backbone of gelatin. He was a very nice fellow, and he certainly didn't hesitate to criticize the United States, but he didn't have very much guts. He didn't take any position at all concerning the Article 19 crisis, which was a most important issue that really involved the future of the United Nations.

The UN is less important to the United States today, I think, than it used to be. The media pay much less attention to the UN now than they did when I was there. Perhaps this is because the UN doesn't deserve a great deal of comment. The Third World plus the Communists can now put through any resolution that they want. The United States now has to rely on the fact that the only thing that really matters is the Security Council. The resolutions that the General Assembly adopts are technically only recommendations. So the United States has to remind the rest of the world that they are only recommendations, and that we don't need to pay any attention to them. When I was there, the United States had confidence in the General Assembly. The General Assembly is now discredited and the Security Council is just hog-tied by Soviet vetoes or by our vetoes. Unless the United States and the Soviets agree on something, it doesn't get done.

Because all of the things that one might like to change involved changing the charter, and you can't do that without getting the approval of the Security Council and the General Assembly, I doubt that there is a way to turn back the clock or change the rules at the UN. Neither the General Assembly nor the Security Council is likely to vote in favor of castrating itself, so I think we've just got to endure the operation of the thing as it is now.

MARIETTA TREE: Delegate to the Human Rights Commission, 1961–65; and Representative on the Trusteeship Council, 1964–65.

The first time that I knew I had been appointed to the United Nations, I was with my husband at our house in Barbados and a telegram arrived from President Kennedy saying, "I hope you will accept the post as the representative of the United States to the Human Rights Commission at the UN." I talked it over with my husband and he said, "Go on, you've got to do it. You'll never forgive yourself if you don't." So a day or so later, I accepted with great pleasure and some trepidation.

A civil-rights advocate and activist in the Democratic Party, Marietta Peabody Tree was named in 1961 by President Kennedy as U.S. representative to the Human Rights Commission of the United Nations, a post she held until 1965. She stated at the time that much remained to be done in the area of human rights. As to the United Nations, she called for support in making "this city of man the most effective instrument of peace." Tree was also a member of Adlai Stevenson's U.S. delegation to the 1961 session of the United Nations.

With her appointment as U.S. representative to the UN Trusteeship Council in 1964, Tree became the first American woman to serve as an ambassador to the United Nations. In 1966 she joined the UN Secretariat as a member of Secretary General U Thant's staff. Since 1968 Tree has been a partner in Llewelyn-Davies Associates, a city-planning firm.

I imagine that it was a combination of my work for the Democratic Party and my work in the civil-rights movement that promoted me to the job of U.S. human-rights commissioner at the UN. But it was my political training, and particularly my training in New York City politics, which taught me the most helpful skills for the UN, because I had learned in New York City how to canvass and deliver votes, how to persuade people to vote—of course, in their best interest—and how to appeal to their ideals.

Mrs. Roosevelt really helped me the most in my UN job. She was on the top of my list for advice when I started out, as she was the first U.S. delegate to the Human Rights Commission, and I wanted to gather the fruit of her experiences. First, she told me to learn the language of the resolutions. That was the hardest part of the job training, as I was not used to precise legal language, and had to memorize it. I had to learn the meanings of words that in normal life mean one thing and on UN documents mean quite another. It was like learning another language.

Secondly, she said, you must learn to know your fellow delegates well and learn who will vote what way in certain situations; who, although he may come from a small country, has enormous influence in his group—say, the Islamic group or the African group; who can be relied on to lie; who will go back on his word. She said the only way you can learn these things is by making friends, and you do that by inviting the delegates to dinner in your own house in threes and fours, rarely in larger groups. The delegates from abroad love to be in someone's house, because in the United States they are generally in some bleak hotel or committee room. They will always accept an invitation to come. Just the meal and personal contact turn you into friends.

Of course, I heeded her suggestions and, as usual, she was right. At this point my husband was away developing a hotel in the West Indies, and so I asked about three or four delegates almost every night for dinner, without fear of boring him with our UN converstaion.

Mrs. Roosevelt was the only person who told me how important it was to meet in a social way with the other representatives. I was very disappointed that the State Department didn't place more emphasis on getting to know your fellow delegates. Indeed, even the career Foreign Service officers at the UN, people who should have known better, did not have the other delegates to their homes. They felt they couldn't afford it on their salaries, but I think that it wouldn't have cost the government very much, and would have been worth a great deal to the United States, to have these delegates go to American houses. You feel more like friends rather than a group of diplomats.

Besides giving me invaluable advice, Mrs. Roosevelt helped me enormously during my first year in the Human Rights Commission. She gave five lunches, for instance, to introduce me to her UN-delegate friends.

On these occasions, I would see sometimes another, sterner side to Mrs. Roosevelt. If after accepting her invitation for lunch, an African or Asian woman delegate failed to show up, she [Mrs. Roosevelt] would ask her sister Africans for an explanation in a nonsmiling manner: "Do you behave like this at home in Lagos?" "Always" [would be] the reply. "Is the food wasted?" "Well, no, Mrs. Roosevelt, it's just kept in the pot on the back of the stove, and someone is sure to drop in." "How very wasteful," Mrs. Roosevelt [would say].

Adlai Stevenson

I worked fervently for Adlai Stevenson in both of his presidential campaigns. He had been a friend of my husband's for many years. They had similar backgrounds. I was one of his loyal supporters and admirers from 1948 to his death in 1965.

Stevenson was the ideal ambassador, at a wonderful time in history for an American ambassador to be at the UN. It was a period, shortly after the war, in which the whole world looked to the United States for its leadership—economic, social, political, monetary, and so on. So Stevenson was also the most powerful ambassador at the UN. Every other ambassador felt deprived if he couldn't see Stevenson at least once a week. When Stevenson's reactions and views were included as part of an ambassador's cable home, it showed his home government that its ambassador was near the seat of power. Stevenson was a passionately busy man [in] all his years there, seeing all of the ambassadors informally; representing the United States on the Security Council at nearly daily meetings; writing speeches both for the UN and to explain the UN to the United States; appearing on television; entertaining and being entertained every night; [making] twice-weekly trips to Washington to see the president and confer at the State Department; and, on top of all the demands of his mission, being a loving man with strong family ties—he also tried to keep in touch with his sons, sister, and his many adoring friends. Overweight at the start, with a compulsion to eat under pressure, and given the opportunity of opulent meals twice a day, it is little wonder that his proportions became ample. He used to say this diplomacy was all protocol, alcohol, and Geritol.

In private he was often worried, always tired, and sometimes depressed because he never felt that he had succeeded in persuading the State Department or the president or his foreign colleagues in just the ways that he envisioned. He always underestimated himself and his effectiveness. But in public his smile, his wit, and his overpowering charm (which, translated, means his ability to give each individual his careful attention and concern) never failed.

Unlike many U.S. ambassadors to the UN, Stevenson had a great effect on making UN policy. For him, that meant tilting the UN toward the Third World. His view was that unless we, the richer nations, tried to tip the balance in a material way toward the poorer nations, conflicts would develop, between the North and South or between the rich and poor nations, which would be far worse than between the East and West. He believed that we should do everything we could to put the less-developed countries on their own feet, not only for their self-respect, but their self-support. Adlai showed more foresight than other Western politicians or Western statesmen had at that time. This included Kennedy, who really was far more involved in the U.S.-USSR tensions—what Khrushchev had to say, or what the German ambassador had to say about the Soviet Union—than in how Africa was developing. But Stevenson believed in diminishing, as much as possible, the conflict between the East and West; not appeasing, but finding the points of difference and trying to solve them through disarmament and trade.

Stevenson also played an important role serving unofficially as a United Nations ambassador to the United States. At the time there were many isolationist groups in the United States. Bumper stickers on cars, particularly in the Midwest, shrilled, "Get the UN out of the U.S. and the U.S. out of the UN." It was only during the Cuban missile crisis, when Stevenson challenged the Soviet ambassador, that he became popular because he was bashing the Soviet Union in public. Stevenson dramatically produced the U–2 pictures of the missiles and, pointing his finger at Ambassador Zorin of the USSR, cried: "Admit that you threatened the peace! Admit that your government has placed its missiles in Cuba. Admit they are there, because I will stay here until hell freezes over until you do so!" This scene on television produced waves of acclaim and applause throughout the country for Stevenson's performance. The UN itself became more popular as a result.

When Johnson became president, he said to Adlai, "I will give you carte blanche at the UN"; so Stevenson more or less had free sailing until the Dominican Republic crisis. I don't think Stevenson was too enthusiastic about the president's overkill solutions. To the rest of the world, we looked like a giant trying to kill a flea with a sledgehammer. But Stevenson went along like a good soldier because in government one can't always agree with the established policy 100 percent, all of the time. Nevertheless, Stevenson had considerable influence up to the time that he died.

Adlai was political by nature and he really liked people; not waving at crowds, but talking to individuals. Having seen the world, and with a passionate curiosity about all the different peoples, customs, and backgrounds, he was well suited to the UN. Adlai Stevenson was simply the best ambassador we ever had at the United Nations.

The Struggle for Human Rights

The Human Rights Commission passed a good number of resolutions and declarations concerning human rights, and there was a general feeling of going forward and making progress. One day when we were working on the Declaration on Religious Discrimination, I was greatly moved by a speech from the leader of one of the nongovernmental religious-freedom groups about the ghastly fate of European Jews under the heel of Hitler. So I wanted to add the words "anti-Semitism" to the banned-forever list in the preamble of the religious-discrimination document. I called my policy authorities in the State Department as well as at the U.S. Mission, to ask their permission to add these words, but everyone was [out] to lunch. Unless the concept could be introduced immediately, I would not have another chance procedurally to amend the preamble. So I took a chance that proscribing anti-Semitism was not debatable in the State Department and raised my hand to introduce what I knew were loaded words amongst the Moslem groups.

The next day I was visited by an angry deputy assistant secretary of the International Organizations Department of the State Department: "How dare you add these words without permission from us?"

"Why should banning anti-Semitism be debatable in the U.S. State Department, and why were all of you out to lunch at the same time?"

"The next time you depart from instructions," said he, "we cannot answer for the consequences. Don't you realize that the Arab and Moslem nations will hold up the vote on the preamble until we take out the offending words? That means that the convention on religious discrimination might never be passed."

His wrath and logic were quelling, but I knew that conventions had to be passed by the Senate, like all foreign treaties. But the Senate had not even passed the oldest UN convention, that against genocide, thanks to the veto power of some southern senators who couldn't put the United States on record against mass murder of racial or religious groups for fear of "foreign dictatorship" on white supremacy in the South. To this day no human-rights convention of any importance has been passed by the Senate, while the Soviet Union gets a lot of credit in the developing world by approving conventions that affect them, for example, on racism.

Fortunately, I had the last word on the International Organizations Division of the State Department, because a week later, in a story on the front page of the *New York Times* (I read it, unbelieving, five times before I understood the good news), President Johnson addressed a powerful religious organization: "As I directed my representative in the Human Rights Commission to say, . . . " and [he] then cited my amendment and quoted from my own emotional [UN] speech against anti-Semitism. A few days later, also in a story on the front page of the *New York Times*, Secretary of State Dean Rusk repeated more or less what the president had said and again used my words in the UN speech. So my own policy prevailed. My only revenge was to send these two clippings quoting President Johnson and Secretary of State Rusk to my friend, Richard Gardner, the deputy assistant secretary of state, without comment.

Probably my best-known achievement in the Human Rights Commission was [the] proposing [of] a world human-rights commissioner, someone of world prestige in the UN Secretariat who would receive complaints on human-rights abuses from governments, individuals, and groups from all over the world. These reports would be read and discussed by the UN Human Rights Commission and published widely. Obviously, the UN could not enforce these rights on governments because it cannot interfere in the domestic governance of countries. But it can publicize, and thereby hold up to the scorn and opprobrium of world opinion, the human-rights abuses of individual governments. I had learned that simply publishing wrongs makes governments feel even more inferior, and they often take corrective action as a result—particularly if the newspapers of the free world, and groups and other governments take up the cry both publicly and privately. I cannot overestimate the power of exposure of wrongs.

Richard Gardner, later to be ambassador to Italy, but then my boss as deputy assistant secretary of state, highly approved of my idea, and together we worked out the details of the proposal. He was most effective on the strategy of selling the concept not only to the

State Department, but to other governments. Indeed, we asked the government of Costa Rica, a small country which was outstanding for its well-functioning democracy and high standard of human rights, to sponsor this human-rights-commissioner resolution, and they readily agreed. If the United States had sponsored the proposal, defeat would have been automatic.

As it turned out, support was surprisingly general, and in some quarters enthusiastic. At the same time, it was a tactical defeat for the USSR because they were forced to oppose it. Making each other look bad is part of "the great game," and with my proposal we forced them to come out against motherhood.

Very shortly after I left the commission, the debate there degenerated into heavy slugging matches between the nations over human rights, or the lack of, in Israel and South Africa. All the delegates did was scream at each other about the sins of these two countries. There was no real concern for human rights in the commission and, of course, this worked to the advantage of those governments that were against human rights. The Human Rights Commission must be a boring and a disillusioning place today.

Representational Activities

Official social events were more important in the 1960s than they are now, but "getting to know you" is always of the highest importance at the UN; one really cannot expect to accomplish much without getting to know the delegates individually. Nearly every day when the UN was in session, I went to one of those awful cocktail parties that each government feels that they have to give. They were too expensive for the less-developed countries, but still, each gave a cluster of them. In some cases governments spent more for official entertainment at the UN than they contributed to the UN budget.

The most lavish and formal parties were given by the delegation of Dahomey. In the ballroom of the Plaza [Hotel], the ambassador received us, resplendent in white tie and tails. There was a large orchestra for waltzing, candlelit tables, and a delicious dinner. Everybody looked forward to the evening, came in their best, and at the same time spoke in shocked tones of the appalling expense for a small country, as they munched their baked Alaska.

The United States should play the role of world statesman at the UN, as it did when Cabot Lodge and Adlai Stevenson were the U.S.

ambassadors. We should propose a host of constructive proposals at the UN that help other nations besides ourselves, instead of assuming a perennial defensive pose, always fending off ideas and looking afraid. Perhaps we should see ourselves as one amongst equals at the UN. We are not the greatest power in the whole world, but we still have huge power economically, militarily, politically. We should use this power to reduce conflict, to increase productivity in all the nations, and to increase the material well-being of people within the UN, as well as their human rights.

Think how difficult it would be were there no UN, and how different history would be without the UN. There would be a great deal more conflict and many more little shooting wars. There would be a great deal more starvation and disease. There would be a great deal more unhappiness with, and more anger toward, the richer countries. Altogether, without the UN, I feel this spaceship world would be a truly dangerous place.

The Reagan administration does not seem to value the UN particularly, nor does it seem to think that as much can be accomplished there as other administrations did. Some administrations, like Kennedy's, thought that it could be positively effective. This is evidenced by the fact that Kennedy put forward a five-point program which he hoped the UN would achieve—"Decade for Development"—and it was mainly the product of Philip Klutznick's thinking. He was then U.S. ambassador to ECOSOC. It was such a good program in the eyes of the world, and of the nations at the UN, that all the five points were put into operation at the UN within a year. That is a statesman-like achievement. It shows what the United States could do then and could do again if [we were] farsighted enough to think constructively, instead of defensively, of the small world we live in.

FRANKLIN H. WILLIAMS: Representative on the Economic and Social Council, 1964–65.

I guess I was the first ambassador to bring in black schoolkids. Every few weeks I would bring classes of young black kids from Harlem down to the mission and have them upstairs on the top floor. I'd have my assistant come up and brief them, and then I'd take them over to the UN and take them right in the delegates' entrance. I'd take them up on the platform and there, up in the balcony, would be all the visitors from all over the world, and here would be these 20 young black kids from Harlem up on the lectern, standing where the president presides. Then I'd take them down to the U.S. delegation and sit them in the seats. I believe that that was one way we should use the mission.

A foundation executive, lawyer, and government official, Franklin H. Williams was named African regional director of the U.S. Peace Corps in 1961. In 1964 he became U.S. representative to the UN Economic and Social Council. His interest in African affairs led to his appointment as ambassador to Ghana (1965–68) during the Johnson administration.

Williams is now president and trustee of the Phelps Stokes Fund and a commentator on radio for Westinghouse Broadcasting Company.

My first exposure to the U.S. Mission to the UN was in July of 1961, when I was appointed as a member of the delegation to ECOSOC, representing the Peace Corps. I was the director of private and international organizations of the Peace Corps, and we were very anxious in those days to try to get the Peace Corps concept adopted by the United Nations. I went to Geneva as a member of the delegation, which was then headed by Philip Klutznick, from Chicago. The number-two man was Walter Kotschnick. It was clear to me even then that Walter Kotschnick was the leader of the ECOSOC delegation. He knew everybody in Geneva, and he more or less ran the delegation. The ambassador was the titular head and gave overall policy, supervision, direction, and tone to the delegation, but Walter was the year-round ECOSOC representative, for all intents and purposes.

A resolution was introduced for the creation of an international voluntary service, which was opposed by the Russians. I did a lot of lobbying on behalf of the resolution and we finally got it passed. In the fall of 1961 it also passed the General Assembly. But back home in Washington, while we were pushing it through, the mood changed—in the Peace Corps as well as in Congress. After it passed the General Assembly, the mood changed there, too. Really, nobody wanted it. The Congress was getting very negative toward the UN in 1961. So all the people within the Peace Corps dampened any effort to implement this resolution, after having initiated it in the first place. Nevertheless, the historical fact is that it did pass the General Assembly, and became a formal UN resolution, but was never implemented.

When I was appointed to head the [U.S.] delegation [to ECOSOC in 1964], I had already gone to Geneva with Walter Kotschnick as the acting head. It was such an exciting thing for me to come to the delegation three years later as the head of it, having just three years earlier been in a delegation of about 49.

My responsibilities covered all of the various and sundry meetings and sessions in between, including [those of] the Economic Commission for Latin America, which met in Mexico City, and the Pledging Conference. The big issue in those years, unfortunately, was an issue that tied up almost everything in the UN machinery, the Article 19 issue.

Our administration [people] in Washington had really convinced themselves of the political and diplomatic correctness and almost righteousness of their position. I happen personally to have disagreed with them. I thought it was ridiculous, and time proved it to be ridiculous, to threaten to destroy the UN over whether or not the Russians would pay their portion of the assessment for the peacekeeping forces in the Congo. This was my first real exposure to policymaking and implementation. Policymaking is a mysterious process. Because it was already established when I got to the U.S. Mission, I could not begin to tell you the genesis of the policy by which we moved to bar the USSR from voting.

In situations like that, you are made to feel that you are almost disloyal if you challenge the policy. Therefore, the only one who really can challenge that kind of policy, once it is adopted, is a person who carries tremendous prestige. I don't know whether Stevenson challenged it with all the vigor and energy he could have. But he certainly had the prestige to do so. I am of the impression that he didn't like it, either, but went along with it as a good soldier, as he was supposed to.

When I was appointed there was a rumor, never confirmed by me in any way, that Stevenson had opposed my appointment because he was not pleased by it. The rumor went, further, that part of the deal for accepting my appointment was that Marietta Tree, who was then head of our Human Rights Commission, would be given ambassadorial rank and become representative to the Trusteeship Council. Of course, that led me to believe that Stevenson's opposition was based on race. There had never been any black at the mission in any significant policymaking position. I was the first black at the U.S. Mission that held the rank of ambassador. It was understandable, then, that I felt that there might have been some logic or some substance to the rumor.

I never did get to know Stevenson very well. I think he invited me to his residence only once, for a luncheon, in the two years that I was there. He never involved me in any of his representational activities, though I happen to know that Marietta was frequently involved in them, even though she was junior to me. At the top of the pecking order was the permanent representative, Stevenson. The number-two person was his deputy, Plimpton. The number-three person was Yost, who was the career officer there. The number-four person was myself and the number-five person was Marietta Tree. Everyone else was staff. That was the ambassadorial delegation.

I'm still under the impression that Marietta was involved in almost all of his activities even though she was junior to me. I do not recall ever being involved by Stevenson at any of his representational activities. If the others were involved, that might make sense because one was [a] political and professional [man] and the other was his deputy.

I also observed, with Yates having left, that there was no Jew in any senior policymaking position at the mission. Max Finger was the highest-ranking Jewish person on the staff, and [his] was not a very high rank. The first confrontation I had with Stevenson was over this question of who would be our representatives in the Human Rights Commission delegation. Morris Abrams was our representative to the commission. His deputy was a black man named Clyde Ferguson, who was then dean of Howard University School of Law. I sent up Clyde's name as the second person. The third person was the general counsel of the NAACP, Robert Carter. I sent his name up, too. I almost did this deliberately, namely, sent Stevenson the names of one Jew and two blacks, because I wanted to see how he would handle it.

Stevenson subsequently called me up to his office. (Whenever he talked to me, he never looked me in the eye. On the elevator, sometimes, he wouldn't even acknowledge my presence. I have no idea whether this was just his manner, whether I made him uncomfortable, or whether he suspected that I disapproved of him.) When I came into his office, he couldn't look up at me. He said, "Franklin, don't we have anyone else?" I was then convinced that it was [a matter of] race and religion. I said, "Why, governor?," and he said, "Well, traditionally, this has been a woman's position." He said, "You remember, it was first Mrs. Roosevelt, and then Mrs. Lord, and Marietta." And I said, "Well, if we can get Connie Motley, fine. But we can't. If I'm to be responsible for the Human Rights Commission, I want the best constitutional lawyers we can find to represent us. And I think I have nominated the three best in the country."

He said, "Well, you know, I need people around me" (and this is a direct quote), "I need people around me who can help me with my heavy representational activities." And a light went on in my head. Stevenson had not cared apparently whether I was black, red, yellow, or green. He was very much concerned that I was poor because all of the people that he brought and surrounded himself with were millionaires: Jack Dick, from Chicago, Marietta Tree, and Francis Plimpton. He used Plimpton's estate down on the island. He would go to his Lake Como home. Marietta Tree would host entertainments for him at her beautiful home in Manhattan. Jane Dick in Chicago was used the same way. Even young David Geyer, whom he brought on the staff as a rather junior person, was a millionaire. So Stevenson surrounded himself with wealthy people. In retrospect, I don't think he cared whether I was black or white. I think if I had been a millionaire, he would have welcomed my appointment.

I never felt that Stevenson had a strong commitment to civil rights. I think he had an intellectual commitment, but not a deep, emotional commitment. For example, when Martin Luther King received the Nobel Peace Prize, I went to Stevenson and I said, "Governor, here's a marvelous opportunity for you to reach out to the black community. Why don't you have a reception for Dr. King as he passes through New York on his way to Oslo?" He resisted that. He did not see the legitimacy of it, or, for that matter, the political opportunity it offered him. The suggestion came about that he should host it jointly with the representative of Sweden, so he then said, "Well, why don't I do that—invite the representative of Sweden to cohost it?" And he finally did. But I felt all along that he was just going through the motions.

I had respect for Stevenson, but I felt sorry for him. I felt that he was not a man of great strengths or self-assurance. I can remember the morning that we were in his office at a staff meeting, when the call came through from Washington, giving him his instructions on the position to take concerning our sending the marines into the Dominican Republic. At best his protest was very low-keyed. Then he turned to us and he said, "My God, when the Indians march into Goa, we raise our voices and protest; and when we march into the Dominican Republic, we're expected to defend it." And I felt like saying at the time, "Well, why don't you protest, governor? I mean, you're a major personality in this country. You could raise your voice in protest." I just had the feeling that he was a beaten man. I had the feeling that he realized that there was nothing else in the public eye for him, and that he dare not take on President Johnson for fear of being removed from his position. He enjoyed the limelight.

He felt that our Article 19 position was wrong, but he didn't fight it very hard. And he let his team—Pedersen, Noyes, and others—buffalo him. I was the only one there who was out on a limb with him and I think I was ahead of him. You have to remember that Stevenson was the Democratic candidate twice. He had quite a constituency in this country and any challenge to the leadership would have been quite effective. But he didn't attempt to use that clout.

Leadership through Friendship

The ambassador essentially places the stamp of his own personality on the [mission] delegation—that is, [in regard to] how disciplined the delegation will be, how the delegates relate to Third World countries, what the mood of the delegation is vis-à-vis the Eastern bloc, and so on. Much of the formal posturing, the coolness, that we were supposed to demonstrate toward Cuba, for example, had no particular appeal to me.

In a lot of issues, Third World countries, small countries, are not instructed. If you have a good personal relationship with the representatives, you can frequently influence their vote. The only time it's difficult to influence their vote is where they have firm instructions from their capital as to how to vote because the issue is of great

concern to their country. But there are so many issues at ECOSOC—
we had 40 to 45 issues that would arise—and many delegates from
smaller countries were simply not instructed on those issues. But
those issues were very important to the Eastern bloc, to the USSR,
or to us, at least most of the issues. Therefore, it was possible to
swing votes in the UN arena. This was one of the reasons I so enjoyed
it; you can influence votes.

I think we're a very arrogant country. When I first saw my briefing book in 1964, and I read each issue with the backup materials in
there, I started out by saying: "How can there be any other position?
Every conceivable argument here has been addressed and our reason-
ing is so impeccable." I got to ECOSOC and I sat there on one of
the very early issues. We had made our intervention and the USSR
had made theirs, which was different from ours, but we had been
prepared for that. Then some young guy from Tanganyika, without
any staff at all (I had a staff of anywhere from 15 to 35), made an
intervention and brought up a view nobody had even thought of.

In our preparation we had considered A to Z and had come up
with the fact that Y was the correct position. The USSR, the United
Kingdom, France, and others had done the same thing and they had
come up with either Y or Z as the proper position. Now, here this
guy intervened and said, "Wait a minute, I think B may be the proper
position." And his logic was very persuasive.

In short, I think it's seductive when you represent a large country
and you have all of the research and background materials prepared
for you that you do have when you represent the United States. The
tendency is to believe that you have covered all bases, and you
underestimate the fact that there is another mind out there which
may have a different set of values and a different set of perceptions.
I think we also tend to believe that we are properly motivated and
our motivations are for the best, that they're unselfish, humanitarian.
The fact of the matter is [that] we are as political as anybody else in
international diplomacy. The Vietnam War is a very good example,
or Article 19; and unless people within our system fight for the right,
such as [being] against the Vietnam War, we're going to continue
frequently to lose our positions.

My attitude to the UN was a very positive one and still is. I was
not very much involved with political issues, such as Article 19, and
the issues which came up in the Security Council. But I was very
much involved with social and economic issues, and but for the

existence of that large number of [UN] organizations and programs, the human suffering in this world would be more intolerable than it is.

They do a fantastic job: ILO, UNICEF, UNESCO, all of the specialized agencies. Those to me are what the UN is really all about. The other [i.e., political aspect of the UN], in my judgment, represents an arena, for the airing of issues, which sometimes can at least take the edge off of things—not resolve them, necessarily, but if we keep talking, at least we're not fighting. Even in that arena, think of the number of instances where UN peacekeeping forces have been sent in, and the only alternative would have been a local war, which could run the risk of becoming a much broader war. There's no question the UN is an extremely valuable institution, and that was my attitude toward it. I was very committed to it and I took my role very seriously.

ARTHUR J. GOLDBERG: Permanent Representative and Chief of the U.S. Mission to the United Nations, 1965–68.

Did you know there is no negotiating room in the UN building? Now, maybe they've changed it since I raised my objection. There is a small room that the president of the Security Council has. Then they have the debating rooms: the Security Council chamber, the trustee chamber, and the General Assembly hall. But there were no decent rooms for negotiating. Nobody ever thought about it until I raised the issue and said, "Where the devil do you sit down across a table? Do you have to go to a hotel, like in my labor days, and rent a room?"

As an attorney and later as secretary of labor, Arthur J. Goldberg earned a reputation for his flexibility and intelligence. His appointment to the Supreme Court in 1962 seemed to put the final crown on a remarkable public career; but in 1965 Goldberg resigned his position as a justice to become Adlai Stevenson's replacement as permanent representative for the United States at the United Nations.

Goldberg accepted the appointment from President Johnson with the stipulation that he be given a major role in policymaking. Goldberg did play a significant role at the United Nations. Hoping to make the United Nations a forum for negotiations instead of debate, he worked on Security Council resolutions calling for a cease-fire in the India-Pakistan War (1965), and recognizing Israel's right to exist but calling for a withdrawal from occupied territories (1967). In addition, he took a harder line on South Africa than the State Department had wanted on the South-West Africa situation.

In 1968, he resigned from his UN post and joined Hubert Humphrey's presidential campaign.

President Johnson talked to me about representing the United States at the UN, but the concept that he pulled my arm or that I was bored with the Supreme Court is nonsense. I was not, and he could not pull my arm because I was a justice. Incidentally, the fact that I made history by leaving the Supreme Court to serve at the United Nations is not entirely true. When the League of Nations was founded after World War I, there was a justice of the Supreme Court by the name of Clark who resigned—not to go to the League of Nations, but to campaign for it. That's generally been forgotten.

I have always been an omnivorous reader and I had read a good deal about the UN. I had made speeches about it and written about it long before [serving]. I knew it was not the UN of 1945; it was changed considerably. But I also felt, in light of the Article 19 crisis in particular, that (1) we ought to save it and (2) we ought to try something different. Every American ambassador before me fell into the pattern of using the UN as a debating forum, whereas I concede that while there is a place for debate, one could practice diplomacy on two levels: demonstrative diplomacy and negotiations. I felt it was important to try to transform the UN [so it could play] its most effective role: to negotiate international differences.

It was my conception and understanding that I represented our country and the president. Interestingly enough, our previous delegates, my friend Adlai Stevenson, Warren Austin, and Henry Cabot Lodge—great Americans—fell into a pattern where the UN representative worked for the State Department. Adlai was a conformist, and he had the State Department prepare his speeches, although he was a really good writer, better than I am. The only speech I took from the State Department—because I didn't have time to do it myself—was a disaster. I was too occupied with the India-Pakistan War of 1965 to write it. That was my first speech in the General Assembly. I just gave it, but I made up my mind afterwards that I would no longer do that. I wrote all my other speeches and sent them to the State Department.

Article 19: The Financial Crisis

Even before I was sworn in, I had a conversation about Article 19 with Johnson and Dean Rusk.* Rusk had told the Congress we would never yield on this point. Adlai had said the same thing, that we would not yield. This became a doctrine of faith in the Congress. A xenophobic feeling in Congress is not hard to arouse. I thought we were off on the wrong tangent. We were right legally, but what provisions were we going to use to enforce compliance?

---

*Article 19 states that a member in arrears for the preceding two years shall have no vote in the bodies of the UN. France and the Soviet Union had refused to pay their budget assessments for the UN peacekeeping operation in the Congo, thus creating a major dispute over whether they should be allowed to vote in the upcoming General Assembly. There was concern that the Soviets, in particular, might leave the UN if they were deprived of their vote.

Studying the matter, I came to the conclusion that the only thing we could do was to yield as gracefully as possible. However, we had to reserve the right to act the way the Russians were acting if we got into a similar situation of not approving of the use of UN forces in the future. That, of course, was essential to getting it through the Congress. The Republicans got to President Eisenhower first, and he issued a statement saying, in effect, the Republicans should stand firm on this issue because we had a commitment.

Even before going down and before being sworn in, I visited General Eisenhower at his farm. I thought he was a peaceful man and a nice man. I had met him many times. So I flew to Gettysburg and we had a talk. I said: "Mr. President, here is the problem. What are we going to do? Are we going to be responsible for dismantling this organization? Of course, we're not responsible in the sense that the Russians are. But in the public eye, it will be our stand that appears recalcitrant." He agreed and he immediately issued a statement, while I was there, saying he had not understood all of the facts and he felt it was necessary to make this concession. Then, of course, [Gerald] Ford, who was the House Republican leader, called me and said, "You pulled the rug from under us." Ford knew he had to follow Eisenhower, and that settled it.

It would have gone to an impasse. The UN had passed up one General Assembly [1964] where it was decided that no decision would be taken regarding a solution to the Article 19 crisis. It's not hard to break up an international group. The withdrawal of either of the two leading powers, as happened at the League of Nations, would have dismantled it.

The India-Pakistan Conflict

I started with the India-Pakistan War in September 1965. Soon after I assumed office, I became president of the Security Council. Joe Sisco [at IO] called me and told me the war had broken out. I convened the Security Council and I knew what would happen next: Pakistan would make terrible speeches and India would make terrible speeches. So I called a meeting of the four great powers in that little room that was supposedly for negotiating. I said, "Frankly, this war is a dangerous one and therefore we have got to try to bring it to an end quickly." So we discussed it. Then I thought we [had] better elevate it above the ambassadorial level, in Pakistan's case in particular. So I got President Johnson to call President Khan and Foreign Minister Bhutto. I rather liked Minister Bhutto, although the State Department did not. He was a very intelligent man as this story illustrates.

We were debating the war in the Security Council and Bhutto announced his intention to fly to the UN to present Pakistan's case. I announced that the Security Council would not reconvene until the foreign minister of Pakistan came, whereupon I received a petition signed by most of the Security Council members, saying, "We're not going to sit around waiting." They wanted to go on and talk. Bhutto, however, was the key to a cease-fire, and I wanted a commitment from him. So I answered my colleagues by saying that I would convene the Security Council as they suggested and express a personal view that the petitioners were putting their personal comfort before settling a war. This put an end to the revolt.

Bhutto arrived at 1:00 A.M. and we had a private talk lasting about 45 minutes. I said, "Look, your air force is inferior to India's and India's other forces are superior to yours." The Indian army had been reorganized after the Chinese incident and they were really winning the war. So I said: "You [had] better make the best of it. Why prolong it? Why waste lives?" He said, "Justice Goldberg, thank you for your candor." I asked him to be equally candid. He said: "Would you do me a favor? This is very painful for me. Would you allow me to make a long speech?" It was then about 2:00 A.M. (We had asked for a cease-fire by three.) "It will be a terrible speech. It's going to excoriate the Indians." And he said, "However, at one minute to three, I'll announce that we accept." So I said, "Sure, why not."

I convened the Security Council and gave him the floor, and he made a terrible speech. He called the Indians "rats" and other equally derogatory names. The Indians walked out, and there were protests by members of the Security Council that Bhutto's remarks were unseemly. Unfortunately, the Security Council has no rule which requires relevancy or permits the president of the council to censor what anybody wants to say. I allowed Bhutto to make his speech and, faithful to his commitment to me, at one minute before three he announced his acceptance of the cease-fire, bringing the war to an end and thus saving unnecessary bloodshed.

The Pueblo Incident

It was obvious what our purpose was with the [Navy spy ship] *Pueblo*. We were at war in Vietnam and could not envision being engulfed in another conflict. There was no question that the *Pueblo* was in international waters [when it was captured by North Korean vessels]. We had taped the North Koreans, so we had these tapes from the National Intelligence Agency.

What happened, there was a typical military snafu. One can argue whether we should have had a spy ship so close to an adversary in international waters, 13 miles out, but the *Pueblo* was there. The North Koreans went out with patrol boats and circled around. Then they called back to their headquarters and said, "Look, they're 13 miles out. What should we do?" The North Korean high command said, "Keep circling. Probably an American plane will come over from Seoul and rescue them. If this happens, return to port." Hours passed and when nobody came to assist the *Pueblo*, the North Koreans decided to capture it and escort it to a North Korean port.

We had a meeting at the White House after this happened, and decided that the best thing to do was to raise the issue at the UN. At least we would satisfy our public that we were trying to do something. We did make a damn good case until Rusk and McNamara messed it up in television interviews in which they said that they could not be absolutely sure that the *Pueblo* was in international waters when captured. But Rusk and McNamara had not listened to the tapes I had. I didn't know that they were going on television, or I would have raised the devil. Our presentation at the UN had been exactly accurate.

Anyhow, the UN served a purpose because after about two weeks, the Hungarian ambassador came to me (I invited him to lunch), and he asked if I knew that Hungary represented the interests of North Korea at the UN. He then said, "I have a message to give you from the North Korean government. They will not agree to appear at the UN or to acquiesce in a UN commission." I really didn't blame them. The North Koreans had not been admitted to UN membership. The Hungarian ambassador stated that the North Koreans were willing to negotiate at Panmunjom. That's how negotiations started. It took almost a year to negotiate the release of the *Pueblo* crew. In addition, although Rusk and McNamara succeeded in obscuring the record a little bit, we did make a damaging case against the North Koreans' interference with our ship in international waters.

The 1967 War and Resolution 242

The Middle East crisis in 1967 was a momentous occasion, and it showed why it is important to appoint to the UN people who have some eminence. This does not mean just personal eminence; it means having relations with the president and not being a secondary figure without such access, as is now the practice.

In 1967, Dean Rusk disqualified himself from handling the Middle East because he had been assistant secretary of state for the Middle East. He made statements which he believed would not be perceived as evenhanded. It was agreed that I would handle the Middle East crisis in 1967. It also suited the purposes of Israel and the Arab states to have the UN as the focal point.

While it was a very tough experience to get the war over within reasonable limits, that [aspect] was really not so difficult, because the Israelis had really won it in the first two days; it took a while for the Arabs to realize it. But fashioning a framework for peace was another matter.

Nineteen hundred sixty-seven was, perhaps, the last year we were able to organize a majority in support of our position, despite the growth in the [UN] membership to 127. We were able to do so as a result of a number of factors: World opinion supported Israel. Also, we gave a prominent role to the Latin Americans. They really are dedicated to international law. I had an advantage there. I could talk to them. The Russians are contemptuous of small powers, and while I recognized that ultimately we would have to get an agreement with the Russians, they were not too polite to the Latin Americans, whereas I treated the head of the Latin American group—Solomon was his name—with deference and subtlety. The Latin Americans offered a basic resolution which I rewrote and which formed the basis for 242. Importantly, our allies supported our point of view. Even Vasily Kuznetsov, then the Soviet first deputy foreign minister, was of great help after he was sent to supersede Fedorenko.

I told President Johnson that I needed the support of the White House, in the capitals of all the countries, to get the resolution passed. For example, we had trouble with the Argentines. They had an ambassador, Ruda, who could not believe that I had reached agreement with the Egyptians and the Israelis and the Russians on 242. He just wouldn't believe it. I finally got fed up with him and I called President Johnson. I said, "Will you call the president of

Argentina to tell his ambassador that it's all set and give him instructions to go along?" And Johnson did. This was a very coordinated lobbying and negotiating effort.

The UN is peculiar. One has to be sensitive to the perceptions of the various members. For example, when the Egyptians, the Israelis, and virtually every member of the Security Council was in agreement on 242, Kuznetsov came to me and he said, "Look, it's all set, but the way we operate, our Politburo passes on every word. I'll have to have a delay." We then reconvened and Kuznetsov said he needed more time. Lord Caradon objected as did the Egyptians. I spoke up and to everyone's surprise said that it was a tradition of the Security Council to honor the request of a member for a short delay to permit him to consult with his government. After the delay of a few days, Kuznetsov received his instructions and 242 was unanimously adopted. It was the end of a long and hard road.

The Value of the United Nations

The UN is not what its founders expected. But the founders expected too much, in retrospect. Archibald MacLeish wrote in that wonderful statement, the [UN Charter's] preamble, that the United Nations was established to protect the world from the scourge of war. There have been about 150 wars since then; one is now going on between Iran and Iraq. However, the American public doesn't realize that despite the terrible rhetoric at General Assembly meetings, like the anti-Zionist resolution at the General Assembly [1975], the General Assembly only makes recommendations. We have the veto power at the Security Council, so that the United States can prevent irresponsible actions such as imposition of sanctions and the like. Moreover, the UN does serve some valuable purposes. One gets a better conception of world opinion at the UN than our country gets in Washington from bilateral ambassadors. Bilateral ambassadors like to get along with their host countries and so they tend to soften the real positions of their countries. At the UN one gets a real picture of the state of the world, sad as it is. Also, just as it affords a forum for our critics, it affords a forum for us.

The staff of the UN [the Secretariat], because they despair of political solutions to world problems, emphasize social and economic programs instead. These programs are all to the good.

But these programs should go on independently at the UN, like the World Bank and the ILO. The real test of the UN is political—what it can do in political terms to assure peace and security. Its accomplishment in these areas is a mixed bag. However, if the UN were junked, we'd have to recreate it tomorrow because there is a need for a world forum.

The UN suffers from bureaucratic timidity. In general, it is over-bureaucratic in its leadership. I would make only one institutional change in the UN since there is nothing wrong with the charter. Implementation is the problem. The institutional change I recommend is to limit the secretary general's term to one term of six years. This would release him from worrying about reelection, and mitigate political pressures, and put more steam into his mediation efforts. On the whole, such efforts in recent years haven't been very effective.

JOSEPH J. SISCO: Assistant Secretary of State for International-Organization Affairs, 1965–69.

> *We were just absolutely the most effective group that you could imagine. We had a good mission, and it was always strongly supported by the active participation of people in what is now the IO bureau of the State Department. I did more work in New York, for example, than I did in Washington for extended periods of time.*

Known by his colleagues at State as "jumping Joe," because of his energy and long working hours, Joseph Sisco joined the State Department in 1951. He became a specialist in international organization affairs, and served as officer in charge of General Assembly and Security Council affairs. He became director of the Office of UN Political Affairs in 1960. In 1965 he was appointed assistant secretary of state for international-organization affairs, whereupon he worked closely with UN Ambassador Arthur J. Goldberg in directing U.S. policy in the Middle East. Sisco took chief responsibility for U.S. negotiations between Israel and the Arabs, after Goldberg's departure in 1968.

In 1969 President Nixon appointed Sisco assistant secretary of state for Near Eastern and South Asian affairs, making him one of the few persons to hold top positions in both the Johnson and the Nixon administrations (and later in the Ford administration). Sisco spent most of 1969 negotiating with the Soviets regarding the conflict in the Middle East. Though he has been described as "a great salesman," Sisco was unable to obtain results in the talks. In 1974 Sisco became undersecretary of state for political affairs.

After 25 years as a diplomat, Sisco became president (1976–80), and then chancellor (1980–81), of American University in Washington. Currently, he is a partner in Sisco Associates, a management-consulting firm, and serves as a foreign-affairs analyst for a cable-television network.

In the 1950s there was a very close coordination between the State Department and the mission. At that time the post of the U.S. representative to the UN was a cabinet-level appointment, and there was a tendency to equate it with the position of secretary of state. Practically every president has made the mistake of telling the U.S. representative at the UN that he would be a major influence on policy, and [of] describing that particular job as tantamount to a second secretary of state. The reality is that there can be only one secretary of state. Kennedy made the same mistake when he appointed Adlai Stevenson, who was disappointed at not having become secretary of state. When Johnson appointed Goldberg, he exaggerated the description of the job, and Goldberg felt that he was going to be an important influence on policy. He played a substantive role in [his] relationship to some policies, but again, the job has always been inflated in order to attract a major public figure to the position. Now, with others that have occupied the job—Mrs. Kirkpatrick, John Scali, Charlie Yost—people not of the same public stature, it is a reflection of the decreasing importance of the UN in the scheme of things insofar as American policy is concerned.

The UN is primarily a public forum. Therefore, the capacities and the limitations of U.S. representatives can be evaluated by seeing how well, how forcefully they expressed themselves. Another yardstick has always been skill at private diplomacy, which is below the tip of the iceberg. The ability to actually negotiate many resolutions is therefore a second dimension. That is diplomacy in the more traditional sense.

Third, in view of the fact that the organization is located in New York and [that] we are the principal architect, what sort of a role could that individual play in the interaction between the external and the domestic? How influential is an ambassador in influencing executive U.S. policy? How influential in explaining and justifying American policy to our Congress?

Those, I think, are very important yardsticks by which to measure effectiveness. I think that is the broad context. You have to really evaluate an individual representative both as the public figure making public presentations and as the more traditional diplomat in serious negotiations.

Henry Cabot Lodge

Henry Cabot Lodge was very effective in his public presentations. He left the detailed negotiations largely to the key members of his staff. Lodge considered himself an equal of Secretary of State Dulles, and he had a certain respect for Dulles's substantive judgment. On the whole, I would say that the relationship between Dulles and Lodge was also very good.

There were a number of occasions where on specific issues, Lodge's recommendation carried very great weight. For example, during the whole Suez crisis he was quite influential in the basic approach that Eisenhower took. Moreover, the principal focus of

American policy was on the UN's effort to achieve a cease-fire and to get the British and the French and the Israelis out. Eventually, as you know, the detailed negotiations took place between John Foster Dulles and Golda Meir in order to achieve the final withdrawal of the Israelis at that time. But Lodge played a very key role throughout that whole period and in getting the UN to decide on a peacekeeping force.

In the initial phases Lodge really didn't quite have any deep understanding of what this big, massive State Department was. We at State got around that by very quickly intermingling with [the U.S. Mission]. In other words, members of the IO, which was then called the United Nations Bureau, began to spend a lot of time with the U.S. Mission in New York and with the UN delegation. Without sounding self-serving, I was a key bridge. Once he developed confidence in me, I represented "the State Department" to him in a very disproportionate way. But that was my function.

We established an office for Henry Cabot Lodge right in the State Department, so that there was a physical proximity to the bureau as well. We developed little institutional mechanisms to make the link. For example, we informally checked with him and got his views on specific policy questions beforehand. We would develop the policy consensus orally. That would be embodied in an approved telegram, which was really sending back to him an approach that we had worked out with him in advance. The IO bureau was the middleman between the secretary of state and the U.S. representative to the UN. Our job there was to anticipate differences between the two and, above all, to work them out, to the degree to which it was possible, before they reached a confrontational stage at the presidential level. That is the test of a good assistant secretary.

In order to keep the positions of the secretary and the U.S. ambassador together, at every opening of a General Assembly [the third Tuesday in September], the secretary of state goes to New York and discusses policies with foreign ministers across the board for two weeks. Then he makes the speech in the general debate. The important talks are the diplomatic consultations in the Waldorf-Astoria, where the U.S. ambassador lives on the forty-second floor, and where the secretary of state and his staff were on the thirty-fifth floor; there we met with foreign ministers from 100 countries in two or three weeks. The job of the IO man was to be sure that both the mission as well as the secretary's staff were on the same wavelength. That system worked, and it has been the pattern for years.

Adlai Stevenson

Adlai Stevenson was deeply disappointed that he didn't become president, and deeply disappointed that Rusk became secretary of state rather than he. He had no real respect for Kennedy. He considered himself a liberal; he considered Kennedy really a conservative, regardless of the fact that they were both Democrats.

Stevenson was very effective in his public pronouncements because, after all, he was a world figure. During the presidential elections, if the votes had been taken outside the confines of the United States, he would have won hands down. He was respected worldwide in that regard as a great American and therefore played a very important role. He did not get himself into the nitty-gritty of UN negotiations, but he played a very significant role at a very key juncture. One of the souring aspects of his stewardship was with respect to the whole Bay of Pigs [incident], and the fact that he was embarrassed by having been provided with the wrong information. It was really a "cover" story, and he hadn't been told that it was. He threatened to resign (as U.S. Ambassador), and he was on the verge of resigning but he was talked out of it with a promise that he would never be misled in that way again. During the whole Cuba missile crisis, he played an important role. But the difficulties came later when he suggested certain substantive positions as they related to an exchange of our Turkish bases for the withdrawal of the missiles— which was viewed negatively by a lot of other officials. That's a story which is well known.

In terms of evaluating Adlai at the UN, he gave the job stature, dignity, respect. But he viewed it largely as a secondary show, which it was. He had a very good relationship with the two of us, namely, Harlan Cleveland, the assistant secretary, and myself, the then deputy assistant secretary. We did most of his staff work on all of the problems because we were much more substantively able to do it with all of the resources of the State Department. He used the UN job as a means of socializing and, therefore, the representational aspect [of diplomacy] was very extensive from Adlai's point of view.

Arthur Goldberg

Goldberg is very interesting. His forte was clearly [in gaining a] consensus, [in] negotiation, and an ability to put together disparate positions. He has never received the credit he deserves. He is the true architect of Security Council Resolution 242, not Lord Caradon [of the United Kingdom]. Eventually, the British draft came out, but the substance was developed by the United States and Goldberg. President Johnson and Dean Rusk, to their credit, gave Goldberg at that time a broad delegation of power. Johnson said, "You will know what the domestic parameters are as to what is acceptable." Goldberg got more out of the Israelis, by way of concessions, than any other U.S. representative could have gotten.

The Arabs, for the most part, respected Goldberg as the U.S. representative to the UN and a powerful force within the administration. Therefore, they took the view that they were dealing with the U.S. government and U.S. policy rather than with an individual. I wouldn't say there was any deep love for him, because of the traditional hostility between Arabs and Jews. But they did not allow that to be an impediment because, after all, these are national interests and governments were dealing with governments. Today every Arab stands [firm] on 242.

In those days Goldberg was damned. Why? Because, quite frankly, in that negotiation the United States prevented the resolution [242] from saying what the Russians and the Arabs wanted it to say: total Israeli withdrawal to the pre-June 1967 line. What it says is: Withdraw Israeli forces to the lines that are negotiated between the two sides. Goldberg made a monumental contribution in that regard.

There were two other big areas of policy that Goldberg sought to influence. One is Vietnam. He regularly sent the president and the secretary of state his concrete views as to what ought to be done. Secondly, he influenced policy very considerably in the area of disarmament and nuclear policy—nonproliferation. I would also add that he made a very substantial contribution to the Cyprus issue, even though others were presumably out on the front line negotiating.

A Continuing Benefit

There is one element of continuity and constancy which has been very important during the period of overwhelming American supremacy in the UN (the 1950s), in the period of equilibrium between East and West in the UN (the 1960s), and even in this more difficult period wherein the United States is in a minority in the General Assembly. The bread-and-butter issues are considered in the Security Council, where we still have a veto. But the positive thread of continuity lies in the ongoing peacekeeping operations of the UN on the ground in Cyprus, in the Middle East, in Pakistan and Kashmir, and so on. This is where I think the positive UN role continues, and, interestingly enough, it continues despite different changes in the organization, simply because there is still the coincidence of interests between the major powers. Where they want to stay out of a situation, the UN provides the mechanism for them to stay out.

FRANK CHURCH: Congressional Delegate to the General Assembly, 1966.

I had always endorsed and supported the United Nations in a state [Idaho] where the John Birch Society maintained a continuous billboard campaign with the slogan, "Take the U.S. out of the UN, and the UN out of the U.S." The anti-UN campaign began before my election to the Senate in 1956 and has continued to the present day.

As Democratic senator from Idaho (1956-80) and a candidate for the presidency (1976), Frank Church's most significant foreign-policy activities concerned the Vietnam War. An early opponent of U.S. support for South Vietnam, he urged a negotiated end to the war once the United States had become seriously involved. In 1966 Church was a member of the U.S. Mission to the United Nations. In 1978 he undertook three days of talks with Cuban leader Fidel Castro, which led to the release of 84 Americans and their families from Cuba. Church became the chairman of the Foreign Relations Committee in 1979, but lost his 1980 reelection bid to his Republican opponent. Frank Church died in 1984.

I was a member of the Senate Foreign Relations Committee, and it was the practice of senators to alternate with members of the House so that the American delegation in each General Assembly included either two congressmen or two senators. In 1966 it was the Senate's turn, and the leadership looked first to the Foreign Relations Committee in the selection of senators who were appointed as delegates to the General Assembly; 1966 was my turn.

When I served as a delegate, the growing disarray in the General Assembly was becoming more apparent, in the sense that those governments which financed the UN and its peacekeeping efforts had less and less to say about the resolutions being passed by the assembly. This gave the smaller Third World countries free rein to exercise their majority at any time they wished, and they did so with increasing frequency.

I believe the financial contribution of the United States then amounted to about a third [31.5 percent] of the general levy for the maintenance of the UN Secretariat. There was a heated argument at the time (the Article 19 controversy) because the Soviet Union had refused to pay its share of the cost of the peacekeeping forces in the

Congo. The United States was trying to force the issue, but the matter was finessed. I took an interest in the system of assessed contributions and the possibility of independent sources of income for the UN, which would give it a modicum of financial independence—for example, securing for the UN certain royalties from the mining of mineral deposits at the bottom of the oceans in international waters. I made such a proposal, upon my return to the Senate, in my report on the UN session.

At first I worked with the Fifth Committee, the Budget Committee of the General Assembly. Then, Ambassador Arthur Goldberg, who followed my work and apparently approved of the fact that I was giving full time to the assignment, shifted me to the First Committee. I preferred the work on the First Committee because it was political in character. It was there that I debated the Korean issue with the Soviet delegate. The United States prevailed again on that issue, as we had in the past. I rather enjoyed the role of being an advocate, in which I simply accepted the position of my government and served as spokesman for it, rather than being involved in determining what that position should be. None of us at the mission appeared to have much influence on what position the American government should take on the issues. As far as I could gather, those decisions were made in Washington. Arthur Goldberg may have had some effect, but I think that he was seldom satisfied that his advice was sufficiently considered.

Contrasting the United Nations with Congress

I think we ought not confuse the UN, either the General Assembly or the Security Council, with a legislative body like the Congress. The UN and Congress are two very different institutions. The UN consists of sovereign nations, and those who represent their respective countries at the UN are bound by the instructions they receive from their governments, with the result that they very rarely have the latitude to change their position on most issues. The representatives are not there to exercise their personal judgment, but to carry out the policy of their governments, as determined elsewhere. This is very different from the duties of a U.S. senator or a member of Congress, who is free to decide his own position on each vote taken.

A second difference to stress is that the UN is not a world government. Those critics who expected the UN to maintain world peace, through the exercise of some kind of supragovernmental authority, ignored the fact that the UN, under its charter, has been given precious little power. Only the Security Council can enforce its resolutions by the establishment of a UN peacekeeping force. In practice, this has been done only where the governments concerned in a given dispute agree to accept a UN peacekeeping force; and then such a force can be constituted only when the permanent members of the Security Council unanimously concur. Any one of the permanent members can veto any peacekeeping proposal brought before the Security Council. The result is that the UN can do only what can be agreed upon by consensus in the Security Council.

The General Assembly has even less power. Although it is principally a hortatory body, it does furnish a safety valve, where governments can find a platform for voicing their views. But a lifelong assignment to sit in the General Assembly would be my idea of purgatory. The delegates must sit and listen to endless preachments, many of which are hypercritical, and do so with the knowledge that the whole exercise is largely a charade.

Even when resolutions are passed by the assembly, they are advisory in nature, and unenforceable. This is not to say that the UN has been useless. I think not. From time to time, it's been possible to form a UN peace force that has had a vital part to play in the avoidance of war. Moreover, the UN has found an entirely different role in the so-called nation-building activities of the many international bodies that have been formed as affiliates of the UN, the various agencies working in such fields as agriculture, health, and economic development. So I would say, in our world and in these times, such an organization needs to function, and one would hope that it might grow more effective over the course of time. On balance, the UN is far more of a plus for the world than a minus.

I don't think that any American representative at the UN, whatever his style, is going to sway many votes. The outcome of a debate in the General Assembly can be forecast, much like the outcome in, say, the House of Commons, where the interchange can be lively and even exciting to witness, but where, once it's over, the members vote the party line—and the outcome is predetermined before the first word is uttered. Now, a feisty ambassador for the United States at the UN is likely to win an appreciative audience out among the American people, who like to hear our representative lay it on the rest of the world. So, I suppose that those whose style is confrontation get more notice here at home and, on the whole, more approval, than those who keep a low profile.

Whether a congressman finds working at the General Assembly a worthwhile experience depends on the blinders he is wearing upon arrival. I had rather expected it to be as I found it. Working at the UN for a three-month period provides a congressional delegate with an opportunity to discover firsthand how the UN functions—a healthy exercise for any member of Congress. So the practice of including two members of Congress in the American delegation at each General Assembly is, I think, worthwhile.

In general, the whole experience gave me a better understanding of both the strengths and the weaknesses of the UN. It dispelled any illusion that the UN might become something other than a looking glass in which one found the reflection of all the members—that it might someday become more than the sum of its parts.

WILLIAM B. BUFFUM: Deputy Permanent Representative to the United Nations, 1967–69.

Probably I've had more time working on UN affairs by now than any American still active in public life. It has covered a whole range of exposures from being one of the most junior officers to being one of the most senior. I came to the job with no prior knowledge or preconceptions about the UN. It was just an assignment from the Department of State personnel division.

William B. Buffum served in the U.S. Army during World War II and became a vice consul of the State Department in 1949. After serving as a political officer in Germany, he returned to Washington in 1958. During the 1960s Buffum worked at the Office of UN Political Affairs of the State Department, becoming deputy director and later director; then he was named deputy assistant secretary for international-organization affairs.

As deputy U.S. representative at the UN, with the rank of ambassador, from 1967 to 1970, he served under Arthur Goldberg, Charles R. Wiggins, George Ball, and then Charles Yost. After three years as ambassador to Lebanon (1970-73), Buffum returned to Washington, where he worked as assistant secretary of state for international-organization affairs until 1976. In 1976 he became UN undersecretary general for political and General Assembly affairs.

My first involvement in UN problems came in 1958 when I was transferred from my post in the embassy in Bonn to the State Department, into an office called United Nations Political Affairs, which is in the Bureau of International Organizations [IO]. This is something that I had not sought; it was part of the automatic Foreign Service rotation system. My entire Foreign Service career up to that point had been in two different diplomatic posts in Germany.

Over a period of time, I began working into a large variety of topics which were on the agenda of the General Assembly. It began, interestingly enough, with disarmament and outer space. In our inimitable way, we in the bureaucracy have duplication of effort many times. We even had a separate office of disarmament affairs, which established the substance of disarmament policy. But since IO is the conduit for all instructions to the U.S. Mission to the UN, the staff in IO is also obliged to keep track of what's going on in New York; funnel that information to the substantive office in the department; help draft instructions in that area back to the mission; and provide whatever is needed by way of procedural or technical input recommending how you go about developing a resolution—what is important in terms of cosponsorship, timing, and that sort of thing.

You get into a blend of substance and procedure in that job, which I found fascinating particularly because it brought me to New York, over a period of years, working as a very junior adviser with the U.S. delegation. That was at a time when Henry Cabot Lodge was the ambassador. There I worked steadily from 1958 until 1967, moving up the line gradually as more senior people moved on to something else. The deputy director of the office at that time was Joe Sisco. We worked very, very closely together, very well together, if I may say so, and as time went by and Joe went up the hierarchy, he asked me to stay on and move along with him.

By 1967 I had moved up to the post of deputy assistant secretary of state for international-organization affairs. Arthur Goldberg, who was then the ambassador, asked me if I would come to New York as his deputy. I hadn't known him terribly well, but it was a new administration here under his direction and he wanted to bring people who met certain criteria.

That was one of the most rewarding, exciting times of my life, because Goldberg is a marvelous human being. He's the greatest negotiator I ever met, he has an excellent mind, and he's a very kind person. He was good enough to tell me that if I took that job, he wanted me to serve as his alter ego—in effect, that I should be in on everything, and if he were not there, that I should expect to take full control.

It was just after I arrived here that war broke out in the Middle East in June of 1967. From then on the United Nations was front page for months. Those debates were televised live. (It doesn't happen anymore; now you get an occasional film clip.) It [the Middle East] was the center ring of the world circus and the most burning security issue of the day. I don't know how many meetings of the Security Council we had. [It] moved into an emergency session of the General Assembly that summer, then back into the council for adoption of the famous Resolution 242, which is still the only basis for an agreed approach to a Middle East peace settlement. The UN in many respects was in its heyday then.

The Middle East crisis was the most concentrated period of work and energy in my life. We calculated, after it was all over, that, at least as far as I was concerned, I had spent four-and-a-half months in the office without a day away from the desk—not a Sunday, not a Saturday, not a holiday; and many of these days ran from early morning until two and three the following morning because the sessions ran so long. Even after the sessions were over, you had your reports to write to Washington, you had planning papers and draft resolutions to prepare for the next day. So it was a period which becomes something of a blur even in retrospect.

A great deal of our effort was in trying to negotiate a sensible resolution of the Middle East dispute, first in the council and later in the General Assembly. Most of my efforts were in [helping] Ambassador Goldberg draft resolutions, contact delegations, lobby, and write papers with policy recommendations; and in serving as liaison with State Department—a variety of tasks that go into representing the United States at the UN.

I worked mostly with Lord Caradon of Great Britain, who was one of the sparkplugs at that time. Of course, we also worked quite closely with the French, although not always in total harmony. Ambassador Berard of France was there at the time. Then, of course, the ambassador of Denmark, Hans Tabor, who was council president during one of the most critical months, was also an important contact outside the U.S. Mission.

We also had to concentrate quite heavily on our dialogue with the Latin American group, particularly [with] the Argentine ambassador, Ruda, who is now on the International Court of Justice. Argentina was on the Security Council at that point. We had a lot of difficulties with their government. It took a lot of effort to try and arrive at a common approach.

Our basic approach was to try and find a formula that both the Arab governments concerned and the Israelis would cooperate in. I think that at that point in time, Argentina and Ambassador Ruda tended to take a more formalistic and legalistic approach in terms of the merits of the case. They felt that international law simply should not countenance the retention of any territory taken by force. The general concept has emerged in Resolution 242, calling for withdrawal from occupied territories, but not saying from all the occupied territories. Our position was that you had to leave room for some negotiation and perhaps rectification of the old frontiers to provide for a new and more stable arrangement in the area. It was very difficult, for a long time, to get some governments, including Latin American governments, to accept that.

If you look at the record of the debate and the resolutions of that time, I don't think one could consider them anti-Israel in the sense that people now see resolutions after a series of events over the past year. It is true that there was a large majority which did not want to acquiesce in Israel's insistence that the borders were subject to renegotiations, and that they would not be obliged to withdraw their forces from all of the territories that they had occupied. Here you come upon a very interesting point. When member states or the assembly as a whole take a position which is not consonant with or identical to Israel's position, can one properly characterize that as being anti-Israel? I think that's too simplistic. There are a lot of elements, including very principled elements, involved here, where governments can legitimately differ in their impressions.

In fact, Israel was blessed, in my view, with one of the most eloquent speakers I've ever heard in this place, and that was Abba Eban—absolutely Churchillian in his approach. It was exciting to work with him. He was a fascinating man of tremendous energy; a brilliant mind. He would arrive after an all-night flight from Tel Aviv with a big yellow pad, and he would sit down in his hotel room at the Pierre. There he would write out his speech for the next day in longhand. Goldberg and I and Dick Pedersen, who was my colleague more exclusively responsible just for the Middle East, would sit down with him and discuss the nature of the debate coming up, the probable course of voting and resolutioneering. He had an extremely penetrating and perceptive mind.

Representational activities were truncated during the Middle East crisis because we simply didn't have time [for them]. But aside from that, when time permitted, [they have] always been an important part of doing that job. The Goldbergs were very gracious and hospitable. Dorothy—Mrs. Goldberg—is an artist and she had devoted great love and care to refurnishing 42A in the Waldorf. They entertained there very graciously. It was an extremely important adjunct, as socializing is to the advancement of most diplomatic and political interests around the world.

On one occasion there was a luncheon given by Ambassador Goldberg in the Waldorf Towers for Security Council members. This was during the time of the 1967 war, after we had gone through the Security Council and then the emergency special session of the assembly that summer. Among the guests was [Soviet] Ambassador Fedorenko. We have a guest book at the mission and people are asked to sign in. Well, he strode through the door and walked past the table that had the guest book. Our chief of protocol, who was standing there, a very conscientious young lady, said to him, "Mr. Ambassador Fedorenko, won't you please sign and indicate your mission?" He stopped and looked around a minute, folded his bow tie a little tighter, took his pen, and wrote down, "Ambassador Fedorenko, mission impossible." True. Absolutely true. If you go back to the beating they took in the General Assembly, I can see why.

Personality makes all the difference. It really does. People will accept [an] unpleasant and diverse policy approach from you if you handle it the right way. In fact, I just recently came across a different definition of a diplomat than I had ever heard before: A diplomat is someone who can tell you to go to hell in such a way that you actually look forward to making the trip.

Over a period of time, I saw in how many ways basic U.S. interests were served by participating actively in trying to improve upon, and take a positive approach toward, UN proceedings or UN programs. It has been a fantastic educational process. If you approach it at any given moment in history and shine the flashlight on this or that aspect, you may see a pleasant scene or you may see a very unhappy scene. But if you look at the whole range of what has happened here over the years, both the good and the negative things, I don't think anyone can leave that examination without being persuaded that the UN is a useful, necessary place in the world today.

GEORGE BALL: Permanent Representative and Chief of the U.S. Mission to the United Nations, 1968.

> *I approached the assignment knowing a good deal more about the UN than most of my predecessors or successors in that job. I had been giving instructions to the ambassadors to the United Nations—Mr. Stevenson and then Mr. Goldberg—for about five years. Besides that, I had some well-settled views about what the UN was and how it could be used. The UN, in my judgment, was a victim of excessive expectations following the experience of the League of Nations.*

During World War II, George William Ball served as legal counsel to the Lend-Lease Administration, and later as director of the U.S. Strategic Bombing Survey, a civilian group established to assess the social, economic, and physical effects of Allied bombing attacks on Germany.

After the war, Ball returned to private practice as a specialist in international trade, serving later as an adviser to presidential aspirant Adlai Stevenson and, under President Kennedy, becoming, in rapid succession, undersecretary of state for economic affairs and then undersecretary of state, the second-ranking position in the department. During the Kennedy years, he oversaw the lowering of trade tariffs and played a crucial role in defending the UN intervention in the Katanga Province of the Congo in 1961. Ball left the Johnson administration in 1966 because he felt he could not influence administration policy concerning the Vietnam War (which he opposed). He returned to serve briefly as permanent representative to the UN in 1968.

In recent years, Ball has been an investment banker at Lehman Brothers Kuhn Leob and an adviser to presidential candidates, including Jimmy Carter.

The Council of the League of Nations was a precursor to the Security Council of the United Nations; the assumption was that if the great powers could agree on some common objectives and on keeping the peace among themselves, they would then unite, through the Security Council, to keep the small powers in line and to settle such local and regional conflicts that might arise.

This was always a foredoomed effort because it assumed that the powers that had cooperated during World War II would continue to cooperate in peacetime. Even toward the latter days of the war, however, it was clear that the objectives and interests of the Soviet Union and the Western democracies were quite at odds with one another. Certainly after the emergence of the Cold War, after Churchill's Iron

Curtain speech and more that followed, it was clear that the under-lying assumption that the great powers could agree to keep the peace was no longer valid.

Czechoslovakian Invasion

We and the Soviets spent a good many hours savaging one another in the UN, following the Soviet Union's push into Czechoslovakia [1968]. Relations were impersonal at all times. I remember one night we had gone on until about three o'clock in the morning. The Soviets had been conducting a real filibuster and the Soviet ambassador, Malik, and I had made a lot of vituperative comments. We appeared to be attacking one another savagely before the television cameras, but when the cameras went off, Malik pounded me on the back and said, "Well, I guess I kept you up late tonight, didn't I?" That was that. He was a professional.

We were going through the motions and putting on a good show, but there was nothing more we could do and the Johnson administration was wise enough not to try to put on meaningless sanctions and make a lot of noise. There was nothing useful we could do other than what we did do: We got the Security Council to pass a strong resolution. That was the only role the UN could play at the time. We didn't go into hysterics and make empty gestures. Economic sanctions would have no effect except on domestic public opinion. The United States had faced this same problem in 1956 as in 1968, and in neither case did we go through with a ritual of sanctions.

We talk far too much about the Soviet threat. The competition between the two major powers today is not so much ideological as national. Gas has very largely escaped from the Soviet ideological balloon, but the power struggle continues. The Soviets are having great problems. Their economic difficulties are horrendous; they've got social problems; they've got demographic problems because the ethnic Russians are not maintaining their share of the population, so that the other nationalities in the Soviet Socialist republics are becoming more dominant. I would hate to be in the Kremlin and have to face these problems.

At the same time, the Soviets continue to allocate a substantial part of their GNP to building up their military forces, so we have to be on guard. I don't believe the situation has changed much. All of these shrill cries about superiority and inferiority are just political and ideological nonsense.

Representing the United States

The American ambassador should be a good professional who understands the job, unlike the present occupant [Kirkpatrick], who doesn't have the vaguest clue as to what her job is in the UN.

The post of permanent representative to the UN has a nominal, honorary designation as cabinet status. But that means nothing. We don't have a cabinet government; we have a presidential government. The idea that the ambassador to the UN, no matter who he or she may be, could be in the mainstream of the formulation of American policy is nonsense. As what is now called the deputy secretary of state, I was in the mainstream of the making of American policy for five years. I knew very well I could never remain in the mainstream with my post at the United Nations, and I didn't even try.

The idea that the ambassador to the UN can develop policies of her own and work them out with the president, and not report to the secretary of state, is a mark of unprofessionalism. It shows an ignorance of the history and the significance of the job and how the U.S. government works. Andy Young was similarly deluded by the thought that he was an independent agent. By contrast, Don McHenry was an extremely good professional who handled the job superbly. He had experience. He knew what he was doing and he knew what the job was.

I recognized the UN for what it is. I knew exactly what I was getting into. My views when I got there were exactly the same as when I left. I am a supporter of the United Nations. I regard the UN as an extremely useful institutional arrangement helping to maintain peace. It has a dozen uses and fulfills them well, but it has always been a victim of excessive expectations. Moreover, our particular, idiosyncratic relationship with Israel has distorted our own position to the point where it has diminished the effectiveness of the UN as an instrument of American national policy.

The UN was never an effective instrument for settling problems among the great powers or between East and West. Its most important achievement has been to serve as a kind of midwife, bringing into existence 100 or 115 new nations; in other words, it has been the instrument to manage, to stimulate, [and], at the same time, to prevent major breakage from, the movement of a billion people from colonial dependency to some kind of independence. That enormous change in the political structure of the world could never have been accomplished if the UN had not been available to play its role, and I think it played it extremely well. At the same time, it has changed politically from a world dominated by a handful of great powers to a scene in which power is shared among 150 nations. That has substantially altered the character of world politics and, at the same time, has changed the character of the United Nations. So long as the United Nations consisted of maybe 50 nations, as it did originally, it was one thing. They were nations that had a more or less common set of objectives. The Third World countries brought into the councils of the UN had objectives necessarily different from the industrialized, advanced powers.

Thus inevitably, the Third World countries have pursued narrow objectives defined in terms of their own particular problems of development and advancement—of modernization and other essential steps to move into a twentieth-century world. These narrowly focused problems often led them to trade off whatever votes they may have for partisan positions on major, cosmic problems—rather cavalierly. When economically advanced nations were the sole members of the United Nations, one could assume that each of them had some sense of the world's scene and thought of problems not only in nationalistic but also in global terms. That is now denied by circumstance to the Third World countries; they basically play no role on the world scene except to the extent they can trade their votes in the UN for something that is specifically of interest to them.

The UN has provided legitimacy for the new small nations. It has given the leaders [the] exposure to international problems which they wouldn't have obtained otherwise. In that sense it has been extremely helpful. The UN has also performed a useful peacekeeping role in many areas of the world.

PHOTOGRAPHS

A general view of the Security Council conference room during the vote of the Sanction Resolution on Korea at Lake Success, New York, June 27, 1950. The seat of the USSR is vacant due to its boycott of the Security Council during this period. (Courtesy of *UNITED NATIONS*.)

127

Big Four of U.S. delegation of 1946 in Flushing, New York. (*Left to right*): Warren Austin, Senator Tom Connally, Eleanor Roosevelt, and Senator Arthur Vandenberg. (Courtesy of *UNITED NATIONS*.)

Abba Eban (*right*) explaining Israel's position to three members of the U.S. delegation. *From left*: Henry Cabot Lodge, Jr., James W. Barco, and Frederick T. Rope, before the opening of a Security Council meeting on January 17, 1956. (Courtesy of *UNITED NATIONS*/pcd.)

Ambassador Adlai E. Stevenson during a press conference held at UN Headquarters on December 18, 1963. (Courtesy of *UNITED NA-TIONS*, YN/ARA.)

The UN Commission on Human Rights considered proposals seeking an end to laws perpetuating prejudice and intolerance. Eleanor Roosevelt and Marietta Tree, of the U.S. delegation, seen outside the Economic and Social Council on March 10, 1961. (Courtesy of *UNITED NATIONS*, YN/ARA.)

Arthur J. Goldberg (*left*) discussing a point with Abdel Monem Rifa'i, Minister of State for Foreign Affairs of Jordan, during a Security Council meeting on the situation in the Middle East, November 9–10, 1967. (Courtesy of *UNITED NATIONS*, TC/ARA.)

Shirley Temple Black, seen here with members of the U.S. delegation at a press conference at the opening of the 1969 General Assembly. To her right is William Coleman; second to her left is Rita Hauser. (Courtesy of *UNITED NATIONS*, Chen/jr.)

George Bush (*right*) conferring with Yakov A. Malik (*left*) of the Soviet Union during a Security Council meeting in Addis Ababa on February 4–5, 1972. (Courtesy of *UNITED NATIONS*, Y. Nagata/ARA.)

Henry A. Kissinger (*right*), Secretary of State, and William W.
Scranton during a meeting of the General Assembly on September
30, 1976. (Courtesy of *UNITED NATIONS*, S. Lwin/ARA.)

Seen here is the U.S. delegation to the 1978 General Assembly Special Session on Disarmament, headed by Cyrus R. Vance (*left*, at table), Secretary of State. Seated next to him are W. Averell Harriman and Senator George McGovern. In the back row are Paul Newman and Ambassador Andrew Young. (Courtesy of *UNITED NATIONS*, Y. Nagata/ARA.)

Secretary of State George Shultz and Jeane J. Kirkpatrick during an official visit to UN Headquarters at which discussions were held with Secretary-General Javier Perez De Cuellar (*right*) on September 27, 1982. (Courtesy of *UNITED NATIONS*, Y. Nagata.)

PART III:
THE NIXON–FORD YEARS,
1969–76

OVERVIEW

The early 1970s began with two major developments that seemed likely to enhance the position of the United Nations as a major factor in international affairs. The first was the election to the U.S. presidency of Richard Nixon, who had campaigned on a pledge to reduce the American involvement in Vietnam through the negotiation of a "peace with honor." Such an agreement would remove a major bone of contention between the United States and the Soviet Union—indeed, between the United States and much of the world, including many of its traditional allies. The second major development was the Nixon-Kissinger policy of détente with, initially, the Soviet Union and then, later, Communist China as well. In theory, at least, the establishment of good relations among the superpowers could only improve the atmosphere at the United Nations.

In fact, however, the United Nations did not markedly increase its role in world political affairs, perhaps in part because of the growing exercise of power by the Third World nations. It was during the 1970s that the Group of 77, as the nonaligned in the United Nations styled themselves, by their very numbers assumed control over the General Assembly. As nonaligned powers, they did not belong to any one camp. Neutrality gave them the potential for acting as a moderating influence on the superpowers, but their votes also allowed them often to thwart the will of the superpowers in the United Nations—which raised the possibility of a stalemated United

Nations: The economically disadvantaged nations had most of the votes, but little real power, and the economically developed nations had few votes, but most of the world's financial and industrial power. As the Third World nations began to intertwine international political affairs and their own economic-development interests in their UN dealings, they came into collision with many developed nations, especially the United States, which tried to keep the two sets of issues separate.

In 1971 a majority at the United Nations favored the seating of the People's Republic of China (PRC) as the sole representative of China, and the assembly voted for the expulsion of Taiwan, despite some U.S.-led efforts to maintain seats for both countries. During this period, Henry Kissinger had made his highly publicized trip to Peking, and the following year Nixon visited China. With Nixon's overtures for normalization of relations with Peking, American policy began to reflect the majority viewpoint toward the PRC at the United Nations.

The Paris peace accords, allowing the withdrawal of the last American troops from Indochina in March 1973, were signed by the United States and the North and South Vietnamese governments. The peace later proved to be short-lived when, in 1975, Communist North Vietnamese forces overran South Vietnam, Cambodia, and Laos.

The process of détente included the successful culmination of the Strategic Arms Limitation Talks (SALT) in 1974 during the Ford presidency. International tensions were further relaxed in 1975 with the signing of the Helsinki accords by 35 Western and Eastern European nations and the United States. The agreement recognized the existing borders of Europe as "inviolable"—thus, in effect, endorsing Soviet hegemony in Eastern Europe while aiming at improving the right of emigration from Russia.

Regional Conflicts

The United Nations proved important when Egypt and Syria attacked Israel during the so-called Yom Kippur War of 1973. When the United States began a resupply of the strained Israeli forces, the Arab states announced an oil embargo against the West. Security Council Resolution 338 called for a cease-fire by all parties. After the Soviet Union hinted that it might intervene militarily, the United States placed its troops on alert, and helped win the Security Council's Resolution 340, which established the 4,000-person UN Emergency Force II in the Sinai. (The force did not include troops from permanent members of the council.) Meanwhile, the Israelis were able to secure a major victory, though at a heavy cost. By the end of the year, Egypt and Israel had agreed to a ceasefire, resulting in part from Henry Kissinger's shuttle diplomacy. Israel and Syria later reached a settlement on May 31, 1974 as well. The UN Disengagement Observer Force (UNDOF) patrolled in the Golan Heights. In 1971 war broke out between India and Pakistan, over the attempt by East Pakistan (Bangladesh) to secede from Pakistan. The United States noted that the conflict "demonstrated again the severe limitations on the [United Nation's] ability to carry out its primary function, the maintenance of international peace and security."

In 1974 the United Nations's attention shifted to the dispute between Turkey and Greece, over Cyprus, and to Turkey's invasion of the island nation. A flurry of resolutions was passed by the Security Council, calling for a cease-fire and criticizing the Turkish action. The UN Peacekeeping Force in Cyprus remained on the island, with only sporadic violence occurring between the Greek and Turkish Cypriots.

At the 1974 assembly, the chairman of the Palestine Liberation Organization (PLO), Yasir Arafat, was invited to participate in a debate on the question of Palestine. Shortly thereafter, in a departure from tradition, the PLO was granted non-voting-observer status by the Assembly, something usually accorded only to neutral states such as Switzerland and the Vatican, by a vote of 95–17. It was also stated that the Palestinians were entitled to national determination.

These issues carried forward into 1975. A Committee on the Exercise of the Inalienable Rights of the Palestinian People was established by the assembly. Advocates of the expulsion of the Jewish state from the United Nations failed to win approval of such a measure in that year's meeting of the nonaligned nations; but 72 countries voted for an Arab-sponsored assembly resolution that "determined" that Zionism is a form of racism. Reflecting the strong feelings of Americans opposed to the resolution, U.S. Ambassador Moynihan vehemently denounced it and its supporters. Nevertheless, some observers believe that Moynihan's vocal opposition and direct criticism of Third World countries may have contributed to the resolution's passage. Later in 1975, the Security Council, as a procedural matter—over the opposition of the United States and its allies—invited the PLO to participate in discussions of Israeli air attacks on Lebanon. The assembly condemned Israel's occupation of Arab territories, but a Security Council resolution criticizing Israel for its retaliatory attacks on Lebanon was vetoed by the United States. Despite the debate in the United Nations over the Middle East, the UN Interim Force in Lebanon and the UNDOF remained in the region as buffers between Israel and the Arab states (Egypt and Syria).

Moynihan's denunciations of the Zionism-is-racism resolution and his other rebukes addressed to the Third World represented the climax of a hostility that had been developing for some years. The Third World, seemingly led by its more radical members, had become increasingly shrill and monolithic in its opposition to South Africa and Israel.

But Moynihan had not been the first American permanent representative to accuse the Third World delegations of acting onesidedly. Moynihan's predecessor, John Scali, had delivered the most articulate warning to the Third World. In his "tyranny of the majority" speech of December 1974, he asserted that the United Nations was losing the support of the American people. He criticized the world organizations for adopting "one-sided, unrealistic resolutions that cannot be implemented." Some of these, he said, ignored the UN Charter. Similar criticisms were made by other Western nations. Scali spoke to the assembly, but the shift in sentiment could be measured in the Security Council as well. Between 1945 and 1970, the Soviet Union cast 105 vetoes, the United States one. In the next six years, the Soviet Union cast five vetoes, the United States 20.

Southern Africa

The United Nations focused increased attention on southern Africa during 1969–76. The major issues addressed were the institution of black-majority rule in Zimbabwe (Southern Rhodesia), the status of Namibia (South-West Africa), and the apartheid policies of the Union of South Africa.

The white-controlled colony of Southern Rhodesia had declared its independence from British rule in 1965, proclaiming the Republic of Rhodesia in 1970. Black nationalists immediately pressed for majority (black) rule. In 1965 Security Council resolutions condemned the minority government and called on all nations to participate in an economic embargo against it.

Although the United States and Britain supported majority rule, joint U.S. and British vetoes were cast in 1970 on a council resolution that mandated the severing of all relations with Rhodesia and the application of mandatory sanctions against South Africa and Portugal. This was the first veto cast by the United States. (The Byrd Amendment, passed by Congress in 1971 [but repealed in 1977] triggered resentment on the part of black African nations by allowing the importation of strategically important materials, including Rhodesian chrome, in contravention of the economic embargo.)

The assembly in 1966 stripped South Africa of its mandate in Namibia. In 1970 the Security Council established an Ad Hoc Committee to consider actions in the light of the continued refusal of South Africa to withdraw from Namibia. Thereafter, the assembly and the council repeatedly passed resolutions condemning continued South African administration of Namibia.

In an advisory opinion issued in 1971, the International Court of Justice declared that South Africa was occupying Namibia illegally. But in 1975 and 1976 the United States, Britain, and France vetoed a more significant resolution that would have declared the South African presence illegal and a threat to international peace and security. A council resolution adopted unanimously in 1976 called for free elections in Namibia. In the same year the assembly gave observer status at the United Nations to the South-West Africa People's Organization (SWAPO) guerrilla movement.

South Africa also came under criticism for apartheid, the term given by the government for its system of institutionalized racial segregation. A voluntary UN arms embargo against South Africa, in effect since 1963, was made mandatory by the Security Council in 1977. In 1974 the United States, Britain, and France vetoed a council resolution expelling South Africa from the United Nations. Despite Western statements pointing out that no legal provision existed in the charter for the General Assembly to suspend membership, and that only the council could expel a member, the assembly voted to reject the credentials of the South African delegation—which marked the first time that a sovereign member state was denied participation at the United Nations.

Arms Control and Disarmament

The 1970 General Assembly recommended passage of the Treaty Prohibiting Nuclear Weapons on the Seabed and Ocean Floors (adopted in 1972), and, a year later, the Convention on the Prohibition of Development, Production, and Stockpiling of Bacteriological and Toxic Weapons. The latter was ratified by the United States, the USSR, and the U.K. in 1975. Also in 1975, the First Review Conference of the Parties to the Treaty on the Nonproliferation of Nuclear Weapons adopted a Final Declaration, which stated that all signatories had observed the treaty. Further, the General Assembly recommended establishing nuclear-weapon-free zones in the Middle East, southern Asia, and the South Pacific.

Economic and Social Issues

The economic development of the Third World became a major UN priority as economic issues came to the fore in the early 1970s. In May 1974, hastily convened at the initiative of the chairman of the nonaligned movement, the Sixth Special Session of the General Assembly called for a fundamental structural change in international economic relations between North and South—developed and developing countries. A declaration and a plan of action to establish a new international economic order were developed, over the opposition of the West, whose cooperation would be needed for realization.

A Charter of Economic Rights and Duties of States was adopted in December 1974, after a series of confrontational debates, by a vote of 120-6-10. The United States and most of the industrialized world voted against it or abstained, objecting that the provisions that concerned compensation in cases of nationalization and expropriation of foreign-owned property called for adjudication according to national, not international, law, which favored the expropriating nation. The Charter of Economic Rights and Duties also recommended the formation of a producer association for raw materials (with OPEC as a model), and this, too, upset many developed nations.

By the Seventh Special Session, it was evident that the United States had become more accommodating and responsive to Third World economic problems, and a broader consensus emerged. U.S. Permanent Representative Moynihan presented Secretary of State Kissinger's proposal for the creation of a new $10 billion fund under the auspices of the IMF. The new fund would provide financial support to help compensate Third World producers for the instability of raw-material markets. In 1975, UNCTAD called for "development of a program for integrated commodity earnings of developing countries." The 1978 UN Conference on Technical Cooperation Among Developing Countries recommended increased cooperation among the less-developed countries so as to reduce their dependence on the West for technology.

Human Rights

Late in 1976, the assembly chose to single out Chile for allegedly practicing torture and using imprisonment for political reasons, and Israel for its administration of the occupied territories. This prompted some U.S. observers to complain in the assembly that the United Nations had become one-sided in its pronouncements on human rights. "Why did the Teheran Conference all but restrict its focus to anti-Israel grievances and the black-white problems of southern Africa, and consciously ignore other obvious and egregious instances of oppression on every continent?" asked former U.S. Permanent Representative William Scranton. "The reason is simply this: human rights are still treated almost exclusively in a political context, even though positions are cloaked in high moral principles." Scranton then asked: "Why is the United Nations so long on declarations and so short on implementations?" He continued, ". . . today the only universality one can honestly associate with the Universal Declaration of Human Rights is universality of lip service."

The U.S. Mission

The year 1969 signaled the beginning of a rapid turnover in U.S. permanent representatives to the United Nations. Between 1969 and 1977, five men served as U.S. permanent representative, with the first three being appointed by Richard Nixon and the latter two by Gerald Ford: Charles Yost (1969-71); George Bush (1971-1973); John Scali (1973-75); Daniel Moynihan (1975-76); and William Scranton (1976-77).

Continuity was maintained by the ambassadorial delegation. Christopher Phillips served first as deputy representative on the

Security Council, and later as deputy representative under George Bush; W. Tapley Bennett served in the number-three spot in 1971–73, and as deputy representative during 1973–77; and William E. Schaufele served as deputy representative on the Security Council in 1973–75.

The congressional delegates included Senators Jacob Javits, Claiborne Pell, Gale McGee, Charles Percy, Stuart Symington, and George McGovern; Representatives Dante Fascell, John H. Buchanan, Jr., and Donald Fraser. Among the public delegates were Shirley Temple Black, Rita Hauser, Daniel Moynihan, Alan B. Shepard, Margaret B. Young, and William F. Buckley, Jr.

SOURCES

General information about the United Nations and the U.S. Mission during this period may be found in *Everyone's United Nations* (New York: UN Office of Public Information, 1979); *U.N. Annual Yearbook* (New York: United Nations, 1970–78); *Issues Before the General Assembly of the United Nations* (New York: UN Association of the United States, 1970–78); Thomas Hovet, *A Chronology and Fact Book of the United Nations, 1941–1979* (Dobbs Ferry, N.Y.: Oceania, 1979); *U.S. Participation in the U.N.* (Washington, D.C.: Department of State, 1969–76); and Seymour Maxwell Finger, *Your Man At The UN* (New York: New York University Press, 1980). Also useful on specific issues are Daniel Patrick Moynihan (with Suzanne Weaver), *A Dangerous Place* (New York: Berkley, 1980), and William F. Buckley, Jr., *U.N. Journal* (New York: Putnam, 1974).

CHRISTOPHER PHILLIPS: Deputy Permanent Representative on the Security Council, 1969; Deputy Permanent Representative to the United Nations, 1970–73.

I think generally the UN is taken seriously, except by such countries as the Soviet Union and perhaps China, which is still not very involved. You could also exclude France, which has tended to look at the UN with a good deal of cynicism. But the Scandinavian countries, the Netherlands, and many of the smaller nations really believe that whatever its shortcomings, the UN should be supported and made more effective.

After stints in the Air Force and as a newspaper reporter, Christopher H. Phillips was elected to the Massachusetts State Senate in 1948. An active supporter of Eisenhower's 1952 presidential campaign, Phillips began his foreign-affairs career in 1953 when he was named special assistant to the assistant secretary of state for UN affairs. "I have always had a deep interest in foreign affairs," he notes. "In fact, I was born in an American embassy overseas (in the Netherlands), and for forty years my father was a career diplomat." Phillips accepted the position as assistant to Robert Murphy. "At that time I also had been quite active in organizing a local United World Federalist chapter in Massachusetts," he recalls. "This was just after the war and many of us . . . were very idealistic about international affairs. We felt somehow we could change things for the better." Phillips later became deputy assistant secretary of state for international-organization affairs, but he left that post to become vice chairman of the U.S. Civil Service Commission (1957). In 1958, he was appointed U.S. representative to the UN Economic and Social Council.

When the Kennedy administration took office, Phillips joined the Chase Manhattan Bank as manager of its Canadian division and as David Rockefeller's adviser on international affairs. In 1965 he became president of the U.S. Council of the International Chamber of Commerce, where he maintained his interest in international economic affairs.

In 1969 Phillips joined the Nixon administration as deputy U.S. representative to the Security Council (1969–70) and then became deputy representative to the United Nations (1970–73)–both posts having the rank of ambassador. He served under Charles Yost and then George Bush. In 1973 Phillips left the

United Nations to become president of the newly created National Council for U.S.-China Trade. He is a member of the Council on Foreign Relations, the American Academy of Arts and Sciences, and the U.S. Committee for UNICEF, as well as a director of the UN Association of the United States.

One of my early assignments at the UN concerned the seating of Communist China in the UN. Originally, American policy recognized only the Republic of China [Taiwan] as the government of China. During the earlier years, because the UN's membership was much smaller, our policy of supporting the seating of the Republic of China was relatively easy to maintain. But by the late 1960s, things clearly began to change—if I may say so, somewhat belatedly.

I think the first visible evidence of a shift in our policy was reflected in a speech that I gave before the General Assembly in the fall of 1970. That was the first time that an official of the United States in a UN body referred to what we used to call Communist China as the "People's Republic of China." The speech was played up in the front pages of many papers and it was interpreted as the beginning of a shift.

By that time Washington was beginning to think in terms of a policy, which we always denied was a two-China policy, but which had many of the characteristics of a two-China policy. We hoped that we could maintain a seat for Taiwan in the General Assembly, while admitting the PRC into the Security Council as well as the General Assembly. We finessed the question as to precisely which entity would be China. It would presumably still be the Republic of China, but since Peking's delegation would have been seated in the Security Council, this would have given them a status which most other members would have accepted as the official delegation of China.

We waged a long and strenuous campaign to try to achieve both of these objectives. We said we were in favor of the admission of the PRC but we wished to retain a seat in the General Assembly for the Republic of China. We felt at the mission that we had a better than 50–50 chance of succeeding because we had mobilized substantial support through careful preparation—a lot of hard work and extensive consultation with other delegations. But what probably pulled the rug out from under our efforts more than anything else was the surprise announcement of Henry Kissinger's visit to Peking. None of us had any advance knowledge of this development; I don't believe even George Bush did. I think the whole thing was held very closely to prevent any premature leaks.

From that point on, our position clearly began to be in trouble. We at the mission did feel, just a few weeks before the vote, that we had a fighting chance but that it would be very, very close. We believed that if we could get all of our [supporters] on the floor to vote, we could make it. Japan worked very closely with us and we also had some of the Latin American countries. The Philippines worked closely with us, too, as did Thailand, but not the Indonesians. In Europe, of course, it differed. In the beginning, Belgium was with us, but at the last minute there was again one of those unpleasant surprises. The Belgian ambassador had to inform us, a couple of days before the vote, that he had received instructions to change his vote from supporting us to abstaining. We then began to see an erosion of support the last two or three days. We did meet regularly with the different regional caucuses of the countries that supported our positions, and in cooperation with them, we worked out our strategy. But when we got right down to the last day or two, and, in particular, the night of the vote, we were simply outmaneuvered.

One of the key tactical decisions was taken during the early evening of the day on which the vote took place. It was getting close to the dinner hour. A well-known UN figure, Ambassador Baroody of Saudi Arabia (one of the cleverest tacticians and parliamentarians in the UN), took the floor and proposed an adjournment for dinner. We fought that hard because we knew that the minute all those delegations left the floor and went to dinner, some wouldn't come back; the votes were so close at that point that we couldn't afford to lose one. We were defeated on the vote for adjournment, and at that point I think most of us felt the game was up. Indeed, when the General Assembly reassembled an hour or so later, several of our key votes were missing; some small delegations just didn't show up and could not be found anywhere. I think the other side had gotten to them, and to avoid embarrassment, they decided to absent themselves. So we lost. The U.S. Mission had done its best, but clearly Washington's decision to go ahead as it did undercut any hopes we had of succeeding.

The Law of the Sea

I was involved, as head of the U.S. delegation, in what was then called the Seabed Committee, from about 1969 through 1971. I think it was in 1970 that we were finally able to get a firm policy statement out of the administration. I have to give Elliot Richardson a lot of credit for this, because he was then undersecretary of state. I worked quite closely with him and urged him to help us, to show interest, and to come forth with an affirmative U.S. position on a good many of these issues. We had been dancing around for quite some time because we had no clear-cut policy. Our policy, to the extent that one existed, was generally negative. It seemed obvious to me that if we were going to try to shape the debate and influence the outcome of what we knew was going to be a long, drawn-out negotiation, we should have a clear-cut policy. Richardson was able to interest Kissinger, then head of the National Security Council, to get the president's support for a policy review.

As a result of these efforts, we did announce in May 1970 a formal U.S. position which I presented to the committee in Geneva. The announcement was made in the form of a presidential statement, I think on May 23rd, setting forth the U.S. position on a number of issues.

At the summer session of the Seabed Committee, we began, for the first time, to discuss concrete issues about the regime, the definition of a boundary which would constitute the limits of national sovereignty for purposes of exploiting and exploring mineral resources, and all of the key issues to which we hadn't been able to address ourselves except in a very general way. The initial statement by the president was the basis of virtually all our substantial positions. I take some satisfaction in having been involved in the work at that time, because there were only a few of us who were really interested. It was at that point that we accepted, for the first time, the "common heritage of mankind" principle, which became the basis for much of the ensuing negotiations. The concept was that the resources of the oceans beyond national sovereignty were the common heritage of mankind. That has become a kind of gospel in the law-of-the-sea negotiations ever since. Of course, the term has been defined differently by different countries.

The issues which have made us take a fresh look at the treaty relate mostly to the mining of deep-sea resources—the character of the Seabed Authority, and things of that kind. People tend to forget there are many other issues involved, such as territorial seas, the right of free passage through international straits, environmental issues, and the management of living resources in the seas. All of these issues are important and they are all interrelated. I think that it is very unrealistic to believe that we could get everything we want and not have to compromise on certain issues of interest to other countries which have needs and demands of their own. The essence of this is compromise, in which one tries to settle for what is the best possible package obtainable.

A UN Critique

I would be the first to admit that if one is to judge the UN solely by the outpouring of rhetoric that takes place every year in the General Assembly, or by the massive production of papers and reports, then one could say it is useless. But that's not an adequate basis on which to judge it. One can admit that such actions are undesirable and not particularly constructive, but the fact of the matter is that they result from the decisions of governments which participate in the UN. It is the collective actions of member governments that establish UN policies.

The UN is not some entity that exists independently on the East River; it is the sum total of the sovereign governments who constitute its membership. So let's criticize those governments. How often in recent years has the United States been willing to use the UN meaningfully? I think we have in one area—the Middle East. Another area would be the multilateral assistance and development programs of the UN, for which the United States is regrettably beginning to reduce its support. After all, if you can get a lot of countries to work together and share the burden, it's less expensive than having to do it alone. As a percentage of per capita income, the United States today is one of the lowest contributors to many of these programs. We have an interest in their success. If conditions in the poorer nations of the world continue to deteriorate, they can jeopardize the financial and economic stability of the rest of the world and directly threaten us as well. What kind of world will it be in terms of political stability and peace if two-thirds of the world is on the verge of starvation?

These are problems that have to be coped with, and we are today not using adequately the institutions and programs which are available. The fact that we are cutting back on World Bank financing, IDA [International Development Association] replenishments, and UNDP [UN Development Program] contributions is, to me, very shortsighted. From a purely financial point of view, much of the money that we contribute to the UN programs comes back to the United States anyhow. Even from a hardheaded businessman's point of view, it's not a bad deal.

SHIRLEY TEMPLE BLACK: Public Delegate to the General Assembly, 1969.

I know that U.S. public opinion tends to rivet on the statements in the Security Council and [on] the parade of diplomatic notables during the General Assembly meetings. The public gives too little credit to the dozens of specialized UN agencies who facilitate international communications, air traffic, postal affairs, and so on. How about the enormously significant, if slow, progress which flows from the world health, food, and agriculture programs? Never mind that the United States comes in for its share of scorn from the assembled nations. Never mind that numerical representation means an obscure Pacific island state votes with impact equal to our own. We should listen and learn. Far better to seek real progress through cordial, open conduct, [being] no less confident because of our egalitarian behavior.

At any rate, this was my public attitude toward the UN, and the way I resolved to approach my task. A mutually respectful and good-natured web of personal international relations was the best framework to play out the drama of our own national self-interest.

Shirley Temple Black began her public career at age three, during the Depression, when she played lead roles in numerous films for the Fox Film Corporation. "I class myself with Rin Tin Tin," she later said. "People in the Depression wanted something to cheer them up, and they fell in love with a dog and with a little girl."

In 1950, she met and married businessman Charles A. Black. While living in Washington, she became interested in politics and in 1967 entered, unsuccessfully, a special election for a seat to the California House of Representatives. She also campaigned for Richard Nixon in the 1968 presidential election, and it was Nixon who named her a public delegate to the twenty-fourth UN session. Her responsibilities as a delegate involved sitting on committees, making speeches, and appearing at diplomatic functions. Black served on the Social, Humanitarian, and Cultural Committee, where she stressed the needs of the aged and the need for international cooperation regarding refugees and ecological problems. She served at the UN Conference on Human Environment (1972) and later as a delegate to the USSR–U.S. Joint Commission for the Cooperative Treaty on the Environment.

In 1974 Black was named ambassador to Ghana, a position she held until 1976. In that year she became chief of protocol for the White House, being responsible for arranging state visits of foreign dignitaries.

Currently holding the rank of ambassador for life, Black is a foreign-affairs officer with the State Department. "One of the things I stress to ambassadors going overseas," she notes regarding the seminars she conducts at State, is, "when you are an ambassador, you're representing the president, the administration, and the people of the United States. You don't have a personal opinion."

I have had a strong interest in international affairs since I was a little girl. I met Eleanor Roosevelt when I was ten. She didn't exactly become a role model, because she had not even started her own diplomatic career. My parents were quietly anti-Roosevelt, but I liked them both, Eleanor and Franklin. When Eleanor became human-rights representative at the UN, what she did and said made a big impact on my teenage years.

I also was indelibly impressed by Adlai Stevenson, whom I met on a train en route to Washington, D.C., where I was to be a hostess at President Harry Truman's inaugural ball. Not yet 21, I wasn't able to vote, but I had a very interesting time passing out programs at the entrance and exchanging small talk with the preeminent politicians who flooded past my door.

Entering the United Nations

When I first arrived at U.S. Mission headquarters, I had ten minutes with Charles Yost, our ambassador, before I was sworn in. In those first ten minutes, he gave me 13 assignments. I remember that I asked, "How many should I have?" He replied that usually there were three, but he suspected I could handle more.

"What do you want me to do?" I asked. "How can I be most helpful?" He replied, "Be yourself." So that's what I was.

Next I was sent across the street to a massive personnel press conference requested by the media, where Soviets, Bulgarians, Byelorussians, Taiwan Chinese, and a really mixed bag of foreign journalists popped questions at me. I chanced to be wearing a bright red suit. "Is that from some expensive designer?" a Soviet asked. "No," I answered, honestly, "off the rack in a store in the Stanford shopping center." His story came out [that] it was Chinese red—a gentle bit of diplomatic protest over my already well-known partiality for inclusion of China in the UN.

At the U.S. Mission, an office was shared by me and Joe Johnson, the senior officer at the Carnegie Endowment for International

Peace, and one of our UN delegates. Like so many others, Joe was skeptical of my appointment in the beginning. He later told me they all thought I was going to fall on my face, and quickly. Thank heavens I didn't know that! Actually, I didn't have any idea that there was anyone seriously thinking that kind of thing. I knew I could handle the job, and I just went to work.

The Regimen

I took a small room in the Waldorf-Astoria Hotel, adjacent to the stylish Waldorf Towers, where Ambassador Yost lived. Living allowances were very skimpy but I resolved to live within the limits. Just behind my closet was a shaft enclosing elevator cables. Every 15 to 20 seconds, . . . my tiny little room would vibrate. It was a very economical room, for good reason.

My regular morning routine began at first light with an instant coffee. I'd walk down the fire stairs, come out on the Towers floor, and ride down a Towers elevator to wait for Yost to hitch a ride to work in his car. Often I looked a little tired because of sleeping all night with elevator cables, but sometimes I'd get into the car and half-drowse while waiting for him. I couldn't be an instant late, or I'd miss that ride and be stuck thumbing a taxi, not an easy task in morning New York. That's how a working girl gets by.

The first assignment that Charlie Yost gave me was on the subject of youth-related activities, and he gave me a stack of speech drafts that the State Department had been laboring over for almost a year. I reviewed them all, made a few notes, and began to write.

What apparently nobody knew was that I write all my own stuff, in longhand. I didn't want to have other people write those speeches. It was neither illuminating nor entertaining to sit through a typical UN speech supporting or attacking such and such for a dreary list of reasons. Most of those speeches are a rehash, something one could play over and over, year after year, with only minor changes. So I tried to personalize what I said, or to use an illustrative story. This was a technique borrowed respectfully from Adlai Stevenson. Writing my own speeches at first threw the standard State Department advisers into a tizzy. The phraseology was strange to them, buzzwords were few and far between, and my speech, heaven forbid, might unequivocably say something. But I stubbornly clung to my pencil and resisted efforts to water things down. Our major allies and

Third World countries later started complimenting me—"We like your speeches because you don't speak governmentese."

Naturally, I was extremely excited when I finally got up to give that first speech, about ten days after the General Assembly convened. Once you've spoken at the UN, I would guess you can speak anywhere without stage fright. Frankly, I was petrified when I gave that first speech. It was not [because of] going public; it was the character of the audience—everyone [was] skilled, all nations and colors, friends and enemies. When many came up to shake my hand and congratulate me afterwards, I was more grateful than they suspected.

One morning [on the First Committee—the Political Committee] I was seated behind my friend and colleague, Bill Coleman, who was the nominal senior representative. Suddenly, the chairman announced we would switch [the] discussion and go immediately to the peaceful uses of outer space. Coleman abruptly rose and said to me, "You've got the chair." I looked around but there were no advisers. There was no one else from the United States. I was it.

In the Soviet chair was Ambassador Malik. Almost all of the chairs in the room had heads of delegations representing each country, and there I was. I briefly caught a glimpse of one U.S. adviser as he dashed out the door to go across the street and get Ambassador Bill Buffum to take over. The United States had coresponsibility for this agenda item, and, of course, he was the expert. I shifted my chair and thought, "Good grief." I had done considerable homework on it, but hardly enough to debate the subject with world experts. When Ambassador Sen from India asked the United States a technical question, I was at a loss for the correct facts and figures, so I filibustered for probably 12 to 15 minutes on all sorts of nonresponsive aspects of the peaceful uses of outer space. One thing was working in my favor: Earlier I had served on an otherwise all-male advisory committee to the vice president's office on what U.S. goals in space should be in the next decade. Pretending I had somehow answered the Indian question, which of course I had not, I said, "Now I would like to turn this question over to my distinguished colleague from Sweden, who will complete the answer." The Swedish ambassador looked stunned. He didn't know I was going to do this, of course. He kind of filibustered along, too. Finally, a U.S. group arrived en masse, led by Buffum, all ashen-faced. Three people squeezed in behind me, including Buffum, so I turned and said, "Will you take the chair?" Buffum whispered back, "You're doing fine; stay where you are."

By this time India was responding again: "It was a very nice answer from our distinguished colleagues from the United States and Sweden, but I don't believe I have received an answer to my question. I'm thoroughly confused." He was not alone.

As the chair called a vote on this particular issue, Soviet Ambassador Malik was smiling, and openly chuckling, perhaps thinking how disastrous this vote was going to be. Did you know that we got everyone voting with the United States on this particular issue except the Soviets and, as I recall, Cuba? But it was amazing. The other states in the Soviet bloc voted with the United States. Confusion was hardly the word.

It was now about a quarter to seven in the evening; the press was long gone—they left at five—and I mused, "Here's an hour of unexpected glory and there's nobody here to report it." Back at the hotel, I was so exhilarated about the event [that] I could hardly relax. The odd final vote could be called a sympathy vote for my ineptitude, but perhaps it was an empathy vote: Everyone gets caught out sometime. Perhaps it was kindness: "She didn't faint and she didn't panic and leave the room, so let's support her."

I only had one bad run-in with my boss, Ambassador Yost, and that was with regard to some aspects of a speech I wrote on the world refugee problem. One of my 13 assignments was [that of] following events dealing with refugees. I was set to give a position speech in the Third Committee. Five minutes before I was due to speak, an adviser tapped me on the shoulder where I was seated in the U.S. chair and whispered, "Ambassador Yost wants to see you across the street." I said, "But I'm due to give my speech." And he said, "That's what it's about."

So I took up my papers and raced across the street, where Yost firmly said, "You can't give *this* speech," shaking a copy provided him earlier. He said it nicely, but he declared it was too radical. I had referred to the American Indians as being our original refugees. I used this analogy as the theme of my speech and Yost felt that I came on too strongly supportive of the Indians. Of course, my husband happens to be one-quarter Cherokee, so I had a personal reason for this. I got kind of exercised and I replied: "What do you want? A puppet in the U.S. chair? Theoretically, I'm representing the president. I'll bet he wouldn't buck at an expression of regret over past history, particularly when it's true and any schoolchild knows it's true."

Yost was taken aback by this argument. At last, he said, "Well, you can give the speech tomorrow, but we will have to launder it a bit." And how they did!

It still had the original thrust but it wasn't quite as fiery. It described how the Indians were rounded up and marched away for a 1,000-mile death march from what is now Knoxville to Oklahoma. Simmered down overnight, I gave it, still a strong speech which suggested U.S. regret over our own behavior might be construed as an asset in our considering the refugee problems faced by Palestinians, Africans, and others displaced in the world.

The day I made that refugee speech, the Saudi ambassador [Baroody] came into the Third Committee with a stack of newspaper articles about the refugees, all uncomplimentary to the United States. He was going to make a full condemnation of the United States. When I got through with my speech, he rose and said, "I can't believe it but I am agreeing with the United States. They've said it all." It was a historical event. He just took his papers under his arm and left.

Developing Relations with Third World Countries

It seemed to me, when I was there, that U.S. delegates, among others, were not spending enough time listening to views of the Third World countries. So this became something that I decided I would try to do. As time went by, I managed to develop cordial relations with many representatives from black, Arab, and Latin-American countries, states which heretofore had seldom had official contact with U.S. representatives, [and had] far less enjoyed the easy personal rapport so vital for useful discussion of issues on which we fall on opposite sides. Bit by bit, this web of personal contacts grew, and before long I realized that it was a specialty in which most of the other members of our delegation had neither inclination nor facility. Almost by default, I became a key link with the Third World countries' representatives.

I found that I could do a lot of useful work with people I had gotten to know. For example, occasionally a small nation could be persuaded to propose something which actually we wanted proposed.

Such surrogate behavior is no secret to anyone at the UN, where appearance is inordinately important. Proposals by big states are often regarded as bullying. Enlisting small-state support is an area where utmost care need be taken lest the big nation talk down to the tiny one. In fact, it seemed to me then, and often since, that intellectual arrogance is a common fault at the UN and a great obstruction to getting things done.

Chance Encounters

Cuba was probably our biggest problem. When I first sat in the U.S. chair in the Third Committee and heard the Cuban female delegate launch a tirade against the United States, I got very annoyed. I intended to reply and started jotting down my notes. Art Stillman, who was my main professional adviser and is now serving in Geneva at the ONU, tapped me on the shoulder and whispered, "It's much better if another country comes to our defense, rather than you speaking back. Silence is much more meaningful than direct debate back with antagonistic delegates." The logic of this escaped me then, and still does to some extent.

I told him I was going to go outside and have a cigarette, so Art sat in the chair and I went to the women's room. There was one other person in there, and by chance it was the female delegate from Cuba. She was brushing her hair, which had pretty blond streaks, and she was humming a tune, an old song called "This Is My First Affair." According to diplomatic rote, nations without diplomatic relations do not speak directly to each other—an instruction emphasized in original briefings at the U.S. Mission. Singing was another matter. So I started to hum the song "It Had To Be You, . . . It Had To Be You . . ." The corners of her mouth just slightly went up, and she shot a friendly glance at me in the mirror. We both played by the rules.

Sometime following the Cuban episode, I unknowingly disobeyed Mission instructions. It was early in the session that the woman representative from Mauritania was elected chair of the Third Committee. That day we all rose to give our speeches welcoming and complimenting her. When we adjourned for lunch, I went up and invited her to go to lunch with me. She was a beautiful, lovely woman, and looked slightly surprised but said, "I'd be happy to."

I didn't tell anybody where I was going and took her in a U.S. car to a lovely French restaurant. We exchanged pictures of our children, laughed, and struck it off very well. Luncheon probably took almost two hours, and when I returned to the mission, they said, "Where have you been? We've been looking all over for you." I replied, "I took Madame Turkia Ul Dada to lunch." Everybody blanched, repeating, "You can't do that. We have no diplomatic relations with Mauritania. You can't take her!" "Well, I did," I replied, "and we had a very nice time." At times the United Nations seems divided by ridiculous inherited habits.

Two weeks later we had diplomatic relations with Mauritania, certainly not because of my luncheon, but this timely event lightened the burden of my goof.

Woman Delegates

There were quite a few of us women at the UN when I was there. I don't think it's a valid assumption, but the Third Committee is where most of the women serve. That was another incentive for me to work on other committees; I didn't want to be just known as Third Committee, although in practice that is where most of my responsibilities lay.

Latin American countries seem very emancipated where women are involved, and there were many women from those countries. Several were also from Africa, including several who became my close friends. There were also women representing Egypt. Being a woman at the UN was neither awkward nor unusual at that time.

I once informally suggested to Soviet Ambassador Malik that the Security Council would be more effective if [it were] comprised only of women. I joshed and teased the Soviets more than a little and they teased back. They were neither stuffy nor inaccessible. Malik shouted my idea spelled disaster—there would be all *nyets.*

Representational Activities

It's not easy for anyone to put in a hard, full day of work and then be obliged to go to a reception every evening. Usually the invitation to such an activity is extended to you personally from whatever country is having the affair. Sometimes it's delivered to your desk, or at your chair in the meeting room. Seldom do you get more than a few hours' notice. For a woman, this presents a peculiar problem of dress. At the beginning, I tried to bring up another outfit, a dress, to my office so that I could change. That scheme lasted about a week. Nothing was possible and practical but to go in your work clothes. Everybody did and it's understood. Rarely was there time or inclination to change into something glamorous. Not every woman would agree. There was one delegate from another country who changed her outfits, I'd say, five times a day. She always made a grand entrance, even in the Third Committee. We'd all play games guessing what she was going to wear next time.

The temptation to drink at an official reception or dinner was, in my case, to be avoided. Not that I am a teetotaler, but representation is no less-official duty than giving a speech in a plenary session. Gracefully decorated dinner tables are no less places of work than a desk. Drink goes with neither circumstance. I followed a rule that one doesn't take anything to drink that's alcoholic at a representational function. I devised, as I guess a lot of delegates did, a stand-in: a glass of water with a twist of lemon. I also learned, from watching Soviet Ambassador Malik, that you don't have to stay at each representational function very long. I would see him come into a reception, only to suddenly vanish. I trailed him once, and found that he would move through the reception room, greet everyone briefly, and then disappear through the kitchen door like a waiter. That was a pretty good thing to do. The longest you had to stay at a reception to be polite was about 20 minutes.

I was very often the guest of honor at another delegate's luncheon. I gained ten pounds during those three months because I didn't want to hurt any country's feelings. As a guest of honor, I always sat to the right of the host or hostess, and was served first. Everyone watched. Not to eat is an insult, and you're always served a second helping. Each chef, I found, was trying to outdo the other chefs. It was, let us say, a broadening experience.

Achievements

I really feel it's misleading to search for dramatic achievements in UN work. As in almost every other aspect of diplomacy, UN work is a process, not a glittering array of triumphs matched to the calendar. Some things finally agreed on during the General Assembly where I served had been grinding slowly in the process for years, and will take further time to bear fruit.

Recent experience tells us again that the task of a UN representative is to represent the views of one's government. There is no place for speaking personally. Instructions must be followed. Policy disagreements must be ironed out inside our U.S. walls before [we address] the world. In 1969 we all accomplished this delicate, often anguished, compromise fairly well. As for me, on more than one occasion, I fervently disagreed with several moth-eaten policies of our government toward world problems. On no occasion, however, was I forced to publicly voice support for something I did not believe in. The constant temptation is to use the UN platform to express one's own convictions, or the UN office to extract personal political mileage for the participant. Either is reprehensible behavior. Diplomatic discipline is a critical ingredient in a comprehensive and coherent program of foreign relations. For any U.S. delegate to the UN who believes otherwise, my counsel is clear and simple: Resign today.

RITA A. HAUSER: Delegate to the Human Rights Commission, 1969–72; Alternate Delegate to the General Assembly, 1969.

It was especially frustrating, being a lawyer and an advocate, to realize that no matter how brilliant your speech was, how great your arguments, how masterful your presentation, you didn't switch anyone's votes, because they were determined strictly on political grounds. The instructions had come from home—"Vote yes. Vote no"—no matter what anyone said. After a while you got to feel, "God—what a terrible waste of time this is; so many endless speeches that influence nobody."

In addition to her activities as a lawyer, Rita Eleanor Abrams Hauser has been active in human rights. She served as U.S. representative to the UN Commission on Human Rights from 1969 to 1972, and was a member of the American delegation to the 1969 UN General Assembly. A Republican, Hauser cochaired the N.Y. Committee to Reelect the President (Richard Nixon) in 1972 and the Coalition for Reagan/Bush in 1980.

Hauser has been a member of the executive committee of the Lawyers' Commission for Civil Rights Under Law (1969–78), vice chairman of the U.S. Advisory Committee on International and Cultural Affairs (1973–77), and a member of the New York City Board of Higher Education (1974–76) and of the Legal Aid Society (1973–76). She has also contributed articles on international law to professional journals.

When I was in college I was very interested in the UN and international affairs. That was my orientation. I was also very active in the International Student Movement for the UN (ISMUN). I became the president of it here in the United States, and the international vice president in my senior year. I went to France after I finished college on a Fulbright scholarship. The first stop I made, I remember vividly, was Geneva, on the way to the Fulbright program. There was a big gathering of the ISMUN that was really my first entree into the whole world of the UN as such. That was in 1954, so obviously it was a very different place than when I served there in 1969. In 1954 it was still very much a Western operation; it was just the bare beginnings of the decolonization and the coming in of the Third World countries. By 1969 it was already a Third World operation.

In 1968 I was cochairman of Nixon's campaign in New York: "New Yorkers for Nixon." After the election he asked me to come to Washington, which I said I couldn't do because of my professional requirements. I had little children (they were ages five and six at the time) and I wasn't inclined to leave New York and go to Washington. I also had a very successful husband, who was moving up in his profession. So I said, "Look, my interest has been the UN and I would like to do something at the UN which would permit me to be in what I am interested in, but also not have to leave home." When Yost was appointed, he called me in and asked me what I would like to do. Human rights had always been an interest of mine, so I said I would like to be the representative to the Human Rights Commission, and to serve on the delegation. That's how my appointment came about.

I was the U.S. representative to the Human Rights Commission during the Nixon period. When human-rights issues came up in the assembly, I was generally a consultant to the delegation on the positions we should take. I would sit in on the meetings at the assembly that related to the human-rights issues that had been on our agenda in the commission. Of course, the commission reports to the Economic and Social Council, and then ECOSOC reports to the assembly. That's the chain of command.

I had two extremely interesting issues both on the Human Rights Commission and in the third committee [of the GA] as well. I was in charge of the prisoner-of-war issue, which is fixed in my memory because the Vietnam War was raging, and we made a very big effort on behalf of our prisoners. That was my subject, and it involved international law under the Geneva Conventions for the treatment of prisoners of war. It was a painful business, because I had to sit there in the chair under enormous attack from the whole range of countries that were opposed profoundly to the war, and who didn't want to make a nice distinction between opposition to the war and the requirement of humane treatment for prisoners of any war.

The second enormous push, for which I got Nixon's full support, was on behalf of the right of Soviet emigration. The Soviet delegate called 12 or 14 points of order during the course of my speech, trying to shout me down. We read into the records some letters from Soviet Jewish mothers about their children who were in prison or couldn't leave, and obviously this was an issue that the Soviets didn't like, so we fought very hard. I never had any compunction about taking them on.

It was also very interesting to sit on the Human Rights Commission in 1971 when the Bangladesh war occurred. We had evidence of genocide on the part of the Pakistanis—who burned Hindu students alive in their dormitories—and things of this sort. I was pressing extremely hard on Kissinger to allow me to make a statement, and he didn't wish me to. I didn't know, and neither did anyone at that time, of the [American] tilt toward Pakistan [that occurred] because Pakistan was helping in the opening to China, if you recall. In the end, I finally made a good speech by using my right of reply, which I found to be very handy. I would say whatever I wanted, and I didn't get bothered again for State Department approval. If you were making a formal speech, it had to be cleared.

Another thing we did was to resurrect the Genocide Convention. That was one of my great efforts, too. It had been dormant for many years, and it took quite an effort to get Nixon to back it. We pushed it very hard, but we never overcame Senator Ervin's objections on constitutional grounds, and to this day it has not been ratified by the U.S. Senate.

U.S. Mistakes and Reconciliations

Two terrible things happened at the UN: one was the first use of the Moynihan-Kirkpatrick approach, which Moynihan started, of outright confrontation in which the Third World is the enemy: that is, we don't recognize them, basically, for their agenda is not in our interest. All of this strikes me as folly, since the Third World exists; it is the source of an enormous amount of the world's resources; it clearly is an enormous market for most of the European countries; it will become ever more so for us; a substantial segment of the population of the world resides there; and it is not something one can ignore easily. This absolute confrontational attitude, I think, is death. Then after that absolute, we oscillated under Carter to the absolute other extreme, which was the Andy Young approach, in which the Third World could do no wrong and the West was the enemy. Between those two, I think the Andy Young approach is by far the worst, because it is basically turning on our own values and interests, and that is intolerable in a political forum. We have swung back and forth like that.

I think the best period that I saw while I was there (actually after my time) was Bill Scranton, who came in and who really picked up the pieces after Moynihan. People forget Moynihan was there only nine months. I reviewed his book *A Dangerous Place* for the *Political Science Quarterly*, and I was very harsh on it because I think his concept of the Third World is erroneous, as I have said. He pretends in his book that he was the first person to discover human rights, which is also utterly erroneous. This "sock them in the nose" approach, which is his manner and way, really left terrible damage in the UN, and it took Scranton a great deal of diplomacy and understanding as well as meetings with these countries to bring them back into a more reasonable posture towards the United States. That doesn't mean they will always vote with you; after all, they have their agenda and set of interests and we have ours. But there is no reason that the UN has to be a forum of complete antagonism between one set of countries and the other.

After Scranton, of course, came Andy Young, and he was terrible. I went over to the mission once for a meeting during his time and I was really shocked. There were Black Power posters on the walls and there were Third World, P.L.O. posters and all that stuff. Now we are back the other way. I gather from what people are telling me that Kirkpatrick is very isolated. Part of it is her personality, which is of the Moynihan school—like that letter on the Non-Aligned Communiqué (1981) that she sent around. I can't understand that. What is the point of insulting all of these countries? If you don't like their rhetoric, you criticize it appropriately or you ignore it, which is what you do most of the time. But to call it rubbish, in effect, and to call upon them to retract their statements and so on, strikes me as a gratuitous act. I think she is playing to the same sort of audience that Moynihan played to, which is the large number of Americans who are very put off by the UN, or are hostile to it. Moynihan had a purpose in mind. It was very clear that he wanted to run for office, and he had a great issue that came his way: Zionism is racism. As I said in *Political Science Quarterly*, I did a lot of research on that and I came up with a conclusion that has since been substantiated by other researchers, which is a very painful thing to say. The Zionism is Racism Resolution had been around for a number of years and it could easily have been buried in the Third Committee, which is what had always happened to it before. It was never elevated to anything. We let it be known that we didn't think this was something that should be promoted, and everybody sort of let it die. Moynihan, instead, seized on it as a direct confrontational "obscenity" as he called it. By doing that he compelled the issue to the table, which to me is a folly when you don't have the votes. He knew perfectly well that he didn't have the votes, and there was no way he was going to have the votes. So, after putting it on the agenda and bringing it up to the table, the United States then engaged in ferocious lobbying in capitals, and I doubt whether we changed two votes. We forced many countries who would have preferred not to cast a vote on this to have to take sides, like Mexico, and others because they were Third World-oriented. When it came to actually voting, Mexico felt it had to vote with the Third World. What good did it accomplish to have Mexico on record against us on this issue? It was not thought through and I criticized Moynihan for it.

The Israelis did the same thing. When I studied the background of it, I found to my surprise that [Israeli Ambassador] Chaim Herzog had also had instructions at the outset to just ignore it, and eliminate it by ignoring it. The temptation is to use that [UN] forum as a medium for political ends. And, of course, Moynihan was elected on it. I don't think there is any doubt that he ran, became a nominee and so on, as a result of that. That's terrific for him, but it is not sound diplomacy and not the way one should conduct oneself in that forum, in my opinion. Now we are stuck with it: it's an official resolution; it's there quoted endlessly and repeated hundreds of times.

The Benefits of Service

I was quite young while at the UN, and I learned a great deal about the world. I saw in three or four years there how the world saw us, which was something of a shock. I had lived in France and gone to law school in France. I wasn't as innocent in that sense as others might have been. But even I, with that background, was shocked at the depth and intensity of the anger toward the United States, the fury the Third World had, in some instances, toward the United States, and the fear that they manifested toward the Soviets.

There were a lot of things one learned in that sense. And with the Third World countries, you met some of the up-and-coming leaders. The UN is an important forum for them, and they often send people for their exposure and learning here and language development. The Western countries, on the whole, didn't have any particularly distinguished people such as they had in the early days.

Personally, the Human Rights Commission was one of the great experiences of my life. I will never forget my French colleague, Rene Cassin. He and Mrs. Roosevelt had drafted the Universal Declaration of Human Rights. He was a towering intellect, and when I got to know him, we became great friends because I speak French fluently and had gone to law school [in France]. He sat on what is the equivalent of the U.S. Supreme Court. You did come across some very extraordinary people, as well as a lot of ordinary people. It was an interesting period. I don't regret it at all. But I did come away at the end fairly depressed, after having started optimistically. I came away at the end feeling not too kindly about the possibilities of the United Nations as a vehicle for promoting peace and understanding.

GEORGE BUSH: Permanent Representative and Chief of the U.S. Mission to the United Nations, 1971-72.

During my early days in politics, I was highly critical of the UN. I felt it was falling short of its promise from the late '40s. I saw it become increasingly unable to be useful in its peacekeeping roles. After I served there, my view changed. I felt that the UN was particularly helpful in the economic and social areas [ECOSOC]. I favored certain of the multilateral efforts in the health field, food field, population field, etc. Sometimes it is much better to use multilateral diplomacy and I saw that clearly after being at the UN.

A former oil-industry executive and Texas Republican congressman, George Herbert Walker Bush was named U.S. representative to the United Nations by President Nixon in 1971. Bush cofounded and developed the Zapata Offshore Company (1956-64), and later advanced to chairman (1964-66). Convinced that businessmen "ought to take an interest in politics," Bush was active in Republican politics in the Houston area. From 1967 to 1970 he served in the U.S. House of Representatives. After losing a Senate race in 1970, Bush was appointed to the UN post. His informal, energetic style, amiable personality, and access to President Nixon won him the respect of fellow delegates. In 1971 Bush advocated the Nixon administration's two-China policy—a compromise under which the United States would support the admission of Communist China while calling for the continued membership of Taiwan. Although Bush tried to win sufficient support for the compromise, the assembly voted to expel Taiwan.

In 1972 he left the United Nations to become chairman of the Republican National Committee; in 1974 President Ford named him head of the U.S. Liaison Office in China. Two years later, he became director of the Central Intelligence Agency, where he instituted structural and procedural reforms. Considered a potential running mate for Nixon and later for Ford, Bush decided to wage his own presidential campaign for 1980. He then became Ronald Reagan's vice-presidential nominee on the Republicans' successful ticket against Carter and Mondale.

I felt [after serving there] that the UN was an extremely useful place at which to conduct bilateral diplomacy. It's a fantastic place for meeting future world leaders—getting to know them on a friendship basis. As vice president, I continually run into people from all over the world with whom I served at the United Nations.

It also found the UN to be frustrating in some ways—the attacks on the United States, and so on. The UN passed a lot of irrelevant resolutions, and I think that diminished its effectiveness. There's an awful lot of rhetorical overkill at the UN. In the General Assembly, the debates were often not real debates, [with] no real give and take, as in giving a speech and [having] someone exercising a right to reply, for example. But it still was a worthwhile forum in which to vent one's frustrations or one's desires or one's goals.

In securing support of U.S. policies, our home mission worked the diplomatic circuit very, very hard. We had excellent political officers, we contacted everyone—no mission was too small. I, as ambassador, would not hesitate to go to a small African country's representative. The UN job is much more than making speeches and posturing. To be really effective in terms of securing votes, you have to get out and work at it. I liked that part of the job; I liked the politics of the UN.

In terms of cooperation or disagreement with the Western allies, generally speaking, we had very close relations and stayed together on most of the important questions. There were of course exceptions. As for the Soviet Union, we had many differences, and they're on the record. I got along with Ambassador Malik of the Soviet Union and made it a point to work with him. But our differences were pronounced on most political issues.

As to the Group of 77, I became frustrated at group positions that I knew individual members did not support. But again, we had to work on various questions to get the support of different members in the group.

As to the tenor of the times, the biggest questions in the political field were the India/Pakistan War, the Taiwan question—entry of China into the United Nations—and certain events in the Middle East. The principal challenge did relate to the Chinese-representation question. Ours was not a two-China proposal in the technicalities of the proposal. There was a dual-representation proposal which was termed "two Chinas" by some. There is a distinction, given the fact that both Taiwan and Peking consider that there is one China. Given the new U.S. opening to China at the time of the UN debate, it was extraordinarily difficult to keep out votes—votes that had been committed to the dual-representation position. The issue was extraordinarily emotional, but when it was over, the United States properly shifted gears and, in the UN context, dealt with the realities at hand.

In terms of tilting toward Pakistan, the U.S. position is on the record there at the UN. We used our best efforts to try to help stop the war between India and Pakistan. But most of the bilateral diplomacy on that one was conducted by Dr. Kissinger in Washington.

I believe strongly in personal relationships in bilateral diplomacy or multilateral diplomacy. I think the United States should not be above going to the smaller embassies, meeting with the ambassadors from smaller countries, working with the regional groups, etc. Some countries' representatives at the UN have considerable flexibility in their positions, and if you have a personal relationship, you find you can get the benefit of the doubt on certain issues. It's not always true, of course, and it's certainly not true with the big powers. But it does work, and in addition, it is important that the human side of the United States is seen through the eyes of diplomats from other countries. I am not naive enough, however, to believe that people would change their fundamental convictions based on personal relationships.

For the permanent rep, access to the White House is important. It's the perception more than the reality, in my view. The relationship between the U.S. perm rep and the secretary general of the UN is an important component. I had many meetings with Secretary General U Thant and Secretary General Waldheim. These relationships do matter a great deal. Word spreads through the UN if there is friction or if there is indeed compatibility. The relations with the secretary of state are of course important. The UN ambassador gets his instructions through the secretary of state, or as the president shall decree. And thus both the access to the White House and relations with the secretary of state are important. It's not always easy—sometimes conflicting signals come forth, and it is then that the perm rep to the UN does a balancing act.

The UN's greatest strength lies in the economic and social objectives, and its greatest weakness lies in its inability to bring instant peace to troubled situations—particularly when the larger powers are involved.

W. TAPLEY BENNETT, JR.: Deputy Permanent Representative on the Security Council, 1971–72; and Deputy Permanent Representative to the United Nations, 1973–76.

We should treat nations fairly and even generously, but, at the same time, defend our own rights. I think we have to stand up for what we believe, and should expect other people to understand our concerns even as we try to understand theirs. I believe in a perfectly honest approach.

Dubbed the "dean of U.S. diplomats" by the *New York Times* when he retired from the Foreign Service in 1983, W. Tapley Bennett, Jr., has had a long and active career as a diplomat, with assignments in Latin America, Europe, and the United Nations. In 1945, only four years after entering the Foreign Service, Bennett served as an adviser to the U.S. delegation at the UN conference in San Francisco. He served again as an adviser to the U.S. delegation at the United Nations in 1950.

He is perhaps best remembered for his part in the American intervention in the Dominican Republic in 1965. President Johnson, fearing that political instability would turn the Dominican Republic into "another Cuba," ordered American troops in to restore order. Bennett, then U.S. ambassador to the Dominican Republic, worked with special envoy Ellsworth Bunker to arrange free elections and the restoration of normal political life.

After serving as ambassador to Portugal (1966–69), Bennett was appointed deputy U.S. representative on the Security Council (1971–72) and deputy permanent representative to the United Nations (1973–76). He became U.S. permanent representative to NATO in 1977, his final diplomatic assignment. During his tenure at the United Nations, Bennett gave special attention to economic and social issues affecting Latin America and the Third World. He chaired a UN visiting committee to the remote trusteeship of Papua in New Guinea in 1972; the U.S. delegation to the UN Development Conference in Geneva (1973); and the UN Conference on Industrial Development in Lima, Peru (1975).

I was at the UN during the Third World's rise in importance, and they were quite unified in the beginning. Now, of course, they've got their own internal differences. But I was there during the period when they were at their maximum of unity, and the Algerians were running it [Group of 77]; Abdelaziz Bouteflika was their foreign minister. They ran it with a whip hand. They'd have these meetings, and if they had trouble, they'd just stay until after midnight, after some of the more comfortable nonaligned [delegates] had gone home. Then the Algerians would ram their measures through; they would tyrannize some of the milder Africans. I would say there was one year—and I don't think this is too much of an exaggeration— when in many ways the single most influential country at the UN was Algeria: more than ourselves, more than the Russians, more than the British, just because they had this vehicle at their beck and call, and used it. And they were absolutely unscrupulous [as to] parliamentary rulings—not hearing a "no," and that kind of thing.

In 1976 we had the Aegean dispute [over rights on the continental shelf] between Greece and Turkey. That was certainly one of my major accomplishments and satisfactions; we worked on that for weeks. We finally got a reasonable resolution out of the Security Council that both countries lived with, and it started them [off] to negotiating again and having exchanges and visits and meetings between the foreign ministers. Nothing really had been resolved, but at least they did not go to war, which they had been close to doing.

I had managed all through the debate, because Bill Scranton had been away. I believe he was at the Republican national convention at one point. And when he came back [to the council], it was the final day [of the debate] and we were going to have the solution. And he said, "No, indeed, I will not take the chance if you've worked this all out. You've worked on it for a month, so you must have the credit—you know, cast the vote." Which was nice. And that was where Bill Scranton was so marvelous. He's really one of the finest men in America's public life.

George Bush was, I think, one of the most popular people at the UN. [Soviet Ambassador] Malik used to say, "Bush, you're my favorite capitalist." He [Bush] just could get along. . . . One day we were in a debate; it was on the Middle East, as they are so often, and old Baroody [Saudia Arabian Ambassador] was orating, and you know he could go on for hours. He'd do it all from a little piece of paper no bigger than a quarter, and talk for an hour and a half. He was berating the Israelis, and berating the oil industry, and so forth— I don't know why a Saudi Arabian should berate the oil industry, but he was. And just at that time Bush came in to take his seat, and without pausing in his oratory, Baroody said: "I'm glad to see you, Mr. Bush. Come in and sit down. I'm having a few things to say about the oil companies. I want you to hear this." Of course, George had been in oil himself.

The relationship with American traditional allies was always very close. The British still thought in world terms and so you could get more support and more understanding from them than almost anybody else. The French also had a world view but it was their own views. When they wanted something and believed in it, their diplomacy was very expert. They could speak on every side of every issue and [could] quite often come out with a dig at the United States. The Scandinavians bore the heavy burden of thinking they were carrying the white man's burden in Africa; they'd be more African than the Africans. I got so fed up once at the Swedish delegate—this was in the Security Council. Time and again, the Swedes would cast a vote which would give away the Western position. They would be the swing vote, and they would consciously abandon the Western position, which in most cases we thought was a reasonable position. So I said to the Swedish ambassador one day, I said: "You know, no matter how hard you try, Sweden is a northern European country. You can't pick it up and move it down to Africa. It's never going to be African."

Of course, we've tangled with the Cubans every now and then. Nobody ever handled the Cubans better than Pearl Bailey. Pearl, you know, has got a heart as big as all outdoors, and she's full of good humor. She was a great friend of President Ford and entertained at the White House. They liked Pearl and so put her on the delegation. I think she was there two years [1975–76]. She was playing in *Hello, Dolly* during one part of that, and she would invite delegates to the show. After the end she would bring them backstage to meet some of the cast. But once the Cubans attacked the United States, and she happened to be sitting in our delegate's chair at the time. Well, she got up and just turned a good old southern frying pan at him. "Now, listen here, young man. You've been attacking the United States. . . ," she said, "I'm 58 years old and you can't talk that way to me." She just gave him some down-home talk, you know, nothing diplomatic, nothing fine or flowery, but just straight. And it brought down the house. Everybody just applauded and the Cuban was heard later saying, "I don't know how to compete with that, I don't know how to deal with that." She said, "I've got no hate for you. I like Cuba. But you ought to behave."

Moynihan and Confrontation

I enjoyed very much working with Pat Moynihan, who was awfully kind to me. He was controversial, you know, and he meant to be. He said things that needed to be said. We were being pushed around and I think what he did was good. I was for that. Then I think toward the end probably he realized that he was carrying it too far, and so I've often said, if people ask me, I think Pat Moynihan came at the right time and went at the right time. Moynihan wanted to weigh the voting record against what we did in the way of aid. That has to be very judiciously done; you can easily overdo that. But that's one aspect. I don't see myself obligated to help everybody in the world if they're busy kicking us in the teeth all the time. I don't feel we have any obligation from on high, or from past history, to take unlimited abuse and bad treatment and still keep pouring out assistance. In other words, performance should have something to do with the state of our relations. I think his tactics were right, but the circumstances just didn't allow for success. I don't think it would've been a bit different if you'd tried other tactics, if you'd follow another course.

We are so often on the receiving end of too much of the invective and polemics, more than we deserve. But then, we haven't always done everything right. There is a lot of [the] double standard at the UN—no question about that; selective indignation and that sort of thing. But the fact that they expect a higher form of conduct from us than they do from themselves, that should be a matter of pride to us.

The UN is blamed for things that are not its fault. It doesn't make these decisions; it's governments that make the decisions, and the UN can only carry out what governments vote. I think this has been one of the problems with the public's disillusionment. At the time of San Francisco, with typical American enthusiasm, we thought, "Well, we've got this marvelous new creation, peace and justice are here forevermore; we can turn everything over to this new body and we'll have no more problems." Well, it never was realistic to think that.

I think the UN was very much oversold in the beginning, and then the inevitable disillusionment came in. As someone said, "The

UN is an institution which became indispensable before it became possible." That's not bad, if you analyze it. I believe you have to have a world organization; at least people can meet. I think the UN mirrors the world reasonably well. It mirrors its frustrations, its sense of grievance; there's no question that the former colonial countries have grievances, and underdeveloped countries do. Many of them are exaggerated; they don't do enough for themselves, and they expect it all to be poured out, if not from heaven, from the United States. And that was the essential unreality of the Third World economic drives, because the more extreme they got, the more they lost the support of the very countries which were in a position to pay the piper. When they passed these unreasonable resolutions, nothing happened. To this day I don't think they fully understood that, although I have the impression it's a little bit better than it was.

Making It Better

I think there are at least a couple of things we [the United States] should be doing. For one, we should be training our representatives as broadly as possibie. There ought to be a mix of career people and people from various walks of life. I think it's better for the perm rep to be a political man. I've never been in any job which is as close to the White House as the U.S. Mission, because day after day you are voting, you are committing the United States, so you are always on the phone to the White House, getting instructions. You've seen some celebrated lapses of that in recent years, and that gets into the press. I think the permanent representative is better off being a prominent American, such as Senator Austin or Senator Lodge, or an outstanding American, such as Adlai Stevenson or George Ball. I think the deputy should be a career man, because he knows the administrative side of diplomacy and knows the State Department well, and it's a good thing. That hasn't often been the case.

The face of America ought to be a generous, optimistic face. After all, we've always thought we were the last best hope on earth, and I think that's still true, if you compare it with anybody else. As Churchill said, democracy is the worst form of government on earth except for all the others.

WILLIAM E. SCHAUFELE, JR.: Senior Adviser to the Permanent U.S. Representative on the Security Council, 1971–73; and Deputy Representative on the Security Council, 1973–75.

The trouble is, the biggest danger is that the game [of diplomacy] can become more important than the substance. The game is very often so invigorating, so stimulating, that you forget about the substance. I fell prey to that occasionally, although once I realized what was happening, I could control myself better. There were sessions in which it was all a game. You knew you weren't going to achieve anything, so it became pure gamesmanship.

William E. Schaufele, Jr., began his more-than-30-year career in foreign affairs in 1950, when he entered the U.S. Foreign Service. After serving in various embassies, including a two-year stint as ambassador to Upper Volta (1969-71), Schaufele joined the U.S. Mission to the United Nations. He served as senior adviser to the permanent U.S. representative (1971-73) and then as deputy representative on the Security Council (1973-75). He attained the permanent rank of career minister in the Foreign Service in 1975. In that year President Ford appointed Schaufele assistant secretary of state for African affairs.

Schaufele's tenure as U.S. ambassador to Poland in 1978-80, during the early days of Solidarity, made him a sought-after lecturer on the situation in that country. From 1980 to 1983, he was president of the Foreign Policy Association.

In my own personal experience, I had had a lot of involvement with African nations, and there were a lot of African issues at the UN. In the 1971 assembly I spent most of my time in the Fourth Committee, which is Decolonization, dealing with African issues and other colonial situations. I began to get a glimmer, maybe halfway through the assembly, why and how one operated in the UN, how important was the actual participation in the debate. I began to get an indication of how different countries voted—it's easy to determine how they will vote on an issue most of the time—and how they would shade their votes.

Then, of course, we spent a lot of time on China. We were making some headway persuading members to vote against the admission of Peking and the expulsion of Taiwan. In the meantime, Mr. Kissinger flew off to Peking, carrying on his own China policy. In my own personal opinion—although I understand that obviously he couldn't tell the world in advance that he was going to do this—his actions effectively killed any chance of success that we had of achieving full recognition for both governments, although I'm not sure we would have made it anyway. Some of the conservative countries like Nicaragua [and the] Ivory Coast were prepared to block Peking's entrance. But I think it's very possible that if the anticipated vote had been close enough, we would have had a resolution. There was a possibility of admitting Peking without expelling Taiwan. I don't know whether Peking would have come to the UN under those conditions, but the idea was that you bow to the tides of history, you allow Peking to enter but don't expel a country which claims its own independence.

We lost on that one. I didn't find it particularly traumatic. Actually, the amusing thing that happened at the time of that vote involved one of our people who was sitting on the side behind a couple of representatives from the Soviet delegation, which had introduced the original resolution on the China issue in 1951. After the vote was over, he leaned forward and spoke to one of the Russians, congratulating them. He said, "You introduced it 20 years ago and you've won now. China is sitting in the U.N." And the Russian said, "Yes, we have won a heavy victory." Because Chinese-Russian relations are not very good.

When [the Chinese] arrived in the assembly, they were very circumspect. Very often at committee meetings they would say that they had not had a chance to study the question and had no experience in the UN. They didn't abstain. They just said, "We are not participating in this vote." But it quickly became clear in the Security Council, where you only have 15 members and where you're dealing with security issues, that the Chinese knew politics; and in many ways it was very comforting to the American delegation that we no longer had to respond to the Soviet Union. The Chinese would respond on somewhat different grounds than we would, but it was no longer a polemic just between the Soviet Union and the United States, or even between the Soviet Union and most of the other members in the UN.

I think it was in that [1971] assembly that we had a meeting of the Security Council regarding the Middle East, in which the Chinese played a memorable role. The Australian ambassador was in the chair and Huang Hua, the Chinese vice minister in charge of foreign affairs, was in the chair for China. Malik was in the chair for the Soviet Union. The first issue that arose was a procedural one. The Soviets called for a vote and the Chinese were inscribed to speak next. I'm sure the Chinese knew the rules—they're very good at this sort of thing—and they started to scream [because they wanted to speak before the vote was taken]. At the same time, Israeli Ambassador Tekoah reacted. So there was shouting going on in the chambers. You had the Chinese shouting in Chinese; you had the Russians shouting in Russian, and the Israeli ambassador loving it all because he was born in Russia, and he, too, was shouting in Russian. Normally, he would never speak in Russian; he would always speak in English, but now he was screaming in Russian, and the Australian ambassador, who didn't like that sort of thing, suspended the meeting.

We were sitting and watching. The Chinese were on one side of the president and the Russians were on the other side. When the Australian ambassador suspended the meeting and asked for a consultation, everybody stood up. The Chinese vice minister came from one direction and Malik came from the other and they started shouting at each other in English. The president resolved the differences between them in consultation, agreeing that the Chinese would be allowed to speak before the procedural motion of the Soviets. A procedural motion is supposed to take precedence over everything, and that's what the Soviets were complaining about—that if you let the Chinese speak, you break the rules. Everybody went back to his seat and the Chinese vice minister started to speak, actually quivering with rage. He stood up, which you didn't normally do in the Security Council, and he said, "Mr. Malik, we know you and we don't trust you," and other words to that effect before he even addressed the procedure issue. That was a good introduction to the Chinese-Soviet relationship in the UN.

You will remember [that] that's when the Chinese started always to talk about the hegemony of the two superpowers. They would take a crack at the United States in one sentence and they'd spend 50 sentences on the Soviet Union. They made their obeisance to ideology by criticizing the great capitalist-imperialist power but they spent most of their time criticizing the Communist social-imperialist superpower. And that particular assembly was mostly noteworthy for that issue, the issue of Peking, and [for] the transfer of Peking and Moscow invective from the airwaves and the newspapers to the UN. Actually, it was very uncomfortable for many

nations of the Third World, because they saw the Soviets as supporters, though many of them had no delusions about why the
Soviets supported them. The Chinese support them on a more philosophical basis, as China considers itself an underdeveloped nation
having more in common with the Third World. Third World members saw these two nations, on whom they could rely, constantly
attacking each other.

As time went on, the Chinese, because of their anti-Soviet stand,
consulted a great deal with the United States. Very often the Chinese
didn't participate in the consultations and negotiations on many
issues initially, but they wanted to be informed and so they would
consult with us, and we would tell them our views of what we
thought the Soviets were trying to do. Of course, these consultations
also infuriated the Soviets. I can remember Malik making occasional
public references to the two other superpowers combining against
the Soviet Union, at which Huang Hua would stand up and say,
"China is not a superpower," and we would say nothing.

The assembly of 1973 was not an unusual one but it was dominated by the Yom Kippur War. The war started when the new secretary of state, Henry Kissinger, was by chance in New York, where we
were dealing with the problem. As usual in that kind of situation,
you couldn't deal with the problem very effectively until there was
some kind of contact between the United States and the Soviet
Union, because anything that we would have proposed probably
would have been vetoed by the Soviet Union, and anything they
proposed would have been vetoed by us and maybe by some of the
other permanent members. Negotiations over the resolution of the
dispute were protracted because of the gains made by the Arabs, although nobody ever said this. It was quite clear, and this is an
important part of the thinking, that the gains made by the Arabs
were large enough so that a successful negotiation of some kind of
UN resolution at this time would have put the Israelis in a worse
position than they had been in before. There was also, initially at
least, a thought on the part of some Arabs, and maybe on the part of
the Soviet Union, that if they held off long enough, the Arabs would
gain even more ground. So initially, there seemed to be a kind of a
general disinclination to get down to the particulars of a resolution
because each side hoped to gain an advantage by delaying.

However, at the time the tide turned, the Arabs and the Soviet
Union became impatient for UN action. When the Israelis finally

went across the Suez Canal and trapped the Egyptian Third Army, the stage was set for serious negotiations of what the UN should do. Most of those negotiations were carried out in Washington and Moscow. The mission in New York essentially worked up the language, depending largely on what was being agreed to in Washington and Moscow, and advised the government of the procedures and some of the pitfalls so that one could get a resolution successfully passed in the Security Council.

A New Bloc

By the time I arrived at the United Nations, the massive new injection of membership was substantially complete. The wave of decolonization in Africa actually resulted in, I think, about 46 new members from Africa itself. So you had a de facto existence of a new bloc—a bloc which could block anything, because we could no longer get the blocking one-third [required] in the General Assembly, which at least we had the hopes of before. This evolution of the UN in turn had an effect on American public and congressional opinion, because over the years, they had just gotten used to the Soviet Union attacking the United States, and now we were going to be subjected to attacks on the United States by small countries very often dependent upon our assistance. I think the mood in the country turned from being mildly neutral, or mildly approving of the UN, to being negative in many respects, and that has effects in Congress and also in the White House. A situation in which we could take the initiative and get a peacekeeping force into the Congo, as we did in 1960, is no longer possible.

The Sixth Special Session [1974] was the first concrete manifestation of what has become one of the preoccupations of the UN ever since, direct confrontation between the North and South, the developed and underdeveloped countries. The Group of 77, we knew, was working on an omnibus resolution which would include all the favorite subjects of debate and complaint that had always been brought up at the UN. As Joan Spero now puts it, the Group of 77 resolutions always tend to be like a Christmas tree because you always have to hang everybody's particular interest on them to get agreement among the 77, who by that time, I think, were 96. That makes it very difficult for them to compromise, because if you take out something that's very important to one country of the 77, then he's [the delegate's] going to say, "Why should you give up what I want when you won't give up what somebody else wants?" The agreement was what in diplomacy is called "fragile" because it has all these things hung on it; at the same time, it became almost unnegotiable because all the ornaments tended to be put on whether extraneous or not.

The West, by its inaction and by the very nature of the system, was in a very defensive position and spent its time trying to improve the draft resolutions by eliminating things which it opposed and by adding some things which it felt should be in there. As a result of this, the group which introduced a resolution could then say that it had made all those concessions. If we and some of our friends had introduced a counterresolution, we could have dramatized, and perhaps reduced, the reach of the Group of 77, perhaps even affected their own tactics so that they would not be so ambitious [about getting] everything in one resolution but [would get] something concrete that we could all agree on. The trouble is that we never make a common proposition of our own. We work on the basis of their [the opposition's] drafts. First we say things like: "Let's not change it because it's so bad; it won't pass," but we try to get it changed anyway. But if we had put our own resolution in, a mirror image, so to speak, of the other extreme, knowing that it, too, was unacceptable, then there would be a basis for negotiating concessions on both sides and perhaps achieving more than we would otherwise. When people want certain things, instead of becoming defensive about them, we should become tactically aggressive.

Now I think there is a greater sense of realism on all sides. I said once, when I took over as assistant secretary for African Affairs, that the days of euphoria, excitement, of dealing with a newly independent Africa were gone, and they should be. They are in the world now, and the days when we could be supportive and even almost sit in for the Africans—giving them advice and more, almost paternalism—were gone. And the Africans that wanted to be treated as sovereign states had been independent long enough to take the consequences of their own actions, and we should no longer make any excuses for them. And I think in that sense, particularly among the Africans whom I know best among the Third Worlders, there has been a maturing, although they probably wouldn't like that term. On the other hand, the North-South differences contain the seeds for a lot of confrontation, and I feel that there is too much of an effort to take on everything at once. With every problem that one faces in foreign affairs, one can make a basic decision to go with the whole issue or to go piecemeal, and sometimes one works and sometimes the other. But a lot of these issues they are talking about will have to go piecemeal.

The Mission and IO

By this time, maybe I should explain, I had become the operational head of the mission. I would coordinate all the mission activities. Nobody else was doing it, so I did it because we had a great problem—people going off in inconsistent directions. Nobody was sitting at the top of the pyramid to see the inconsistencies, or to see that maybe if we wanted something in the political sphere, there was something we could give away in the economic sphere. I noticed this the longer I was there, so eventually I ended up coordinating the running of the mission and operations. I made the assignments to the committees and [put] the items on the agenda, kept up with the progress of each of the committees, determined which ones were troublesome, which were not. If anybody had ever told me, before I arrived there, that I could sit down in the morning for 15 minutes with six people (the basic professional people for each committee—a permanent staff person is assigned to each committee to follow it in detail) and discuss 15 agenda items, what they were supposed to do that day, just hopping from item to item, I would have said they were crazy. You [can] only do that after you [have] gained a certain amount of experience and know the basic items so [that] you don't have to go into a long discussion about what's involved. That's what we used to do every morning.

We often felt that Washington was dilatory in issuing instructions, because the period before the debate opens can be terribly important, and we would get some very vague and general instructions which very often were not sufficient to really conduct an effective predebate consultation which had some hope of succeeding. Too often, also, it was the other extreme—we got very specific instructions: "That resolution, as we understand it, is unacceptable." You [then] go to everybody and say it's unacceptable, and then they ask, "What has to be changed?" We would say, "Don't worry about that, it's just unacceptable." Actually, it's a good tactic up to a certain point. You don't offer any amendment, you just tell them [the opposition] it's bad and you're not going to vote for it and you're going to encourage everybody else not to vote for it. That starts them on the procedure of trying to find modifications or amendments which would make it acceptable to us.

The relationship with Washington had a somewhat difficult aspect during the years that I was there because there wasn't a whole lot of enthusiasm for the United Nations in the Nixon administration. They realized they had to cope with it, but they were not inclined to make any significant departures from past factors or even to take any initiatives.

The biggest problem to this day in our relationship with the UN is getting people who can make decisions to focus soon enough on what's coming up. We knew the assembly was coming every year [in September], we knew what 95 percent of the agenda items were, and what the differing viewpoints would be. Every year we would send a message to all embassies abroad to discuss, in various degrees of detail or intensity, the issues of the next General Assembly. These things never went out, at the earliest, until the middle of August, and by that time most of the other governments, especially the smaller ones, had pretty well done their analysis and made the decisions as to where they were headed. It was a little too late for us.

It's partially bureaucratic inertia, and partially because when the telegram goes out [to the embassies], there are certain issues that have to be cleared at a higher level because they may be troublesome issues that present problems in terms of precedence. In other words, there might be an unprecedented effort to make an unprecedented decision. Also, it is the feeling among many people in the foreign-policy establishment that the basic important decisions are not going to be made at the UN. That isn't true in certain issues like the Middle East, where we have traditionally agreed to UN consideration of peacekeeping functions; but they tend to come up without warning, and we don't have to plan for them long in advance.

I thought that the people in Washington were extremely sincere and highly motivated, and a lot had experience. But as far as our own tactics were concerned regarding bureaucratic struggles in Washington, it was not always clear to me how those were carried out. When it was a very hot issue, there was a lot of direct telephoning and talking with the undersecretary of political affairs, the deputy secretary, and the secretary himself, not to speak of the White House. On those very hot affairs, it didn't always mean that the assistant secretary was cut out—he was not; but the kind of preparatory and analytical work that is done at the working level of the State Department did not get done. The basis of general policy was made in this way, and then you would try to shape your tactics, your words, and proposals to the general policy.

President Nixon did not like to be bothered with more minute issues, and I think that shows up in the studies I have seen of his administration. It had to be pretty important for him to get interested. Some perm reps did not like to use whatever clout they had with the White House—they did not want to waste it—so they tended to be sparing. Others would turn to the White House, whenever they got resistance from the State Department or someplace else, and [would] try to get a White House decision, which overrides everything. Very seldom, in my knowledge, did any of them talk directly with the president. I should add that while the perm rep is a member of the cabinet, in every administration so far, meetings of the cabinet have tended to decrease in frequency, the longer the president is in office.

Andrew Young had direct access to the president, and I think that was unusual for two reasons. If you look at the Carter administration, Andy and the president had a relationship before he took office, and Carter was very interested in details and so he didn't object to being talked to about detailed matters. Andy was a very unorthodox politician. I am not saying that he didn't think things out in advance, but he would be more willing to depart from past practice in how he handled his bureaucratic or White House relations. I think Young was almost unique, because Adlai Stevenson didn't have it, Cabot Lodge didn't have it, George Bush didn't have it—I don't know what Moynihan had—John Scali didn't have it; so I wouldn't know of anybody (certainly Yost didn't have it) who had that almost immediate access to the president and on detailed matters simultaneously.

Personalities

George Bush is a politician's politician. He has a very deep sense of responsibility, and he places a great deal of emphasis on his relationships and contacts. He didn't always follow the issues as closely as other people did, but whenever one of us pointed out to him that we had to get deep into an issue, he was very good. The only question about George Bush is: Did he waste time in building up personal relationships with people who perhaps didn't always count so much in terms of what actually happened at the UN? I should say that Bush was very reluctant to involve the White House. He tried to get his recommendations accepted through the normal chain of command in the State Department and [to] involve the White House only rarely.

Scali was not a politician and was not a man who was patient of hierarchy or the system. He was very conscious of image, and I am not just talking about personal image, but about his public image and position as the U.S. representative, and how it was perceived. He did not have the wide range of contacts with as many people as Bush did. Consciously or unconsciously, he picked out the important people and those are the people he dealt with. Scali liked to talk rough, he was a little bit like Moynihan that way; but obviously he didn't have Moynihan's ambitions. So Scali would listen, and when you said, "Look, talking tough is the way I feel, too, but this is the reaction you are liable to get and it might not be so good," Scali would listen to that. He was a good listener despite his kind of brusque—some people would say abrasive—manner, because he didn't want to be caught off-base by not knowing something he should know.

Kurt Waldheim was very much preoccupied with the change and nature of the composition of the UN. How did the secretary general function in that atmosphere which was new in UN history and certainly was a completely foreign element to Mr. Waldheim, who was a traditional—overly traditional—European diplomat?

The relationship with Waldheim at the beginning was not an easy one. We saw him as sometimes bending over backwards and submitting to pressures which he didn't have to submit to. On the other hand, he probably felt that he was establishing his credibility as a secretary general of all the members of the UN and had to take their views into consideration. All UN secretary generals are subject to a lot of conflicting pressures, and I think there was a general feeling, at least on the American side, that he submitted too easily to such pressures. The Soviets have a way of pounding on the desk, and that may have had an effect on the Third Worlders—not [issuing] threats, but warnings about what would happen, could happen, to the UN and maybe would happen to Mr. Waldheim if he didn't have their support. Maybe they threatened to withdraw their support.

The assumption was that in 1971, when he was elected, he hoped to use that as a stepping-stone to the Austrian presidency. Once that plum was no longer available to him, he stayed on. He sometimes had the ability to say some things he shouldn't have said—for example, on the South Africa issue. Everybody is against South Africa at least in theory, but he seemed to say some things that he didn't have to say, which he knew would alienate at least the British and Americans. He must have known that if there was going to be any solution down there, the Americans would have to be one of the instruments [used for] the solution, and that used to get some people in Washington very upset. Anyway, [Waldheim's predecessor], the inscrutable U Thant, was also subject to such pressures, but as a Burmese he could use his inscrutability to good effect. Mr. Waldheim's constitution was not to be inscrutable. I'll say two things: One is that he may have had an exaggerated opinion of the power and influence of the secretary general, and, secondly, he tended to get involved in some things gratuitously. My own feeling is that the UN should not get involved with things gratuitously, because if the issue doesn't develop naturally, or as part of the political ideas of the nation or nations which bring the matter to the UN, it's going to be a troublesome issue, because there's no other initiative to bring it to the UN. That means that once the UN gets involved, it's going to be a troublesome issue. You know that in all the time I was there, only one African issue, outside of southern Africa, was brought to the UN. It was something between Senegal and Guinea. It was settled in consultations and there was never a debate on it. That's because the Africans never want to bring African issues to the UN. I often used to wonder why Waldheim didn't get involved in more African issues on his own initiative, but he was sensitive to the Africans not wanting to bring their issues to the UN.

Moynihan and Confrontation

Partly, I liked Moynihan's approach to the extent that I think the tone of the debate has importance—not necessarily in our relations with the other UN reps at the UN, where presumably even the perm reps gradually realize that a lot of this is for show, but because of the effects on other diplomats, on the White House, the secretary [of state], or even the general public. I can admire the gall, if you will, of a UN ambassador getting up and—this has happened—really blasting the United States all across the board at the UN; and, since he was also accredited to Washington, coming down the next week and asking for umpteen million dollars in aid. He [then] says that shouldn't affect anything. That may be a nice theory but it doesn't work in practice.

I think that tone has importance and effect. If you pick your spots when you come out with very sharp dialogue [*à la* Moynihan], you have much more effect because you don't do it all the time. If you do it all the time, people stop listening. Then if they complain about it, it does have an effect on our relationships at the UN. I don't think my attitude toward the UN was changed much by my UN experience. I was pro-UN and yet had great respect for the use of power in foreign relations. I always used to say that after four years, my tolerance for frustration had decreased to the point I was glad to leave, but that doesn't mean I didn't like the four years I was there. There's a type of repetitiveness but that's not unusual. Most legislative bodies have that to a certain extent. The General Assembly debate in many ways is a necessary mechanism for everybody to be given the opportunity to have his say, no matter how big or important his country is, or whether it's in the center of things or on the fringe. But I don't think that the general debate really adds much to the worth of the UN except an opportunity for all the members to get on the record on any issue they want to get on record with.

The Security Council, too, is frustrating in many ways but it really is operating the way it should. I know what people say. They go back to the birth of the UN and talk about the Security Council being a peacekeeping body because it can take mandatory actions under Chapter VII, with the built-in protection that you have to have unanimity of the great powers, the permanent members. For a long time there's been a movement to do away with the veto. I think that would be a great mistake because if there were no veto, the permanent members would conduct even less of their business in the UN. If they didn't have the veto, they wouldn't even let the UN discuss the issues in any meaningful way, with the chance of doing something mandatory on which all the members would have to follow up. There's talk of a few changes in the charter, that the Security Council membership [should] be increased. There are pressures, as you know, to add Japan as a permanent member and to add a Third World permanent member.

The committees tend to work the same way the assembly does— but at least they're working on specific, proposed resolutions with specific problems and are supposed to stay within the framework of those specific problems. All the general debate you have in the committee has very little importance until you get down to the actual wording of the resolution and the proposals for modifying it, because originally there is always one text down on the table, proposed by somebody. Sometimes there are opposing or alternate texts. That's where the debate really starts to count. The environment is always interesting because you see people doing things that, by our standards, don't seem to make much sense. I found in my files memorandums of conversations with the Dutch government in The Hague on the question of should you vote "yes" on a resolution which contains one or more operative paragraphs which you oppose? The United States, and I think it's still true, is generally of the position that if you vote "no" on any one operative paragraph or more, the best you can do is abstain on the resolution—that it would be inconsistent to vote "yes." The Dutch in that conversation did not see any particular value in that kind of formalistic position, but I do find it somewhat surprising that people will vote "no" on important parts of the resolution and then turn around and vote "yes" in order to satisfy their relationship with other countries who favor the resolution. That's a way of evading the issue and that leads into a discussion on the value of hortatory resolutions.

It's true what the General Assembly does is not mandatory. It has no legal force, technically speaking. But the fact remains that if you pass a resolution which includes a particular paragraph, and that paragraph is picked up and put in another resolution on a similar subject and then is picked up again by another organ of the UN discussing the subject, the constant repetition tends to give that paragraph some status, even though it's not mandatory. It does not have the status of international law, but nevertheless, the constant reiteration of a particular sentence, or a series of sentences, which perhaps [had a vote of] 110–25 in such and such an assembly and 90–36 in WHO, tends to give it a certain amount of status which comes very close to being international law. People will say that the United States, for instance, has violated international law as based on the repetitive acceptance of some particular paragraph. They will say that the United States, or whatever country, is violating the spirit of the views of the world community, and that's one of the things that worries me about consensus. I see a value in consensus if, indeed, the consensus is real and the differences among the members are differences of degree or differences of emphasis, but not real differences of substance. The trouble is there's been an effort to get consensus on things in which there are real differences of substance, and I think sometimes we've agreed on consensus even though we've had real differences in substance.

I feel that the UN is an instrument of U.S. foreign policy, as it is an instrument of every other country's foreign policy. It's something we should use for best effect and something we should do positively, even knowing that we will never be in a position where we will ever control it again, and that we will not be in a position of perhaps getting resolutions adopted which completely meet our needs as we perceive them. But there's a follow-up which is also an important mandate. When we vote for a resolution in a positive spirit, even a spirit of enthusiasm, we should do what that resolution says UN members should do. We don't always do that. We vote for it when we're in favor of it, but then the enabling legislation or regulations or actions required in Washington don't come through. We voted for the Convention against Genocide, but no administration has been willing to spend the political capital it costs to push that through ratification in the [U.S.] Senate, because they know they'll have to make concessions on something else.

As a great power, as a superpower, and as a power for 35 years with the ability to intervene almost anywhere in the world, we do not regard the UN as so important. But the fact is that things do get debated in the UN, and the words get out to the public in the United States by various means. The UNA [UN Association] does it, the FPA [Foreign Policy Association] does, other organizations do it. People learn there are other points of view that can even sound reasonable. A smaller country in Africa sees the UN as a vehicle for getting the kind of assistance and interest which it might not be able to get in bilateral relationships. They [smaller countries] are looking for something different and to them the UN is more directly important. There is a UNDP in most of these countries, a UNICEF program, a World Health Program, a trade program, or maybe an FAO program in a lot of these countries. In the United States we don't need it, but that doesn't mean we should deny it to other people.

Actually, in some respects, the presence of the UN in the United States creates political problems. Its presence here makes people more conscious of it. When the UN is doing something that we don't like, whether officially or in public opinion, then you get bad reactions, which make it difficult. Just a little issue like the parking—you should have seen the letters I used to get about the parking violations.

I have always felt that international organizations are most successful in the functional areas. When it becomes necessary for states to regulate an international postal service, they find a way to regulate it. It's when you get into issues that threaten the security—real or imagined—of states, that international organizations are least effective. Security can be an awfully big blanket, depending on how you interpret it, and if the Third World countries are interpreting deep seabeds as part of their economic security, then they treat it almost as a security issue. They would never say that but that's what they may be looking at. When environmental protection has a common element among enough countries, you will get international environmental controls. The underdeveloped countries don't mind having a little pollution because that means that they will be gaining some industrialization. Nevertheless, the pollution will become a problem for them eventually.

Economic issues are a mixed bag. When the Western world controlled the economy of the world—[by] the Bretton Woods Agreement—and the world was essentially run by those rules, it was a pretty stable world and it wasn't so bad in retrospect, despite what people say. At that time a lot of these countries were colonies and may have been badly treated by their colonizers. Nevertheless, they were part of the international monetary system. Now they are not—at least most of them aren't.

Benefits

I would [cite] first the functional things which have a potential to cause disputes among nations. I think the food bank—although I don't think it has worked out as well as it should have—is a step in the right direction; it does eliminate potential disputes among other countries. The second tangible benefit, strangely enough, I would put in the area of peacekeeping. You can be terribly disappointed with what the Security Council does or doesn't do, but at the same time, without the Security Council, the successful peacekeeping operations would never have occurred, and there have been some successes. I am not saying that people don't criticize what happened in those operations, but the fact is that they did relatively well in keeping peace, or at least [in] providing an atmosphere in which other avenues of settlement could be pursued and, one hoped, succeed. The Congo peacekeeping operation, I think, will be looked back on as something that a lot of people viewed as a mess; but it not only preserved the territorial integrity of the Congo, but also forestalled perhaps the tendency of tribal groups in other African countries to spin off and to try to form independent states. I think that various operations in the Middle East have often kept the pot from boiling—never kept it from simmering, but kept it from boiling. When the wars in the Middle East occurred, there was probably nothing that could have headed them off. But when I think of all the wars that could have happened in between, such as what's happening in Lebanon today, the UN has been helpful. It's also true of Cyprus with its very small peacekeeping force, and the fact that the UN is involved helps keep the parties apart.

The third thing, perhaps, is not so tangible, and that is the public education which has resulted from having viable and growing international organizations. Nevertheless, the public education which I see in the United States—it's hard for me to measure in other places— makes for greater understanding, if not always sympathy, for the values and benefits to be gained from cooperation.

JOHN A. SCALI: Permanent Representative and Chief of the U.S. Mission to the United Nations, 1973–75.

I went to New York as a skeptic. I was all too familiar with the number of times that the United Nations had dealt with problems unsuccessfully and had wound up giving many speeches that were stirring calls to action which, unhappily, produced few if any results. I did feel that one of my most important roles was to be a more effective public spokesman for the United States in responding to critics. I must say, too, that this is not any criticism of any of my predecessors; I just felt that at that time the degree of criticism that was emanating particularly from the assembly was reaching a new level.

John A. Scali spent 16 years as an Associated Press diplomatic correspondent (1944-60) before becoming foreign correspondent for ABC News in 1961.

Except for service as an unofficial liaison between the White House and Moscow during the Cuban-missile crisis, Scali did not hold a government post until 1971. In that year, President Nixon appointed him his special consultant for foreign affairs. Scali, a Democrat, was considered a "vocal critic of the Nixon administration's press policies" and thus a surprising choice. According to Scali, Nixon "nonetheless felt that I had been very fair in my reporting of all his activities."

Scali's appointment was seen as an unsuccessful attempt to ease tensions between the media and the administration and to close the so-called credibility gap by facilitating disclosure of the administration's activities. After the 1972 elections, the former journalist planned to return to ABC, but he was offered, and accepted, a new post as U.S. ambassador to the United Nations. Scali denounced the passage of "one-sided, unrealistic resolutions that cannot be implemented" and that disregarded the UN Charter, such as the General Assembly votes to grant the PLO observer status and to limit Israel's right to respond during debate on the Palestinian question.

In 1975 Scali returned to ABC News as a senior correspondent.

After 18 months of serving as foreign-policy consultant to President Nixon, I had decided to return to ABC News. After I had negotiated my contract with ABC News in December of 1972, the president called me into his office and asked, "Have you signed your contract with ABC News yet?" I told him I had not. He said, "Well I have something I would like to have you consider. . . ." He then without further ado offered me the position of U.S. ambassador to the United Nations. I was thunderstruck that he thought that I could perform the task.

I told him, at the time, I was honored, but I also noted that he knew, from his previous discussions with me, that the United Nations was not necessarily my favorite organization, and that I was very skeptical about the possibility [that] it would ever succeed in promoting the world-peace objectives that we all had shared back in 1945 when it was founded.

I remained a friendly skeptic up through the 1972 Israeli-Arab war. I had a role in drafting and pushing through the United Nations Resolution 338, which is now one of the bedrocks of U.S. policy. This was a follow-up to Resolution 242, which was an earlier [1967] UN effort to develop a substantial foundation for bringing peace [to the Middle East].

I wish I could say that Resolution 338 came into being because of my eloquence and my incredible negotiating talent, but that would be untrue. Resolution 338 was born out of direct discussion between the Soviets and the United States in Moscow, between Henry Kissinger and Foreign Minister Gromyko and other Soviet leaders. The fundamentals were something that we had already discussed in the United Nations, but the brevity and the balance were put together with great care and detail by Henry Kissinger and Joseph Sisco, with assistance from the U.S. Mission operation in New York. One of the beauties of that was that it really avoided most of the passionate, controversial, inflammatory issues, and concentrated on making sure that both sides understood the very simple language of how each combatant was to stop shooting and to stay in place while we put together a United Nations peacekeeping force. This force would be inserted between them to enable them to stop shooting while the diplomats tried to put together the same thing—peace, a permanent settlement in the Middle East—that had eluded them so often.

My role was exceedingly difficult because we went through three stages in that discussion. Many of the sessions lasted until two and three o'clock in the morning. In the first phase, the Arab countries, in informal discussions, made it clear that they did not wish to talk about a call for a cease-fire, because not only were they sympathizing with the Egyptians, but for the first time, the Egyptians were making substantial territorial gains. They had moved into very important parts of the Sinai while the Israelis were in a state of shock and, eventually, retreat.

As the Israelis succeeded in stabilizing the front, and as the United States, in one of the giant, successful airlifts of all time, rushed more than $2 billion in weapons to Israel, it became more and more possible to think of not only stopping the Egyptian forces, but staging a counterattack to recapture the territory already given up, and perhaps do something about destroying the Egyptian army.

Then came phase two. After it was clear that the Egyptians had gone about as far as they could, they and their various friends were interested in seeing that the United Nations Security Council pass an immediate cease-fire resolution which would leave everyone in place, which meant that the Egyptians would be in possession of all of the territory that they had already captured. The Israelis in turn were preparing for a massive counterattack, and it then became my role to stall until they were ready, which I did.

I talked about the need for further discussions. I pointed out that the secretary of state was undertaking an emergency mission to Moscow to discuss new ideas. I also noted repeatedly that even as the Arabs were previously unwilling to agree to cease fire, the Israelis were unwilling now to agree; and that no matter how much we sought to persuade them, they wouldn't accept our advice. Of course, any advice that we gave—along with the enormous amount of weapons we supplied—would have been, and probably was, to decline to stop, and indeed to stage the successful counterattack which they eventually did [stage]. As the Israeli forces began to move forward, it was clear that they were going to regain more than just the territory in the Sinai they had lost initially. While the Israelis were in the process of entrapping the entire Egyptian Third Army, we moved to phase three, which was to put pressure on the Israelis to stop before they not only surrounded, but could even have destroyed, the Egyptian Third Army.

At this stage, many of the Arab countries doubted that we were really interested in stopping the Israelis. We were, and it required considerable diplomatic pressure not only behind the scenes in the United Nations, but in direct discussions between Washington and Jerusalem on the imperative need for them to stop. The Israelis, as you recall, finally did stop, but only after they had successfully surrounded the Egyptian Third Army and were in a position to destroy it if fighting resumed. At that point, the formula for ending hostilities and allowing a United Nations peacekeeping force to intervene became the primary objective; and then I was finally able to concentrate on the wording, the timing, and all of the other problems.

U.S.–Soviet Conflicts

You have to remember that during all of this period, there were other major developments such as the Soviets threatening to send their own forces into Cairo to stop the Israelis if the United States declined to join with them in this two-nation, superpower peace-keeping effort. We not only declined, we thought it was a very bad idea, fully realizing that the Soviets might then decide that this was something they would do alone. Sure enough, the Soviets did fly an advance contingent of something like 50 Soviet officers into Cairo without notifying us, making it clear that they were serious about acting unilaterally if necessary.

At that time, President Nixon put into effect the nationwide nuclear alert which was meant to make it very clear to the Soviets that if they moved further, despite our strenuous objections, there could be a much larger war.

I believe that this was easily the most dangerous confrontation with the Soviets since the Cuban-missile crisis of 1962. We were not sure that even the obvious display of American readiness to fight would persuade the Soviets not to move unilaterally, because they had the advantage of logistics: They were much closer [to Cairo] and could move far faster than we could to stop them. We were very sure that they had mobilized at least two armies in the Ukraine and ad-joining areas, and [they] gave every evidence of being serious about all this. This is why the action by the president, of ordering the nuclear alert, was of such enormous significance, and indeed decisive enough to persuade the Soviets that it would be too risky to move into the Middle East because they would risk a head-on clash with the United States. But I must say that for 48 hours we were very nervous, almost as nervous as we were during the last stage of the Cuban-missile crisis.

During the time Kissinger and Gromyko were talking about a potential compromise resolution in Moscow, I chatted informally with Soviet Ambassador Malik on several occasions in one of the little anterooms off of the United Nations Security Council chamber. I sought, as best I could, in general terms, to find out whether he thought a compromise was possible, since that clearly was the objective of Kissinger's mission. He dodged the question and instead kept on insisting, as he did for days previously, that the only way to settle this was for the [UN] resolution to reflect the Arab viewpoint. He spoke without too much enthusiasm about the possibility of Soviet-American cooperation to buttress that possibility. He indicated very strongly that this was as much as he thought could be done. I concluded that he really didn't know, and that Moscow was not keeping him informed about the possibilities that there could be, or indeed at that time probably already was, in existence the draft of a jointly sponsored resolution. I knew that when he flew there, Mr. Kissinger had brought with him a copy of that resolution, which was changed only slightly in Moscow.

I was sent a copy of a proposed draft of the resolution. Malik was also sent one from Moscow. We then got together through our aides, compared drafts, and made sure that they were identical, word-for-word. And then we jointly introduced the resolution in the Security Council and, with a minimum of discussion on the part of either the Israelis or the Egyptians or any of their friends, got a quick vote that was unanimous, ending one of the more agonizing crises that has beset the United Nations.

In the Cuban-missile crisis, by comparison, despite the fact that I was a diplomatic correspondent, and not a government official, the formula that the Soviets discussed with me actually became the basis of the settlement. Curiously, I had far more to do with making sure that it was an acceptable compromise, word-for-word, during the Cuban-missile crisis, than I did in making sure that the resolution which ended the Middle East fighting was acceptable to all sides. In my non-diplomatic role, then, I was far more directly involved in the backroom negotiations. For example, I personally knocked down three of the Soviets' unacceptable conditions, such as the idea of swapping the American bases in Turkey for those in Cuba; the idea of allowing international inspectors to examine the coast of Florida to make sure that we were not planning a secret invasion of Cuba at any point; and the third, a curious proposal that Mr. Aleksander Fomin made later, which was that the secretary of state and Ambassador Dobrynin should meet three times a day, once the Cuban-missile crisis had ended, to make sure that there was never again the kind of dreadful crisis that both our governments had just survived.

Relationship with the State Department

Being a member of the cabinet while serving as ambassador to the United Nations in New York is one of the great illusions. No one in that position, no matter how close he is to the president, can hope to play a meaningful role in formulating foreign policy. The demands of the position in New York are such that you cannot spend enough time proposing and arguing for your view within the structure of the government in Washington. It just takes too much time; so you may intervene, argue, plead, and forcefully explain a specific point of view over a period of a few days, but unless you're there to see the debate through to the final conclusion, you wind up only an occasional voice. Eventually you wind up with a final decision which reflects only part of what you believe the situation demands. As an instructed ambassador, it is your duty to carry out this policy just as enthusiastically as you would a decision that you had decided by yourself. An ambassador in that position faces many and many a difficult moment when he must swallow hard and accept the view that wound up being put together in Washington, particularly if you had a very determined, assertive secretary of state.

My relations with Mr. Kissinger in that position were very professional. I think he recognized very early, somewhat to his surprise, that I could be, and was, an informed and effective voice at the United Nations. I didn't have any major fights with Kissinger during that time. I found that I received far less information than I would have liked on important issues, however. But I was not the only one. Many of his own colleagues in high positions in the State Department often were not privy to important developments that were happening around them. But that's part of Henry's style of operation. This meant, however, that as ambassador to the United Nations, I was flying blind on more occasions than were necessary, relying on my own overall understanding of policy, and not on detailed or even general knowledge of important decisions that influence the policy.

UN Deficiencies and Achievements

I was among those who witnessed the birth of the United Nations in San Francisco. I was a reporter who covered the initial conference sessions. I shared most of the dreams and the hopes that somehow this new organization could become a splendid shining light which would guarantee that the major powers would work not only in their own interest in the future, but to help others. Gradually, year after year, I've watched it fall short a little more until now, [when] I am not at all sure that we can do much to discourage an era of angry confrontation which is going to inevitably make more and more Americans angry and disenchanted with this organization.

I tried very hard to moderate the extreme demands of the Group of 77 and the others in the Third World who had decided the time had come to redistribute more of the wealth of the Western world to the Third World. Despite numerous discussions, we found that the minds of the radical leaders had been made up, and that the most that we could do to deflect what appeared to be a very determined drive, the most that we could hope for, was to call for further discussions and refer it to study groups, with the aim of impressing upon them how impractical their proposals were. I was so dismayed at the unwillingness, particularly of the Yugoslavs, to listen to advice of this kind, that I decided to give a speech that I still remember: It was the address before the assembly where I warned of the tyranny of the majority. I consider that speech the most significant and the most far-reaching of the many, many remarks that I made during my stay there.

I think the tyranny of the majority has now become not just a possibility, which is what I warned about, but a fact, and it is one of the major reasons why some of us who once supported the United Nations believe that this great international organization is dying. Unless we do far more than has been done to moderate the extreme demands and the angry rhetoric of the more radical states who continue to demand redistribution of wealth, who believe only in bloc voting, and who continue to insist on controlling the key organizations and committees, we are witnessing unhappily the demise of a great and noble dream.

One of the remaining great achievements of the UN that I always had pointed to is even now in grave peril, and that is the success of the UN peacekeeping forces in at least keeping combatants apart long enough so that the diplomats can discuss a permanent peace. I think that the developments in Lebanon particularly have dealt a very serious blow to the concept of international peacekeeping forces. I must also say that I am deeply disappointed that the Israeli government has persisted in its policy of opposition to cooperation with the UN peacekeeping units. Increasingly, the Israeli policy has become one of disregarding and opposing UN peacekeeping, and it is an attitude I have never understood.

If the concept and the role of the United Nations peacekeeping forces dies, the United Nations will die with it. It will be an international crime of massive dimensions because this has been perhaps the most successful achievement of this organization, thanks mainly to the great talent, the genius, and hard work of UN Undersecretary Brian Urquhart, who by any measurements is a great international public servant. He has pioneered, masterminded this idea [and made it] an actuality, despite the hazards and the problems and the almost impossible difficulties. If there were more Brian Urquharts, there could be a renaissance of hope that somehow we can still make the United Nations the meaningful leader for international peace and harmony that it should be.

The United Nations Security Council has proved repeatedly something that I have grown to understand and believe very firmly— namely, that it is the single most important reason why the United States has to remain in the United Nations. Without a Security Council, without the built-in veto power of the five major powers, there is no sure-fire, swift way to move peacekeeping forces into crucial areas to separate the combatants while the diplomats argue about what the more permanent peace should be.

I believe very strongly that the Security Council works not only to lessen the possibility of a larger war developing, but that it is vital to American security interests, and a positive addition to the many bilateral steps that we take to try to insure a peaceful world.

Nothing will hasten the demise of the United Nations more than a slavish band of reporters who are so captivated by the United Nations that they can see only good. We have to have a goodly share of skeptical, objective newsmen who can see the problems, the disappointments, and the inadequacies of the United Nations as well. Those within the United Nations structure, and, indeed, particularly the Third World governments, who believe that the answer is to have a trained and faithful band of reporters who will write only good about the UN, I believe, are doing more to hasten the death of the UN than even its more bitter foes.

When I speak about those who are blind to the United Nations's shortcomings and its failures and disappointments, I'm talking mainly about the large apparatus within the United Nations which is geared to spreading the word around the globe about the achievements of the UN. I agree that the achievements oftentimes have not been sufficiently recognized, but you cannot force-feed them to a skeptical world solely by rhetoric or by the number of publications which present a special version of what has happened.

I am impressed generally with the caliber of the journalists who cover the United Nations for private news organizations. They do a remarkable day-in, day-out job of not only reporting what is happening, but relating it to the problems that exist outside the United Nations's world.

I don't for one minute share the view of some Third World countries that somehow American and Western reporters are unfairly reporting, or failing to report accurately, the achievements within their borders. I don't believe for a second that passing a resolution in UNESCO, or any other part of the United Nations family of agencies, will in any way guarantee more international attention to their own successes and some of their problems.

The Western concept of journalism always has been to report both sides, and objectivity somehow conflicts with the news standards in many of the authoritarian nations, which wish the world to know only of the positive developments. The idea of creating a whole new information order, I believe, is doomed to failure because in the final analysis, the Western journalists will find out more or less accurately what is happening in even the most remote countries. Propaganda in press releases from their government-information ministries won't hide the truth.

I would like to see more ambassadors appointed from the ranks of newsmen who are foreign-policy specialists. As a result of years of experience, most of them have developed the kind of practical expertise which can assist a government not only in expressing its point of view, but in quickly recognizing public-relations traps which are often as important as substantive problems. I also believe strongly that any experienced foreign-policy reporter who spends time within the government, helping to discuss, debate, and put together a controversial policy, inevitably winds up being a far more informed and compassionate human being once he returns to his role as a journalist. Clearly, this experience also gives added depth and insight into his reports on policies and problems thereafter. I would like to see some kind of international exchange whereby newsmen, for a limited period of time, are welcomed into the top ministries to serve as government officials, with the idea that sometime later they would return to their chosen professions. I think it could make both sides far more aware of the inherent problems that each other faces, promote more understanding and more accurate information.

DANIEL PATRICK MOYNIHAN: Public Delegate to the General Assembly, 1971; Permanent Representative and Chief of the U.S. Mission to the United Nations, 1975–76.

I didn't go to the United Nations and say what I said because I thought the place was unimportant, but because I thought it was important. If we don't start holding our own there, make our case there, it will get to the point where two-thirds of the U.S. Senate will say—as it did say this year—Stop paying our dues. Ambassador Lichenstein (Alternate Representative for Special Political Affairs) would say, Leave the United States; off into the sunset. You know, into the land of Hoboken, but oh, well.

This morning (November 4, 1983) the president spoke about the Grenada episode and the fact that we were voted down in the Security Council by eight votes, but that it didn't bother his breakfast one bit. It's one thing to defy world opinion but it's another thing to be dismissive of it. We will pay a price for that, if we think it doesn't matter. We used to think it mattered a great deal, until it stopped being favorable to us.

Daniel Patrick Moynihan, currently the Democratic senator from New York, has had a long and controversial career in government and academia. He has been a member of four presidential administrations, and is perhaps best remembered for his brief tenure as U.S. representative to the United Nations.

After joining the U.S. Department of Labor in 1961, Moynihan rose to assistant secretary by 1963, and in 1965 achieved notoriety for *The Negro Family: The Case for National Action*, a Labor Department study that posited a connection between the "breakdown" of the black family and growing poverty among blacks. Moynihan later left government to become director of the Harvard-MIT Joint Center for Urban Studies and professor of government at Harvard University.

Under the Nixon administration, Moynihan returned to government as presidential assistant for urban affairs. Moynihan soon became involved in controversy again, as a result of one of his memorandums, which advised President Nixon that "the time may have come when the issue of race could benefit from a period of benign neglect." Replying to critics who accused him of recommending neglect of racial problems and minority advancement, Moynihan said he was referring to the use of racial issues as a polarizing force by extremists. Shortly thereafter, Moynihan returned to Harvard.

During the early 1970s, Moynihan began to focus his attention on international affairs. He was a U.S. delegate to the twenty-sixth General Assembly session in 1971. Two years later, he became ambassador to India, a post he viewed as a challenge, given the strains in U.S.-Indian relations that developed as American policy tilted away from India and toward Pakistan.

In 1975 President Ford named Moynihan permanent representative to the United Nations. In his new role, Moynihan quickly established himself as a highly assertive and aggressive figure. He is especially remembered for his strenuous efforts during the debate in 1975 over the UN resolution equating Zionism with racism. After the Arab-and-Communist-bloc-sponsored measure was approved, Moynihan stated, "The United States rises to declare before the General Assembly of the United Nations, and before the world, that it does not acknowledge, it will not abide by, it will never acquiesce in this infamous act." Critics argued that his combative attitude during the debate on the issue had actually alienated some Third World delegates, but Moynihan contended that the main goal of diplomacy at the UN was "not to paper over differences, but to make their existence known and to make them clear, to define these differences so as to reduce the possibility of misunderstandings between countries."

As a result of tension between him and the Kissinger State Department, Moynihan resigned in early 1976. He went on to wage a successful campaign for the U.S. Senate that year. In addition to his other activities, Moynihan is the author of several books on domestic and foreign affairs, including *A Dangerous Place*, in which he discusses the United Nations (1978).

I didn't go to the UN [in 1975] to get into arguments with anyone. I went because of the upcoming Seventh Special Session of the General Assembly, which would be focusing on economic matters. There had been two previous [UN] meetings on North–South Economic Issues, and they had failed dismally—but utterly. Meanwhile, returning from India, I had published an article in *Commentary* ["The U.S. in Opposition," 1975]. Kissinger read it and decided I could handle this upcoming special session at the UN.

(I should note that I've actually had a fair background in foreign affairs. I'm a graduate of the Fletcher School of Foreign Diplomacy. My doctoral dissertation was on the United States and the International Labor Organization. Of the two organizations in the League of Nations that were established—the World Court and the ILO—the ILO was the one the United States was least likely ever to join, but we did join it in 1933-34. My dissertation asks how that could have happened, and I untangled a fair number of things.)

The seventh special session [of the UN] met on the first of September, 1975. We adjourned at 11:30 AM on September 14, and the General Assembly met that noon. A few will recall, but I will record, that the assembly reached unanimous accord on what had been discussed in the special session. There had not been unanimous agreement on that subject previously, and there has not been any since. Tom Enders, down here in Washington, was very good. I had enough of a sense of how to use their [the assembly's] language and, when language was the problem in the discussions, to find agreement.

I served in the UN twice, as public delegate in 1971 and as permanent rep in 1975. A lot happened between those two dates. During 1971 the United States formally lost its majority of the General Assembly. In 1971 the Third World countries were mostly new and caught up in the euphoria of independence. I recall Harlan Cleveland, who was assistant secretary of state for IO under President Kennedy, telling of one Asian prime minister (who was the second head of government in his country) who said his predecessor had had a wonderful time: "All he had to do was go around and shout 'freedom!' For me, he continued, 'it is all statistics.'"

Then came 1973 and the oil crisis. There was the gradual realization, by some of the less-developed countries, that things weren't going very well. The oil-price increases were a tremendous blow to them. A huge economic transfer from North to South had taken place, only some [the oil-producing countries] got it all and the rest got nothing. There was no longer any great point in talking to the West about transferring more to the underdeveloped countries: The oil producers had spun us into a decade of stagflation, inflation, and, through OPEC, the most incredible transfer of wealth to underdeveloped or developing countries that ever could have occurred. It did not go to India, and did not go to Bangladesh, and did not go to Ghana. That's the way the world is.

The second change was that the Soviets had begun their campaign to delegitimize Israel. This has dominated the United Nations ever since; about half the events at the UN and its agencies deal with Israel and are extensions of this Soviet campaign, which had begun in 1971.

The proposition of Zionism as a form of racism first appeared at the International Women's Year Conference in Mexico City, which wound up around July 5, 1975. The pattern of UN and Soviet behavior has been to put propositions forward at some peripheral event or at some specialized agency, and then move them into the center at the General Assembly.

I could see that, as early as 1971, the Third Committee was beginning to acquire the political culture of, I don't want to say the Third World, and I don't want to say the Soviets—but a political culture that was accommodating itself to nondemocratic forms of government in a way the United Nations was never intended to do. The charter of the United Nations assumes that the member states are democracies. It says so. It talks about human rights and was written by British and American lawyers who, when they said "human rights," meant what we think of as human rights.

In 1972 something was put out called the *United Nations World Social Report.* I got hold of this thing and I looked at it, and I was appalled. The *World Social Report* was the first indication of the kind of problems that UNESCO would have. Its measure of how good or bad things were going in a country was the degree of opposition to the government that was to be encountered. If the government had a lot of people shouting at it and holding rallies and denouncing it and so forth, it was to be assumed that things weren't going very well in that country. If, on the other hand, everything was peaceable and there were no protest rallies and such, evidently things were going pretty well. The *World Social Report* concluded that things were pretty bad in the United States and were really good in Czechoslovakia. No problems at all in Czechoslovakia because no one was protesting, and you could tell that because in the newspapers, everyone thought that everything was fine; but in the papers in the United States, people thought that the government was terrible.

The United States [and the Western Europeans] did not understand the situation well enough. [They] did not care enough to say, "Hey, stop right there. The social systems in the world are too much at variance to allow any such comparisons." Nobody is ever going to get a report out of a place like the UN in which these subjects are treated [fairly], because there are polar differences in standards and values. We should avoid such subjects altogether—we should say we will not talk about these things because there is nothing to talk about. All we can do is get mad, or make concessions which we should never in any way consider making.

The *World Social Report* is an antecedent, you might say, of UNESCO's decision to inquire into freedom of the press. If we had any sense in these matters, the minute the subject arose in UNESCO, we would have said there is nothing to discuss because there are only about 35 countries which have freedom of the press, and the rest don't. There is no point in talking about it—not even to get started, because we will have to start making compromises which will only end up to our disadvantage.

If we're trying to use the UN for what it can be used, there's no point in letting it be used against us in these ways. We never spotted this tendency. The problem was that in the Department of State, these things had had a low priority. People did not understand how powerful such matters are in the end—who controls the symbols of progress in the world. We never made a decision that this was serious, and so "damage control" became the operative term: See to it that it is no worse than it has to be.

We are now in opposition in the world, and we have to act that way and not act like somehow the world hasn't shifted any. The old days won't come back. And now the question is: How do we behave in this new situation?

We can use the UN optimally by using it minimally—attending to the things it must do, such as the atomic-energy agency; things which we might as well do at the UN, like the World Health Organization. We should use the ILO in ways that it can be used and use the General Assembly as little as possible, because the outcome is always going to be adverse to us.

But more importantly, the United States has still not learned multilateral diplomacy, partly because we are quite an old country. Almost our entire experience in diplomacy has been bilateral. When I went to the UN, I started out by asking, "Do we have any voting records?" It turned out we [in the government] didn't, but somebody did. In an odd way, it was a formative event in the career of an assistant professor at Annapolis. He was teaching international organization to the cadets, and had the voting records of the UN on a computer. We learned this and said, "My God, that's what we need." And so we got it and someone at the Naval Academy found that this assistant professor was working for the U.S. Mission, and that got him a much deserved promotion.

We sat down one weekend and said, "Let's make a list of five criteria for countries that are important to the United States in our bilateral relations." For example, we buy $100 million worth of goods from them or sell $100 million worth of goods to them, or we import a significant amount of oil or a critical raw material, or our investments are over $100 million, or any other reason that seems relevant at the time. And we'll call them "bilateral nations." The [U.S.] ambassador in that country has to be thinking about the bilateral relationship. For the other countries, the single most important relationship we have with them is in a multilateral context: They have one vote in the General Assembly and so do we. Our ambassadors in these countries must understand that behavior in the UN is the most important relationship that they have got to try to influence.

When you try to measure the performance of an ambassador in country x, in which we really don't have any affairs at all, let him see if he can't get their UN voting record down from 93 percent against the United States, to 91 percent. Chalk that up as good for him; better job next time. I mean, learn multilateral diplomacy.

It is an institutionally difficult thing to do, and would require some coordination, but not beyond our capacities. We must, for example, realize that the nonaligned, by the time they reach the General Assembly in September, have already gone through a series of decision-making processes in the spring and summer, such that their vote is fixed and there is no point in talking to them in September. You have to talk to them in April, and talk to them in their capitols.

One did find that an awful lot of these countries really were surprised to find that it mattered to us how they voted. No one had ever told them beforehand, and no one had ever told them afterwards. We had not learned multilateral diplomacy, whereas that's the only diplomacy most of them know. They came into the world [recently], and in a sense, they are more modern than we. The world they entered into as independent entities was a world of party systems, these caucuses. You have the Soviet bloc, they vote their way, and you have the nonaligned, and they vote their way; and the Western nations, and they vote their way. It works rather like parties in a parliament. And I think about it in those terms.

It's hard to think that you go to the UN and you argue your position with a lot of strength and a lot of energy, and then someone says the place is not worth a damn anyway. If we throw the UN out of New York and it ends up in Vienna with Soviet troops on its borders, it would change the whole symbolic configuration of the world; it would mark the onset of the decline of the United States as a world power.

It was my view that the place was a very important one and you had to have the American people believe that they were being represented there, not that it was an unimportant place. If it's an unimportant place, don't bother with it. It's a very important place.

WILLIAM W. SCRANTON: Permanent Representative and Chief of the U.S. Mission to the United Nations, 1976–77.

The caliber of the representatives to the UN is very high. The Third World ambassadors are frequently among their very best professionals, and they often return to their countries to become foreign ministers. Americans generally don't realize this—how much the UN means to the Third World.

William W. Scranton entered government service in 1959, as press secretary to Secretary of State John Foster Dulles. Previously, he had been active in business and industry in his native Pennsylvania. During 1959–60 Scranton represented the United States in conferences of NATO, the United Nations, and Latin America. Secretary of State Christian Herter, for whom Scranton served briefly as press secretary, once commented on Scranton's ability to grasp complicated issues quickly.

A Republican in party affiliation, though with a liberal bent in civil-rights matters, Scranton became governor of Pennsylvania in 1963, and in 1964 entered the presidential race as a moderate Republican alternative to Barry Goldwater. After completing his governor's term in 1966, Scranton left politics for business. Ten years later, however, he agreed to serve as U.S. ambassador to the United Nations, following Daniel Patrick Moynihan's resignation. He left his UN post when the Carter administration assumed office.

To start off, I must tell you what the situation was when I arrived. Pat [Moynihan], a good friend and a man I like very much personally, had done an extraordinary job of pointing out to the American people some of the many difficulties America faced at the United Nations, and also some of the really substantive defects in the UN system. On the other hand, at the mission itself, there was almost no understanding of the techniques of administration. Moynihan apparently dealt with relatively few people—some of his own friends from the outside and some from the inside. His influence didn't seep down into the core of the personnel there very much. They didn't really know what they were supposed to do or what was going on.

Secondly, strong antagonism to the United States emanated from almost all the other delegations, not so much on policy as on style. That affected us in one vital way: There was almost no communication or coordination of effort between the U.S. Mission and others, with the major exception of Israel; the Israeli Mission worked very closely with the U.S. Mission.

I saw my immediate task to be twofold: first, to organize the mission and its management so that the personnel knew what they were doing and why; secondly, to start, as quickly and as thoroughly and as intensively as I could, to communicate with many of the other delegations [so as] to work toward our objectives with their help. That took a great deal of time and work, and I was very fortunate to have a good staff at the mission.

At the outset, I spent a great deal of time with social occasions—attending all the dinners and the receptions. That was very time-consuming. I used social occasions for one-to-one talks and group talks. I had groups of delegates at our apartment, including some of the Africans, some of the allies—the NATO group—some of the Europeans, some of the Asians. We had lunches together and we discussed many policies very openly. That went on for at least a couple of months. I called on a number of the ambassadors, which, I guess, hadn't been done for some time. That made a good impression, at least in some cases.

In the meantime, we were structuring what we were going to try to accomplish in that year. I don't want to oversimplify this, but I think it came down to the following main issues: We would make a strong, coordinated effort on the Korean issue. Second, we would work hard to minimize the number of altercations involving Israel. Third (it wasn't in this order, incidentally), we would try to achieve a much more cooperative effort with our friends, particularly the Europeans, but others, too, on all of the issues that were expected on the agenda. Fourth, we wanted to implement a change in our African policy. Last but by no means least, because I am a very strong human rightist, I thought the United States should take leadership in that field and make progress there.

Anti-Israeli Rhetoric

There was relatively little anti-Israel effort in the 1976 General Assembly. I think the reason for that was that we organized the whole mission to talk with all of the various other missions at the UN, so that they were all thoroughly contacted on this issue. I had long conversations with the Egyptian ambassador, Meguid, and a number of others. The Egyptians were not pro-United States in those days. We made an enormous effort to make sure that if anything did come up at the General Assembly, it was relatively unimportant.

One of the things I did which was helpful, I think, is that I fostered a pretty good personal relationship with the Syrian ambassador, who was a semi-demi-leader of the anti-Israeli Arab group. We had two or three long sessions. He listened to me and reported back to his government. You can point out to them what they lose. They need the help of the United States in many different ways—economically, for food, and in some cases militarily.

It always worried me terribly that there are three million Jews in Israel and 100 million Arabs surrounding them. If they tried for too much territory, I thought they would be overwhelmed. And yet, they must have security. How do you have security for a nation that is but 13 miles wide at one of its most populated spots, on flat terrain? There are people living there, just north of Tel Aviv, who are subject to anything at any moment. I believe the only way Israel can ever attain real security is to have at least some friends on the Arab side. That's why I felt we had to make friends on the Arab side and see if we couldn't persuade them to be reasonable about the entity that is Israel and its security.

About five weeks after I arrived, the council encountered the first major problem, the Israeli settlements in occupied territories. It was one issue on which the administration, generally speaking, and some people in the Congress disagreed with the Israelis. I made the speech outlining our differences. Personally, I thought the settlements on the West Bank and in the Gaza Strip, etc., would be a long-term problem, and that the Israelis were wrong in increasing their numbers.

The other big event which came up in the Security Council with regard to Israel was the Entebbe raid [to free Israeli citizens held by terrorists in Uganda]. I felt strongly that the Israelis were right, and that they had a right to protect and save their people in Uganda. Fortunately, so did Washington to a degree. But Henry Kissinger was worried, and for good reason, because he was then in the middle of his Middle East shuttle diplomacy and he was concerned that if we were too pro-Israel in our UN handling of this matter, it would hurt his relationship with the Arabs at a critical time in his effort.

An event took place then which was the only time he and I had a major disagreement. The State Department sent to the mission a statement for me to make at the council—a normal procedure. I often changed such statements a good deal and sent them back for approval. I made some changes this time and added some strong personal comments addressed to both the Arabs and the Israelis. I sent the personal comments to Washington.

Just after I addressed the Security Council that afternoon, I was given a message saying, "Secretary Kissinger is on the phone." I said, "Tell him I'll call him back as soon as this is over."

Henry was very upset. He thought I had gone too far in praising the Israelis and being electrified by what they had done. I think that was exactly the word I used: "electrified." I said: "Henry, there's a very simple answer to that. Your work in trying for peace in the Middle East is far more important than anything I say about the Entebbe raid. If you feel my statement has been a deterrent to that work of yours, I will resign. I made it very clear to the president that I would only stay here until January, whether he is elected or not, and you know I'm not looking for governmental jobs."

"Well," he said, "let's wait—overnight. What's the reaction up there?" I said, "Henry, I don't know, I just made the talk."

The next day he called me rather early in the morning and asked again, "What is the reaction up there?" I said: "Henry, you're asking the wrong person. Obviously everybody is going to say nice things to me, and they have. What you should do is talk with the British and the French and the others. You probably have done that."

He said, "Yes, I have talked to some of them, and they all thought it was excellent." And I said, "Well, what's the reaction down there?"

He said, "Well, very frankly, the reaction down here is fine." I said, "Well, then all right. But if you find that this is really a deterrent to what you're trying to do, you know right now I will leave anytime." And that is the only personal problem I had with Henry Kissinger.

Korean Question

Korea was a great big problem at the UN. [Korean reunification has been a perennial item on the assembly agenda since 1947. North and South Korea have distinctively different views on how to reduce tensions. Thus, there are both North and South Korean Resolutions.]

I worked out the strategy with Henry and with the president. This was not all on my initiative, but partly so: that we would make an all-out effort about the Korean matter because the vote on this issue at the UN was becoming very close. In fact, most experts predicted that the so-called South Korean resolution would not pass in 1976.

We organized the entire [friendly] diplomatic service of the UN on this subject. The working group started [its] work early at the UN. It was made up, as you might imagine, of France, Britain, South Korea, Japan, Australia, and so forth. It met every week. We worked out what the resolution would be and assigned various delegations to various missions. Meantime, the State Department was very helpful, and we coordinated the assistant secretaries in the various territorial areas to work with our ambassadors all over the world on this subject, to call on governments to which they were assigned and discuss the problem. When any of us went on trips, we discussed this subject with the heads of state. Henry did the same thing and so did all the other major officials on their trips around the world.

One morning I received a telephone call [if my memory is accurate, it was early in September] from the Romanian ambassador. He said, "I have a very important matter for you. Can you see me today?"

I think it was about 8:15 A.M. He came over and outlined the following: "If you can have the South Korean resolution withdrawn, I will guarantee that we will withdraw the North Korean resolution."

I said, "How can I make sure of that, that you can arrange it?"

He said, "Well, you talk with your group and, if you can get it, call me back as soon as possible. Meantime, I'll talk with my group."

He called me back (I think it was two hours later) and said it was arranged. I said, "I can guarantee to you that ours will be withdrawn." And the Korean subject never came up at all.

Frankly, the reason for this was that we had done a very good job of preparation. I think they knew they were outvoted. Maybe both resolutions might have passed, but the South Korean resolution clearly was going to pass.

Secondly, we had worked very hard to do a little splitting among their group. I talked with the Polish ambassador at some length. I talked with the Romanian ambassador at some length and to a number of others about all of this. It became quite clear that there was a difference of opinion within their ranks about the North Koreans. We used this difference to hold down their strength. It worked very well, and I was very grateful to the Romanian ambassador and some of the others.

Human Rights

When I went to the U.S. Mission, I formed a team to work on this. I was very disappointed that we did not produce a major step forward on this issue, but there was some progress—for example, a speech I made to the Third Committee.

I was determined to name countries that were denying human rights. To the best of my knowledge, that had not been done very often by the Americans at the UN and it had not occurred in the Third Committee, particularly with regard to the Soviet Union. I will never forget the day I did that because I could see the Soviet representative while I was talking, and his mouth and his whole jaw dropped. He was so flabbergasted that he didn't reply at all that day. The next day they sent up the Czechoslovakians to say something, if I remember correctly. It was obvious that they were waiting for word from Moscow as to how to handle this. Then when they finally did talk back, it was not very effective.

Frankly, even though I went to the Third Committee, it didn't stimulate immediate results. I was disappointed that we didn't come up with anything more striking than what we did, although it was an unusual approach both personally and for the mission. Yet there was a purpose in it. I thought if I didn't go there personally, it would look as if we were just talking; but if I did go, maybe it would impress them. My speech did have specifics in it and it did name specifics in it and it did name specific countries including the USSR.

I had a theory which I worked out with our close allies. I said: "Let the United States go out front, and all the antagonists who don't like us will begin to jump on us in various ways—people who are really worried about too many laws on this subject. Then one of you start working it quietly. Over the next couple of years, maybe you can do something about it." Rudy von Weckmar, the West German ambassador, who is a super person, took it up. We made the initiative and they all jumped on us, but it finally began to take hold.

I think that's a very good technique for America in the UN: to get out front on something and let those who will, attack us on the subject, and then let one of the other countries take the constructive leadership on the issues while we aid and abet them all the way.

I'm still not happy about the extent of U.S. efforts on behalf of human rights. I'm glad there has been some progress, but I feel so strongly about this that I think we ought to be right out there in front as much as we can and keep right at it. I understand that from a political standpoint, as well as for effectiveness, you can't be totally moralistic on this subject and totally high-plane. But it is the single, not the only, but the single most important difference between the free world and the totalitarian world. If we don't believe in that and we don't espouse that cause, then I think we are not standing up for what we believe in and for the main difference between a republic and a totalitarian state.

The Soviet Union

We were able to prevent a major struggle between the Soviet Union and ourselves on any particular issue. I don't mean we voted together, but we didn't come up with a major altercation which split the whole place between them and us.

When I first got there, Malik was the ambassador. I remember that he came to see me in the spring sometime. He was very upset because he said the United States wouldn't support their plan that they had had before the UN, for two or three years, for a world disarmament meeting. I said: "You know, it isn't just that we don't think much would come out of such a conference, but it seems a little impractical to us to have such a conference when you can't get the Chinese and the French and so forth to come. After all, you and I can agree on something, maybe, but what good would it do if the other nuclear countries didn't?"

We went back and forth on this; they were trying to make a propaganda thing out of it, knowing full well that nothing would occur. Finally, I became a little exercised and I said to the ambassador, "I'll make a deal with you." The minute I made that comment, he became totally interested. He said, "What's that?" I said, "Well, I don't think I'd have too much trouble getting the British to come to such a meeting. I might have a great deal of trouble getting the French, but I will do my level best to persuade the French that they ought to do this—if you can get the Chinese." Whereupon he practically went through the ceiling, he got so mad. He said, "I can't get the Chinese," and that broke up that problem.

The second thing was that the Russians habitually attempt one highfalutin propaganda effort every General Assembly. That year they presented [a resolution] "outlawing the use of force." As you undoubtedly know, the UN Charter outlaws the use of force. So there was no reason to cite it again by resolution. I kept pointing this out to them, but they were interested only in a big propaganda effort.

Malik and his wife were in an automobile accident, and so they returned to Moscow. Malik was replaced by Kuznetsov, who was the deputy minister for foreign affairs and a far better man. He and I had seven meetings alone, lunches and one thing or another, in that fall. We didn't agree on the systems or anything of that sort, but I think that he respects me and I certainly respect him. I think it's fair to say that because of that personal relationship, there was never a major knock-down-and-drag-out fight on the floor of the assembly between the Soviets and the Americans.

Multilateral Diplomacy

An idea which I advocated to Washington often was that the UN should be handled differently than our bilateral foreign policy. I preached in Washington and everywhere else even, before going to the UN, that multilateral diplomacy was already more significant than we realized. None of the developed nations are prepared for this at all, either psychologically or organizationally. We and all the other countries—France and England and Germany and the Russians, particularly—are still organized almost totally for bilateralism in our foreign affairs. The dominance of the Soviet Union or ourselves or any one power or even group of powers is less likely in the future even than now. We ought to be prepared for the multilateral era.

We ought to change the setup in the State Department. I have suggested many times that an undersecretary for multilateral diplomacy ought to be established at DOS. We should have a clear understanding of what the relationship is of the UN ambassador to the secretary of state, to the president, and how to handle that relationship so that no embarrassments occur. I think we did this successfully.

I went down to Washington (except when I was out of the country) every two weeks, quite regularly. I set up that arrangement, had an agenda, took the agenda with me, and the agenda was accepted and followed. We had constant communication.

I always saw Henry and the president separately. He knew that and so did the president. If Henry and I disagreed on an issue, I would tell him I was going to talk with the president. Whatever the president finally decided, I abided by, but he always listened to my views first.

I had no political ambitions. When the president asked me to take the job, I told him, "Don't appoint me except under these conditions: that is, that if I have a major difference with you about a foreign-policy matter, a matter of vital importance, I will resign."

I think the personal relationship, as it worked out, was very good indeed. Besides, I was working with an individual who was extremely straightforward: Jerry Ford was about as straightforward an individual as you'll ever meet. He told me just when he did agree, just when he didn't, and why in each case.

GEORGE McGOVERN: Congressional Representative to the General Assembly, 1976, 1978.

The UN has never had the kind of respect in the Congress that one would wish. As you know, there's a certain amount of anti-UN rhetoric that turns up in Congress regularly. They reserve the right to scold the UN, to treat it with a certain amount of contempt. Still, Congress has always supported it.

George S. McGovern, known for his liberal stands on major national and international issues, has been a representative in the U.S. House, senator from South Dakota, and Democratic candidate for the presidency. During 1976 and 1978 he served as a congressional delegate to the United Nations. After losing his bid for a fourth term in the Senate, in 1980, McGovern joined a Washington law firm.

There is an established tradition now that each year, two members of the House or two members of the Senate are named as members of the American delegation to the UN. In the election years they name two senators who are not running for reelection that year. In 1976 it was Howard Baker for the Republicans and myself for the Democrats. In the odd-numbered years when nobody is up for election, they appoint two members of the House instead of the Senate, again one Democrat and one Republican. Those are presidential appointments, but as a practical matter, you're recommended for the appointment by the Senate or the House leadership. The majority leader recommends someone on the Democratic side if we're in the majority, and the Republican leader recommends somebody on the Republican side. You always end up with a bipartisan pair of either senators or congressmen. It's a very popular tradition in the Congress, and I found that it worked very well as far as the delegation in New York was concerned. It gave them an insight into the congressional side of U.S. policy that I thought was important. The ambassador recognizes that it is somewhat of an honorary position and tends to let you set your own schedule.

I was on the political committee at the UN, and I was also on the social and humanitarian committee that dealt with economic problems: foreign aid in the developing world, trade relations, and the world food problem. I was also concerned about the Middle East.

I was struck by how isolated the United States and Israel were in their positions on the Middle East. We really were almost alone in the world, and virtually all the rest of the world was sold on the Palestinians' cause and the necessity of addressing it. They seemed to be puzzled as to why the U.S. policy was so completely oriented around the desires of the state of Israel. I was dimly aware of that, but to see this idea so universally held and expressed at discussions at the UN was something of a shock to me.

I began to recognize the need for a broader, more evenhanded approach by the United States. I was glad to see Carter negotiate the Camp David accords after he was elected and start to deal with the Arab world as an equal to Israel—treating Sadat and Begin in a more or less evenhanded way. It still didn't mean that we had addressed the Palestinian question, but at least we were recognizing that the Arab world was a constructive partner.

The other area where I began to get new perspectives during my service at the UN was Africa. I frankly hadn't focused on Africa, but it seemed like a third of the delegates at New York were out of Africa, because a third of them are. As a matter of fact, Kissinger, who came to the UN while I was there, recognized by 1976 that we had to shift our policy in Africa away from automatic endorsement of ruling regimes to the concept of majority rule. He made an important speech at the United Nations where he underscored U.S.-Third World concerns and indicated a much more advanced posture. He really anticipated the Carter policies that came in 1977 in that regard. I talked to him directly about the necessity of affirming our support for majority rule, if not black rule.

One delegation that is overlooked in New York is the Cuban delegation. They're boycotted up there by the United States. On the opening day of the session, I saw the Cubans sitting back there and nobody paying any attention to them. I had been to Cuba in 1975, and I saw a couple of people that I recognized. I just walked back in the UN General Assembly and shook hands with them, and they were very moved by that because no American had shaken hands with them in years. It set off quite a stir. You could hear audible comments, not critical, but just sort of a buzz running through the whole area and I became aware that I was being discussed. I didn't know why, but later on I saw one of them alone over in the lounge. I had a cup of coffee with him and he said, "You know, that was a very nice thing you did."

It's a minor point, but it just struck me that the United Nations is a place where the United States ought to be big enough to talk to everybody. I don't think we ought to boycott representatives there like the PLO observer, the Cubans, the Koreans, or other people. The fact that we don't have relations with them, in my judgment, doesn't mean we can't have a certain informal, unofficial contact with them.

The United States has to rise above the Third World antagonisms and resentments and not engage in the kind of confrontational tactics that some of our ambassadors have doubtless called for. I don't think we ought to worry about every Third World country that takes a poke at us, speaking out in their anguish and frustration. If you're going to live in the best house in town, you're going to have a lot of the neighbors resentful and jealous.

I was always encouraged by the knowledge that the United Nations is in the United States, so we don't have to talk about the diversity and glories of our system. New York is one of the great cities in the world, maybe the most fascinating city in the world. I never heard anybody seriously propose that the United Nations be transferred, let's say, to Africa or to the Middle East or to Latin America or wherever. Virtually every delegate that I talked with up there seemed to be having a marvelous time in New York.

Of course, they see the bad parts of it, too. They occasionally get mugged on the streets of New York. They know about rape and drugs and all of that stuff that all of us are so distressed about. They see that and they recognize we are struggling with it, but that we also have this marvelous cultural diversity in our great cities that they can enjoy.

I don't know why we instinctively think that the State Department is the first resort [for] resolving international crises. We ought to automatically think in terms of the United Nations. We don't because neither we nor other great powers have invested the UN with that kind of prestige and power.

I don't know any quick way to do that, other than starting to use it. But I don't suppose there's much hope for it unless the great powers decide that it's a vital forum that they have to use for resolving disputes. I think you could sell the Third World countries on that. These Third World countries send the best diplomats they have because it's their one showcase, their one mouthpiece to the rest of the world. As a general rule, I think you could say we send our second-level people to the UN and our sharpest people to London, Paris, Rome, the State Department, and the National Security Council.

Even though we don't always use the UN, it is true that when a problem develops, people wonder what the UN is going to do and they grumble that they don't do more. I've heard people say, both in the Congress and as private citizens, that the UN ought to be doing more in the Middle East; the UN should have been more active on the Falkland Islands crisis; the UN ought to be doing something about Poland. At least the expectation is still alive.

In the absence of some kind of international organization of that kind, you've got 150 disorganized countries, each seeking their place in the sun without regard to the well-being of the rest. It's only at the UN where they all come together and look at the world from a standpoint of an international community. So it serves various valuable purposes: One, it is a pressure-release valve. Secondly, it is a forum for airing differences between countries, and hopefully suggesting a way to reconciliation. Thirdly, it's an absolutely indispensable outlet for the Third World even if we could get along without it, which we probably could. As a great power, we might be able to make our way without the UN. The Third World countries could not. They have to have a forum of this kind where they can voice their special concerns, which are so urgent, problems of economic development, of trade and aid, resource development, population, food—the UN is the best focus for dealing with problems of that kind.

I would like to see the UN steadily elevated as a useful forum in which the United States participates. I think its peacekeeping functions ought to be enhanced. I've been very disappointed that the UN hasn't strengthened its peacekeeping functions over the last 30 years. I think it has not lived up to the hopes and anticipations of the founders. One of the reasons is that the great powers have used it when it was convenient and then bypassed it when it wasn't. It's only through the habit of use that the UN is going to develop the precedent and the prestige to be accepted as an important peacekeeping instrumentality. But if we could create a situation in the next Falkland Islands crisis, or the next Beirut crisis, or the next Afghanistan crisis, where the UN automatically is the agency that we turn to for a resolution, I think it would do more to the cause of peace and understanding in the world than anything else.

PART IV:
THE CARTER YEARS,
1977–80

OVERVIEW

The Carter administration took office in 1977 with a fresh and hopeful approach to foreign policy, characterized by an emphasis on human rights, renewed efforts at improving relations with the Soviet Union and the Third World, and the appointment of a secretary of state (Cyrus Vance) and a permanent representative (Andrew Young) who were committed to the use of the United Nations. The important role that Carter accorded to the promotion of human rights abroad was underscored by the appointment of an assistant secretary of state for human rights and humanitarian affairs, Patricia Derian, and of the first full-time U.S. representative to the UN Human Rights Commission, Edward Mezvinsky.

Middle East

Given the historic Egyptian-Israeli hostility, the unprecedented trip to Jerusalem in 1977 by Egyptian President Anwar Sadat signaled that the Middle East impasse might be broken. Under U.S. auspices, Egypt and Israel signed the Camp David accords of 1979 that provided for gradual Israeli withdrawals from occupied territories and laid the groundwork for a peace treaty. Thereafter, the United States sought to bring other Middle Eastern states into the peace process, but Egypt was ostracized by the Arab world for its initiative. At the

United Nations the predominant position remained: that there could be no peace without a final settlement of the Palestinian issue. The General Assembly passed resolutions stating that any peace efforts "must be based on a comprehensive solution under UN auspices" and "could not be established without the achievement of a just solution to the problem of Palestine." A Special Unit on Palestinian Rights was created by the GA in 1977.

Meanwhile, Israel moved troops into southern Lebanon in 1978 in response to raids by Palestinian commandos based in Lebanon. The Security Council called on Israel to withdraw its forces. The United Nations, embarking on the most dangerous peacekeeping mission since the Congo situation, established the UN Interim Force in Lebanon (UNIFIL), which operated in a volatile atmosphere of continued hostility between the Lebanese Christians and Moslems and which was itself the subject of hostility. (Previous peacekeeping forces were based upon the agreement of the adversaries to cease hostilities and establish a demilitarized zone between the factions.)

In a number of other world crises, the United Nations was less able to play a decisive or even significant role. A change in the regional balance of the Persian Gulf area occurred early in 1979 when the Shah of Iran fell from power and was replaced by the Ayatollah Khomeini. Late in the year, Iranian militants took as hostages more than 50 Americans at the embassy in Teheran. The Security Council unanimously called for the release of the U.S. diplomats, and the World Court ordered Iran to release them, but to no avail. The United Nations played only a minor role in the year-long negotiations that led to their release. In a somewhat related matter—an invasion by Iraq into Iran and the ensuing bloody and inconclusive border war—the UN Security Council recommended to Secretary General Waldheim that a mediator be appointed with the consent of Iran and Iraq. The former Prime Minister of Sweden, Olaf Palme, served in this capacity but with little apparent success.

Little effective UN action came out of yet another war, this time in Afghanistan, where Russian troops had entered at the end of 1979 to prop up a shaky pro-Russian government. The Security Council debated the issue and voted on a resolution calling for Soviet withdrawal, which met with a Soviet veto. The assembly, under the "Uniting for Peace" provision, also demanded the immediate withdrawal of all "foreign troops" from the country. The principal result of the UN actions was to diminish Soviet stature in the eyes of the World community.

South Africa: Decolonization

In southern Africa, free elections in Rhodesia (Zimbabwe) in 1979 and 1980 established black control. Majority rule—the principle that the General Assembly had insisted must be implemented before independence—had been achieved, and independence was declared in 1980. Progress was slower in Namibia. At a special session on the Namibian question in 1978, the assembly adopted measures calling for South Africa's withdrawal from Angola and Namibia. Progress seemed to have begun that year as a Western plan for Namibia was submitted to the Security Council, which called for a cease-fire and the suspension of free elections by the United Nations. In 1979 the assembly called for economic sanctions to be used against South Africa unless it accepted the UN plan for independence. SWAPO, the South-West Africa People's Organization, a Marxist guerrilla group, was recognized as Namibia's "sole and authentic representative." South Africa initially agreed to an election and independence for Namibia, but then rejected the role prescribed for SWAPO in the election. With independence still in the future, South African troops and guerrillas continued to engage in periodic fighting.

The United Nations and the Organization for African Unity (OAU) sponsored the 1977 World Conference for Action Against Apartheid, which called yet again for cessation of arms sales to South Africa. The next year, the World Conference to Combat Racism and Racial Discrimination called for broader measures against racist regimes and for the prevention of investment by multinational corporations in those countries. In 1979 the assembly reaffirmed its 1974 decision to bar South Africa from participation in the United Nations.

Human Rights

The condemnation of human-rights abuses throughout the world became highly selective and politicized in the late 1970s, with a continued and consistent focus on Israel and the occupied territories, southern Africa, and, more recently, on Chile, to the exclusion of any discussion of flagrant and gross violations elsewhere.

In the late 1970s, Southeast Asia became a focus of debate. The credentials of the Pol Pot government in Kampuchea (Cambodia) were accepted by the General Assembly in 1980, in spite of the fact that the Chinese-backed Communist regime had been ousted by the invading Vietnamese Communist Army. While supporting the vote, UN Ambassador McHenry stated that the American move did "not imply United States Government recognition of the Democratic Kampuchea regime, support for the regime or approval of its heinous practices. We condemn unequivocally the savage human rights violations that have taken place under the Pol Pot Regime." The United States, in other words, was supporting Pol Pot solely to prevent recognition of the Vietnamese-backed government that was then being installed in power by the invading forces. In 1979, the assembly had adopted a resolution calling for the "withdrawal of foreign forces," that is, the Soviet-backed Vietnamese.

Arms Control and Disarmament

A special session on disarmament (SSOD) was held at the United Nations in late spring 1978. Particularly noteworthy was the end of France's 17-year boycott of UN disarmament negotiations: It joined the Disarmament Commission, which has universal membership, and the Committee on Disarmament, which has a membership of 40 and which, of the two organizations, tends to be regarded more seriously by the nuclear powers. By 1979 the People's Republic of China had also joined. The SSOD produced a final document consisting of general recommendations on slowing the arms race and, for the first time in UN history, some statements on the problem of conventional arms. But generally, the many UN efforts toward disarmament were hampered by substantive differences between the nuclear and non-nuclear nations as well as between the superpowers. Thus, major attempts to reach arms-control agreements—such as SALT talks—were initiated on the bilateral level, with the General Assembly urging ratification of Salt II by the United States and the USSR.

Economic Issues

The most pressing economic issues of the United Nations continued to be those involving developed versus less-developed nations or, to use the current shorthand parlance, between the North and the South. In 1980 the less-developed countries proposed the establishment of the Third Development Decade (1981–91), which was inaugurated at a Special Session of the General Assembly. As a way of urging the developed countries to devote a greater share of their resources to international development, the LDCs had written into the Development Decade resolution the requirement that each developed country begin, no later than 1985, to devote 0.7 percent of its gross national product to international development. (Since 1970 the actual proportion of development aid had been about 0.34 percent of GNP, although a few developed nations had actually exceeded the 0.7 percent target set in 1981.) The Development Decade was intended as the first step in negotiating a new international economic order that would redefine economic relations between North and South. The actual negotiations, however, could not begin as scheduled because of disputes over whether the negotiating instrument should be a specialized agency, such as the IMF (which the North preferred), or the United Nations as a whole (which the South preferred).

The Third Conference on the Law of the Sea (UNCLOS III) was convened in 1977 and met frequently thereafter. Its guiding principle proclaimed that the seabed and its resources were "the common heritage of mankind." The complex issues before the conference included fishing rights, conservation of the marine environment, overlapping national boundaries along continental shelves, and the mining of the seabed. The negotiations ended with a document signed by 118 nations in Japan in 1982. As the spirit of détente faded, the Law of the Sea Treaty became a partial casualty of the growing strategic concerns of the newly elected Reagan administration. The United States, protesting against some of its restrictions on mining of the ocean floor, and citing the voting formula for the 36-member Seabeds Council (which did not earmark a spot specifically for the United States), refused to sign.

The Fading of Détente

In its later years, the Carter administration was faced with a series of unwelcome events that triggered a reassessment of its foreign policy. The seemingly intractable and interminable hostage crisis in Iran brought home sharply to the American people, and the world, the vulnerability of the United States in an increasingly hostile and violent world. The Soviet invasion of Afghanistan drew strong measures from the administration, including the imposition of a grain embargo that angered American farmers and was not widely supported abroad, and a somewhat more successful boycott of the 1980 Olympics. The abortive rescue of the Iranian hostages in spring 1980 and the subsequent resignation of Secretary of State Cyrus Vance further contributed to the perception by many observers that the administration did not have a coherent and decisive foreign policy.

Against the backdrop of heightened international tension and the use of military solutions by the Soviets in Afghanistan and later in Poland, the administration began to abandon detente. Cold War tensions surfaced and the arms race resumed. Salt II, although concluded by Carter and Brezhnev, was later shelved by Congress in an increasingly confrontational atmosphere. In the United Nations the United States and the Soviet Union could agree on little besides their common desire to slow the growth in the UN budget.

The decline in relations between the two superpowers would not have been so discouraging to the administration if it had been accompanied by an improvement in U.S. relations with the Third World, especially in the United Nations. Unfortunately, resolutions passed in the world body continued to be of a nature that many Americans regarded as contrary to U.S. interests, particularly those pertaining to South Africa and the Middle East. Thus, the United States continued to appear isolated in the General Assembly.

On the other hand, the Carter administration could point to improved relations with the People's Republic of China and to the fact that the United States remained at peace—no small boast considering that memories of Vietnam were still fresh. The human-rights policy, although selectively applied due to the constraints of national security and domestic politics, represented a noble attempt to reflect the best of American traditions and values in an imperfect world.

The frustration and disappointment often felt by the Carter administration was mirrored in the United Nations as well. Despite all the resolutions about economic development, self-government for black South Africans, and self-determination for Palestinians and others, the United Nations had ceased to play a major political role in world affairs, except in a few special cases. Increasingly, the superpowers relied on the more traditional methods of bilateral diplomacy to conduct their relations, perhaps in part because so much real power in the United Nations had gravitated into the hands of the Third World, specifically the Group of 77. United Nations affairs became dominated by countries whose immediate interests seemed quite divergent from those of the superpowers, and debates in the General Assembly and even the Security Council often were exercises in bombastic rhetoric. Camp David occurred outside the United Nations; when the Carter administration sought a meaningful sanction against the Soviet invasion of Afghanistan, it acted unilaterally, with its grain embargo and Olympics boycott, because no serious United Nations action seemed likely. By 1981, when Ronald Reagan assumed the presidency, American foreign policy, especially regarding the United Nations, had already begun to shift, and the main question was simply how far in that direction the new president would go.

The U.S. Mission

In Andrew Young, Jimmy Carter found an articulate instrument for his ideas about the world. A minister in the United Church of Christ and a leader in the civil-rights movement, Young was also a congressman from Atlanta who had been one of Carter's closest political supporters. He shared Carter's belief that the United States could exert a stronger moral force on the world scene and welcomed appointment as the first black U.S. permanent representative to the United Nations. He worked closely with Carter and with Secretary of State Vance, notably in efforts to hasten the day for independence in Zimbabwe and Namibia. Young swiftly improved relations with African states, in particular, and with many other Third World nations. He attended cabinet meetings and traveled extensively, to the detriment, it was said by some, of the day-to-day administration of the mission.

Young resigned as U.S. representative to the United Nations after revelations about his unauthorized meeting with a PLO leader. As a successor, President Carter selected the soft-spoken Donald McHenry as the fourteenth and youngest UN representative.

The first major international crisis to confront McHenry was the November 1979 takeover of the U.S. Embassy in Iran. McHenry's evenhanded tone helped secure two favorable Security Council votes, though a Soviet veto precluded the enactment of economic sanctions.

On March 1, 1980, McHenry voted in favor of a UN resolution condemning Israeli settlements on the West Bank and Gaza Strip. Two days later, Carter disavowed the controversial decision—the United States previously had abstained on such votes. Secretary of State Vance took the blame for the reversal, though McHenry was criticized by some Jewish leaders in the United States for being anti-Israel.

The Carter administration was represented by two separate and distinct delegations over its period of four years. The resignation of Andy Young in September 1979 was followed by a turnover in the ambassadorial representation. James Leonard was succeeded by William vanden Heuvel as deputy representative. With the assumption of the perm-rep position by McHenry, Richard Petree, a career diplomat, became deputy representative on the Security Council. Melissa Wells, a career diplomat and the first woman to serve as representative on ECOSOC, was later followed by Joan Spero, a former political science professor from Columbia University. The post of alternate representative for special political affairs was held first by Allard Lowenstein, then by Richard Petree, and finally by H. Carl McCall, a former New York state senator. C. William Maynes, the assistant secretary of state for international-organization affairs, was followed in that post by Richard McCall.

During these years, the congressional and public delegates to the General Assembly included Senator Abraham A. Ribicoff and Representative Benjamin Rosenthal; Coretta Scott King, Marjorie Craig Benton, Howard Rosen, and Esther Coopersmith. An illustrious delegation to the 1978 Special Session on Disarmament was headed by W. Averell Harriman; it included Senators George McGovern and Charles Mathias, and actor Paul Newman.

SOURCES

General information about the United Nations and the U.S. Mission during this period may be found in *Everyone's United Nations* (New York: UN Office of Public Information, 1979); *UN Annual Yearbook* (New York: United Nations, 1978-81; *Issues Before the General Assembly of the United Nations* (New York: UN Association of the United States, 1978-81); Thomas Hovet, *A Chronology and Fact Book of the United Nations, 1941-1979* (Dobbs Ferry, N.Y.: Oceania, 1979); *U.S. Participation in the UN* (Washington, D.C.: Department of State, 1978-81); and Seymour Maxwell Finger, *Your Man At The UN* (New York: New York University Press, 1980).

ANDREW YOUNG: Permanent Representative and Chief of the U.S. Mission to the United Nations, 1977–79.

> *The most important thing about the U.S. ambassador is the ability to go to Washington once a week and talk with the secretary of state and the president. If you can't do that, the forum will only get you fired, or it will create problems. I really had few if any problems with the president and the secretary of state. I had problems with the press because they didn't appreciate my understanding of my role.*

Trained in the ministry at Hartford Theological Seminary, Andrew Jackson Young, Jr., became a minister in the United Church of Christ. After serving in churches in Alabama and Georgia, and then working for the National Council of Churches in New York (1957–61), Young joined the Southern Christian Leadership Conference (SCLC), becoming executive director in 1964.

In 1970 Young entered the U.S. House of Representatives, where he served the first of three terms as representative of a mostly white district in Atlanta. He supported Jimmy Carter in that fellow-Georgian's successful presidential campaign, and late in 1976 was named U.S. ambassador to the United Nations.

Beginning the day after taking office, the outspoken Young frequently became the center of controversy. He said that the Cubans had brought "a certain stability and order" to Angola. He embarrassed the Carter administration by angering the Russians, Sweden, Britain, and the New York City borough of Queens: He called the Russians "the worst racists in the world"; claimed the Swedes were "terrible racists who treated blacks as badly as they were treated in Queens"; and then asserted that the English still had an "old colonial mentality." His call for negotiations in Zimbabwe and South-West Africa irked African revolutionaries, while the South Africans were miffed by his call for economic boycotts by South African blacks to protest apartheid.

Carter did not waiver in his support for his UN representative until 1979, when Young resigned under heavy criticism after revelations of his unauthorized meeting with a Palestine Liberation Organization leader. He was replaced by Donald McHenry. In 1981 Young was elected mayor of Atlanta.

I believe in the United Nations, and I have always felt that it offers the world's only hope of peace. President Carter had campaigned publicly in support of the UN and made one of his first presidential foreign-policy speeches at the UN. He was committed to trying to do something about the world in which we live, and he understood that you couldn't really solve domestic problems unless you had some impact on the problems of the world.

I was able to talk freely with the president, and that was one of the things that made it very comfortable and appealing to me. I also had something that, I think, even Henry Cabot Lodge didn't have; that is, I had an active public constituency. I felt that my appointment represented, first of all, the black voter that gave President Carter about 29 percent of his votes in the course of the campaign. Add to that the peace movement and the student movement and the labor movement, all of whom I had campaigned amongst for President Carter, and I felt that I represented an important part of the Democratic Party's constituency, and that if I had not gone into the cabinet, it would have been a much more conservative cabinet than it would be with me there.

Striving for World Order

The most valuable aspect of the UN experience was the opportunity to build bridges to the developing world, and that was Africa, the Caribbean, and the Middle East.

When I first got there, the president asked me to take a plane to Africa and to visit African heads of state to see just what it was that they wanted the United States to do. In fact, we systematically looked at the world. The president had a concept of world order that depended on strong U.S. leadership, which fit right in with notions [held by] Roosevelt and Truman when the UN was founded. Those notions have not been shared by too many presidents since, and the need for world order has not been understood, but I think President Carter understood that if you didn't have an aggressive peace policy and progress in the Middle East, you were going to have chaos and war. The world either moves toward peace or it moves toward war and chaos.

Panama was a place that could have been very explosive had we not moved ahead aggressively and developed a treaty with the Panamanians. Southern Africa was another place where there clearly were difficulties, in Zimbabwe. That southern African belt contains many of the valuable minerals that the United States needs for its continued growth and development. It was in the process of becoming more and more under Soviet influence because Africans perceived that the United States was not interested in independence movements or liberation, because we did not support their liberation movement and the Russians did. When we established the fact that we did support self-determination and independence by democratic means, and that we could deliver on that through free and fair elections in Zimbabwe, they clearly understood that it was in their interest, too, to do it that way.

One of the great benefits of the UN is that people get a chance to exchange ideas with others in direct negotiations. In fact, the U.S. secretary of state meets more diplomats at the UN than in the entire course of service otherwise, because we have what we call scheduled bilateral meetings. Cy Vance used to meet with as many as 35 or 40 foreign ministers. One year he had 60-some meetings, and he stayed up there two weeks, and then he extended it awhile because he found it so valuable. The interesting thing was, none of this was in the press. He had a suite at the UN Plaza Hotel, and about every half-hour, another delegation of ministers would walk over. He'd talk a little bit with the Europeans, and then people [with] whom he had a lot to talk about he would probably schedule longer. But he got to meet face-to-face with so many people that he really built up a great deal of credibility and integrity for the United States in those meetings.

I took the role of talking about the U.S. position and its weaknesses myself, in order also to talk about the strengths of the U.S. position. That was the way I think I deflected criticism. If a Russian ambassador talked about Russia like I talk about the United States, he wouldn't be fired, he'd be killed. And they know that at the UN, so they don't expect them to be suicidal and martyred.

During the entire time I was there, we didn't have embarrassing, condemning resolutions in the Security Council at all, and we had very few in the General Assembly, mainly because we talked to people and we negotiated reasonable language. The key to it is, we talked with everybody about everything. You get in trouble at the

UN when you won't talk to people. But you get in trouble in any political body when you don't communicate. I'm in trouble with the City Council here in Atlanta because I don't talk to them as much as I should. It's a hard thing to put in your schedule, you know, talking to people. Where you know you disagree, you do it. The problem with the City Council is I think we agree on too much, and we do agree, but there's no substitute for personal contact in any political forum.

My understanding of my UN role was that President Carter campaigned on a platform that said he wanted a foreign policy as open and honest as the American people. Carter felt that the open and honest discussion of foreign policy, however controversial, was important to a democratic process. And so I didn't hesitate to talk about issues, and I usually knew what I was talking about, and knew how it would contribute to the public debate. I also knew it would be controversial, but there's no learning without controversy, and so a certain level of controversy in a democracy, I think, is necessary to bring about change.

In the context in which I made them, all of my controversial statements had a relevance. Sometimes that was distorted. I had a discussion with a British journalist where he was asking me about the civil-rights movement and race relations in the South, and I told him I thought we had moved a long ways toward solving these problems in Atlanta. He said he was glad that America had finally realized it had this problem and was doing something about it. I said, "Well, we're not the only ones. Britain's got a few race problems." And he said, "Oh, now, come on. We don't have a race problem in Britain." And I said, "What do you mean? You invented it!" It was on camera, and I said it humorously, but the headline the next day was: "Young Attacks British As Racists." All I was saying was that they were going to have problems with their immigrant population because they are not integrated. He said, "How can you say this?" I said, "I watch soccer on British television, and I see all these British teams, and I don't ever see anybody black. You can't tell me that West Indians and Africans can't run and can't play football. You all are where we were 30 years ago." It was an intelligent argument, but by the time the Conservative Party got through with it, it was an attack on the honor of Great Britain.

I think that the whole purpose of U.S. foreign policy has got to be to provide peace and stability in the world, and you can't do that without protecting human rights. Where human rights are being denied, and where repression is in place, revolution and bloodshed are inevitable. Either we provide for respect for human rights by democratic means, or we see the world disintegrate through violent means.

The [UN] Human Rights Commission was a very weak commission, and there again it was partially weak because of the United States. We didn't want to discuss problems of Palestinian rights on the West Bank. We didn't want to do too much about Chile, about Argentina, about the Philippines. And because we didn't want to do anything about our problems, we had no incentive, no credibility to push the Soviets to do anything about their human-rights record, or raise with the Arabs the question of the rights of women. The most controversial thing I did inside the UN was to make a speech on women's rights, and I got cussed out for it by the Saudi ambassador, Baroody. Even Waldheim got mad.

Lessons

I think that the first thing we can learn is that the UN does respond to U.S. leadership. In fact, it only works when the United States gives leadership. The second thing we can learn is that it's a political process. The democratic process doesn't work automatically. You have to make it work. Whenever I knew the United States had a sound, fair position, I could go to the Europeans, the Africans, the Latins, and even the Russians, explain it to them privately, tell them why we wanted to do it, and most of them would go along with us. Quite often the Russians didn't agree with what we were trying to do in Zimbabwe, but when you lined up the Africans and the Arabs and the Latins, the Russians didn't want to be opposing the whole Third World, so they would not veto the things that we did; whereas normally, if you just bring up a resolution without lining up your votes and your support, there's too much distrust for people automatically to vote for a resolution on its face. You have to take the time to discuss it with people, to answer their suspicions, and to convince them of the rightness of a position. But that's what you had to do in Congress: I mean, you couldn't get anything through the Congress of the United States without talking to key leadership.

That's why I say politicians have fared much better at the UN than most folk. Lodge was a politician; Stevenson [was]; Scranton.

But the career diplomats and the academics have not done as well. I've often said I would like to see Moynihan go back to the UN, now—after he's been in the Senate. He'd be a different kind of ambassador, I think.

Confrontation is counterproductive. We have the most to gain by the UN working, and we have the most to lose by the UN being disruptive, because our country's place in the world depends on a certain amount of stability. Our national interests are tied with free trade, free access to minerals, free access to markets. We can prosper in a world that's stable and secure.

JAMES F. LEONARD: Deputy Representative to the United Nations, 1977-79.

I think that the Third World failed to realize what a good thing they had in the Carter administration, and how fragile it was. They really thought that they could keep pressing, and demanding more and more, and that the American political system would respond and give them more and more, because they were so convinced that they really did deserve it. And that was a bad misjudgment.

James Fulton Leonard joined the Foreign Service not long after World War II and served in posts in Damascus, Moscow, Paris, Taipei, and Washington. In 1969 he became assistant director of the Arms Control and Disarmament Agency (ACDA). He resigned from that post in 1973 in the wake of the Nixon-administration purges of the ACDA. "Those who could be fired were fired. They couldn't fire me, but they could give me back to the State Department," he recalls. "I was disguested with the way the whole thing was carried out. ... It was part of Nixon's desire to get rid of all the moderate elements in the government, the more liberal elements."

He became vice president of the UN Association of the United States in 1973 and president in 1974. In 1977 President Carter appointed him deputy permanent U.S. representative to the United Nations.

Leonard served as a deputy special representative to the Middle East peace negotiations (1979-81) before his retirement from government service. He is the chairman of the Committee for National Security and a consultant to the Aspen Institute in Washington, D.C.

We at the mission were delighted with Andy Young; he is the most marvelously personable character. We got to know him and became aware of some of his talents. The tenor of the times, in 1977, was extremely buoyant. We all really had the feeling that we had come through an extremely bad period of Watergate and Vietnam. We were very hopeful that the new administration was going to be a great success, including [efforts at] the UN. The basic attitude of the principal figures—Carter, Vance, Brzezinski—toward the UN was extremely favorable, and they were all on record in good ways about it. I don't think they exaggerated, either. I don't want to suggest that they had stars in their eyes over the UN. They'd been observing it, especially Vance, over a long-enough period to be realistic about what it might be able to do, and not do. But they wanted to use it to its maximum, and I think that's what the administration did set out to do in the early months. The policies which Secretary of State Vance intended to carry out were basically those of the liberal center, the establishment, but the liberal establishment. It was a moment of very great hope.

It didn't go so well, as you know. We had underestimated the difficulty, and really had not correctly judged how much political capital we would have to expend in the American domestic political system in order to attain these objectives. I would have to say, even though I was very disappointed at the outcome, that a great deal was accomplished, especially in the first year and a half or two years, which, just by coincidence, is the time I was there. I left in May of 1979.

The 1977 General Assembly was something of a honeymoon for the Carter administration. Andy Young had done enough by then to get a lot of credit. Don McHenry had Namibia moving. The Gang of Five, as we called the Western members of the Security Council, was at work on the matter, and there was hope that solutions could be had within a year. We instituted the ban on the purchase of Rhodesian chrome [in 1977] and, in other ways, showed the Africans that we were on their side and trying to get independence for Zimbabwe and Namibia. The Africans gave us a great deal of credit, therefore. The Panama Canal treaties had been negotiated and the Latin Americans gave us enormous credit for that, and deservedly so, because Carter spent a great deal of political capital in getting that through. We hadn't done much for Asia, but the Asians reflected general satisfaction.

In retrospect, I feel that we didn't get from the nonaligned [nations] generally in the General Assembly, and certainly not from the Russians, the kind of reciprocity that we should have. Most of them were genuinely grateful for the important things we did, but they tended to be prisoners of positions that were taken, in some cases, under direct Cuban and hostile-nonaligned influence. Very early in the Carter administration, the nonaligned showed a weakness and a willingness to be led by their worst elements. I've held this against them ever since. It's because of the way they worked. The nonaligned movement has a caucus, and they have the leadership group—the steering committee—which is more or less permanently in session.

The dynamics of personalities and of issues within the group is such that bad money drives out good, as they say. The most radical elements run the group. The more positive persons tend to be quiet and sit there and don't object. The result is that countries like Cuba have a disproportionate influence that is regretted by the more moderate members. But other countries will not stand up to these characters.

The nonaligned in the UN allowed themselves to be led by the nose by a small group of extremists. Compare that with what Andy Young and Cy Vance and Jimmy Carter were trying to do for these same people. If the United States was not able to come through at that point with a lot of things the nonaligned wanted, like millions of dollars more in economic assistance, it was very understandable, it seems to me, in the light of the absence of reciprocity on their part.

It got worse in the 1978 General Assembly. We were treated very badly on the Middle East, the whole Camp David business. The result was just a steady deterioration. The honeymoon was over, say, in early 1978. Things just went along with one incident after another that kept making this relationship worse.

Mishandling of Camp David

The Arabs' initial reaction to Sadat's visit to Israel in 1977 was that they really wanted it to succeed. They felt that this was the only way to avoid disaster in the Middle East. Yet they weren't willing to declare themselves. They would only whisper this privately to us, in part because we on our side—and here I speak rather bluntly—mishandled our end of the whole Camp David operation.

It goes back not to the way we handled the aftermath of Sadat's visit—that all went very well—it's what happened at Camp David itself. We thought we had some elements agreed to in the Camp David document, including the halt on Israel's West Bank settlements. But we were ready to interpret them one way and [Menachem] Begin had a different interpretation. Specifically, he denied that he had agreed to a halt in the settlements. That was the breaking point. If only Carter had won in his dispute with Begin over that—Vance assured us, you see. We were in touch with Vance. We said, "Here, look. Here are these two interpretations. Which is right?" Vance said that "there's no doubt at all which is right: We are right and Begin is wrong." Two weeks later Begin had won. The whole UN was watching and the Arabs, in particular, took that as a manifestation of weakness and that the United States could be bullied, in this case by Begin and the American Jewish community.

American Jews had mixed feelings. Most of them didn't like the settlements program but they also didn't like to see Israel pushed around. But when Carter in effect said, "O.K., I guess we haven't got Begin's agreement, after all," and he turned to Sadat and asked him to continue to observe the rest of the terms and to go forward with the negotiations for the peace treaty, then that did it. The secret supporters of Camp David at the UN all said, "No more. That's it." From then on it was all downhill.

In retrospect, one can argue that the response by Begin was really not a big surprise. The United States was advocating a comprehensive solution to the Mideast problem, but any Israeli government is going to be unhappy with such an approach because it seems to call for Israel making a lot of concessions to everybody rather than a procedure, which is obviously favored by most Israeli strategic thinkers (if you want to call them that), that is to take the countries one by one and make peace with them one by one. Therefore, when the administration's approach didn't succeed, or was going so slowly that Sadat became exasperated and switched to the other track, made the trip to Jerusalem, and then did everything that led on to Camp David and the Arab-Israeli peace, that really pleased most Israelis. But to go back to the UN, a majority there feel that the comprehensive approach is the right one. And so the administration had a very favorable reaction in the UN to its Middle East policy all through 1977. The only real complaint was that it wasn't moving fast enough.

And, of course, the complaint of all of the Arab countries was that not enough pressure was being put on Israel to make concessions. There was a very considerable dismay among them, when Mr. Begin was elected [prime minister], because they saw his as a harder-line government. Although few of them really had a great affection for the Labor government, when they compared the two, they could see there was a difference. Though I must say that quite a number of Arab governments had grown so angry and talked themselves into such a state of indignation over Labor-government policy that at first they took the line that, "Well, nothing could be any worse, and probably Begin will be better, he'll be a deGaulle; he'll be of the courage and political strength to settle with us when a Labor government never would do so."

So the initial reaction even to the election that brought Begin into power was not all bad. But then, when the comprehensive approach got into trouble, you remember the sequence: First, there was a moment when it looked like it was about to succeed, and this was expressed in a communiqué, after a meeting between Vance and Gromyko in late September or early October. This contained some phrases which were perhaps incautious, and the Israelis reacted very strongly. The result was that Vance met with Moshe Dayan, who was also here in New York for the General Assembly, and issued a strong statement with him which, to the Arabs and the Soviets, looked as if it took back what had been stated in the joint statement [by] Vance and Gromyko. Vance didn't feel that these two statements were inconsistent at all, and was very put out at the negative reaction. But as a result, at that point the process which had been under way—moving toward a reconvening of the Geneva conference and the adoption of a comprehensive agenda with all the principal Arab countries participating, and the Israelis in a specified way, and the PLO as well—that all came to a halt.

Sadat saw this and became utterly impatient and took the decision to go to Jerusalem. The Arabs and the Soviets thought that this was a conspiracy between the Americans and Sadat, when in fact it was as much a surprise to the Americans as it was to anybody, including Sadat's own cabinet. I think Ambassador Eilts, who was our ambassador to Egypt at that time, was sitting in the room off the Parliament, where Sadat was to make a kind of a state-of-the-nation speech. The people there were discussing whether Sadat should announce that he planned to go to Jerusalem. All of the cabinet was arguing against it, and Eilts had no instructions. He couldn't argue one way or the other, of course, but was listening very attentively, and as he went out the door, Sadat said, "Well, I don't know; I'm not sure whether I'll do it or whether I won't." And Sadat turned and went out the door and began to make his speech. Well, we know what happened. He decided, while he was up there at the microphone, that he would do it. So he did.

It was not plotted with him by the Americans, but the Soviets, in particular, could never be persuaded of that. Many of the Arabs were the same way. From that moment the Middle East policy in the UN, from the U.S. viewpoint, was in real trouble, and we never really recovered from that. We began to work our way back a little bit, and when [the] Camp David [accords were] being negotiated, I think the possibility had again appeared that we could [come back] with the efforts that were going on between Begin and Sadat. By then it had become possible again to get enough other Arabs to support Sadat while [they were] making their own reservations about particular positions. I think the possibility was there that some of them would support Sadat and we could then have a revival of the sort of honeymoon that we had during the first year [1977]. But, as you know, Sadat himself did not handle his brother Arabs effectively, bitterly antagonizing both the Saudis and [Jordan's King] Hussein, even the Moroccans, who were probably the closest to him and were trying to stay in step with him.

From that time on we never really had much of a chance. The effort, after Camp David, to negotiate the bilateral peace between Egypt and Israel was regarded with indignation by most of the countries there, and they hoped it wouldn't succeed. That view was shared by an awful lot of Egyptian officials as well: Sadat barely dragged his government along with him on all of that.

That was not our problem at the UN, except that so many countries, both the other Arab countries and the Third World generally, knew how little support Sadat had, not only in the Arab world but even in Egypt. That led them to resist totally our appeals to get on board the Camp David accords.

I was still at the UN when that happened. It was a tragedy because I really thought we were on the road to getting a peace in the Middle East that would remove one of the two most fundamental obstacles to a total repositioning of the United States in the eyes of most of the world. If we had been able to do that and also settle matters in Rhodesia and Namibia, we would have developed a totally different relationship with the other UN members. We would have had no major political questions between ourselves and any important group in the Third World. And we would have, I think, come close to recovering the automatic majority that we had in the early years. Instead, we lost on Namibia, and Rhodesia had to wait for a tough Conservative government [Thatcher] in Great Britain to push that through. And the Middle East, you know where it is today as well as I—nowhere.

Andrew Young

Our traditional Western allies were, of course, very disturbed by the way Andy talked. They were worried that all of this focus on the Third World would mean a sacrifice of their interests. But they found, as they worked with us, that Andy was not the person that they had feared from some of his statements. As they got to know him, they realized that a lot of it was that he simply misspoke. He used words wrongly, not realizing the implication that a particular phrase had. For example, he was charging the British and the Swedes with racism. He really seemed to be charging all white men with racism. Well, I think Andy genuinely feels that. But it isn't that he feels they're sinful; he feels that's just a part of human nature. From his own experience, he feels that race is a deeply held attitude, and [that] people who claim they are not in any way racist simply haven't looked into their own hearts. It's easy for Swedes to claim they are not racists because they have almost no blacks in the country. But when you look at the way they treat Turks, the guest workers, then by golly, color makes a difference. Coming from the Mediterranean area, Turks are looked on as different people. When he would explain this to the Swedes, the better Swedes would say, "O.K., now I see what you are talking about." But just the naked charge that Swedes are racists set them into headstands.

The Europeans didn't really think that the United States was going to be irresponsible. They know that we have our own economic interests, and that we were not moving in a rash and heedless fashion to put those interests in jeopardy for the sake of the political objective of getting an independent Namibia and an independent Rhodesia. But they did feel uncomfortable until they got to know Andy personally. It wasn't all that easy because he traveled a lot in his first months there. He was somewhat careless or short on the protocol side, and never did make the calls on other ambassadors that were appropriate. Many of them were quite offended and would say to us, "I've been here six months, and I met Andy at some reception over at an institute somewhere, but I've never been able to sit down and have a serious talk with him." You would get that complaint from the representative of an important country. He'd say, "I see him all the time with the African group" or whatever, "but my government can't understand why I can't see the American ambassador." It was a genuine and strongly felt feeling. We presented it to Andy and he'd always agree, saying yes, he was going to do it, but then other things would take priority. I don't think, by the time he left, that he had made more than four or five of these obligatory calls.

Andy would often speak in a way that was not totally in line with the positions of the State Department, and at times in a way that was utterly inconsistent with policy—resulting in heavy phone calls from Washington, sometimes at 7:00 A.M., from someone wanting to know what on earth was going on. Andy would talk to some reporter, it would come out in the press the next morning, and I'd start getting calls on the gravity of the thing, as did Andy. But sometimes Andy wouldn't be there. He'd make a statement and go off to Europe, and then I'd get the call from the British or the Swedes or just the press wanting to know if we could explain the statement that Mr. Young made yesterday to the reporter of the *Wall Street Journal*, or whatever. But that wasn't making policy. That was manifesting an attitude which, in the end, we simply had to explain, was Andy's own attitude.

Daily Routine

At the mission I would have a staff meeting first thing every morning at a quarter to nine or nine o'clock. And by that time, all of the key people should have read the telegrams from the day before. They should know what's going on. That's during the General Assembly. The pattern is similar for the rest of the year except there's a lot less formality to it. You don't have nearly as many people to work with as you do during a General Assembly or a special session. But even so, there is business to take care of until ten or 11 o'clock at night. Some committee will be meeting, and a report on that has to go to Washington. All of this has to be absorbed and in the heads of the people by the time they meet there at nine o'clock the next morning.

I would go around the room and try to find out what the priority items are that must be dealt with on that day. Usually, before that meeting, I would speak with Bill Maynes and find out his priorities. He would have had his staff meeting. He would have been to the secretary's staff meeting at 7:30, believe it or not, and he would have read his telegrams before he went to that meeting.

There would be cables from all over the world—reactions to the disaster of the previous day, and that kind of thing. They got surveyed in about 45 minutes by our staff. Then assignments were handed out: One person would meet with such and such a committee; another person had the text for a statement that the United States must make on a certain topic—perhaps it had been received in draft but there were problems with it and it was necessary to go back to try to get them straightened out. You just make sure that the machine is in motion for the day, and then everybody goes off to do his job. Mine was to sit there in the office and act as a communications center so that there would be somebody that anyone could get in touch with.

I would usually have a list of calls from other missions. The Indian ambassador, the Greek ambassador, etc., would want to discuss certain issues and I would spend most of the morning on the phone dealing with these problems, one after another. I might respond in whatever ways I could to the people who called. I might say, "Well, I don't know the facts on that, but let me get so-and-so to call you. He's got more information on that than I do; he talked to Washington yesterday and I didn't." So that would pass off one of the problems, and I would go on to the next one.

There would often be a lunch, [involving] 20 or 30 representatives of different countries, that might be organized by some country around a particular theme. Foreign ministers might attend, or perhaps it was useful to go just to have a lunch and talk over what was going on. You could do a lot of lobbying on these occasions. Then about seven o'clock it all calms down. There is a sort of floating crap game in the delegates' lounge, and I might well go over there and try to do some lobbying. But most of the lobbying was done not by me but by other people.

Then in the late afternoon, early evening, I would sit down and start to read the cables. That would go on until seven or eight or nine, whenever I got done. That was the quiet time of the day. Other people had more or less that same pattern except that toward the afternoon they would begin to write reporting cables. About five o'clock or so these would start to come up from the different sections for review. I would look at one, it would be O.K., and I'd just initial it and off it would go. Or I'd notice that another cable wasn't seen by such and such a section: "Why the hell would you write a cable and not show it to so-and-so? You're trying to pull a fast one here," and so forth. We got all of that working so that by the time people would go out for dinner, these reporting cables were done and on their way to Washington.

We also had the Datafax, a machine that will reproduce a document in Washington, or reproduce a Washington document in New

York, more or less instantly. It normally takes hours for a cable to go through the code room and get deciphered and delivered. A cable in the State Department is reproduced in 50 to 500 copies and sent all over the place. Mechanically, that takes time. Even a high-priority cable wouldn't get to Washington until maybe the next morning, or until 11 o'clock at night, so you would put something like that on the Datafax and then Washington would have whatever they needed in Xerox form. They'd only have the one copy but they could work with that.

That's sort of the way it ran, and it was admirable and fun—a good show. I know of no other mission, except possibly the British, that comes close to it. God knows how the Russians operate. They have a system but it's all behind closed doors.

Disarmament Conference of 1978

In the fall of 1977, about the time the General Assembly was winding up, we discussed with Washington the fact that we were going to have a major conference [the first UN Special Session on Disarmament]. God knows, I would have preferred to avert it. I argued with people that it should be put off a year or so, to give Carter a chance to really do something; I argued it would [then] be a more realistic and meaningful conference. But the nonaligned were adamant. They had fixed 1978 as the date and they were going to have it no matter what. So we tried to organize for it. Between Bill Maynes [assistant secretary of state] and ACDA, we organized a team in Washington to prepare the U.S. positions. That team worked all through the spring trying to put together an agenda. We knew we couldn't negotiate a treaty all of a sudden, but we could perhaps come up with some ideas for things that a huge body like the UN might be able to tackle, or that the United States might set forth at that time and [as a result] gain rightly some credit for declaring a new posture on one or another issue. But unfortunately, exactly through that period of, say, February to May, our relationship with the Soviets was getting worse and worse, and the team that we had working was just not able to get its way. It didn't have effective White House backing, which is needed to overcome resistance in the military or in the economic departments or wherever. Therefore, they came up to the special session really very short.

An attempt was made, I think, by the White House to compensate for this by naming a very illustrious delegation [to the conference], with Averell Harriman at the top of it, and we began having meetings with him, but we had to make it plain that we were trying to make bricks without straw on this conference. Our strategy, therefore, was to try to avoid being put under pressure to produce things in haste, and to get people to understand. The SALT talks [in 1977] had gone badly and it wasn't our fault—we had come forward with a very strong proposal and the Russians had simply rejected it. You remember the famous March '77 proposal that Vance went to Moscow with, the so-called comprehensive proposal. That was welcomed in New York, where the disarmament community, the non-aligned, thought it was wonderful. They were very upset when the Russians turned it down, but true to their principles, or their lack of principles, they wouldn't back us. They would mumble quietly to the Russians that they had made a mistake. But they didn't come out and say anything. Nevertheless, we were able to work with the non-aligned and the others on this great document that they produced, the so-called final document, which they attached a totally dispro-portionate importance to. "But never mind," we said, "we don't think it's all that important but we'll see what we can do to help you." And in the end we were able to compromise everything—fine language—and it came out as a consensus document. So relatively speaking, the disarmament community looks back on that first special session as a good thing. The classic conventional description of what happened is that it went to pieces after the special session. In fact, however, [while] the special session went all right, people didn't fulfill their promises, and, in particular, the two superpowers didn't with SALT.

The Value of the United Nations

Under good circumstances—and I think in some areas we were close to that in 1977 and 1978—the UN can also be a means of mobilizing world opinion: It was used exactly that way, in spite of the disappointments that I referred to, when, after I'd left, the Soviets invaded Afghanistan. The UN was the one place in which we really did succeed in getting a very clear manifestation of how out-raged the entire world was. In spite of the fact that a lot of these governments were very angry at us about a whole set of other issues, they nevertheless came through. It wasn't to do a favor to the United

States; it was to show their real opinion. All the Moslem countries, who were also very angry at us about our Middle East policy and support of Israel, didn't allow that—except in a very few cases—to stand in the way of their condemning the Soviet Union for its invasion of Afghanistan.

There's another set of problems where, in fact, the UN machinery can address the problem to some degree. We all know that peace-keeping has a demonstrable role in the mediation of disputes. The fact that the secretary general came so close to mediating the Falklands dispute, even after the American secretary of state had made a major effort at it and failed, shows that there is something to be said for the machinery that you've got there, where an individual who does the mediating—in this case the secretary general—comes at it with no prejudgments. He doesn't bring the interests of any great power or alliance, or a particular outlook, to it.

The Nature of Diplomacy

To me, diplomacy is politics—politics carried on in formal fashion between governments, but it's politics. It's not giving toasts at luncheons and dinners; that's not diplomacy. The U.S. delegates who seemed to understand the UN best and were most effective here were generally congressmen, because they were used to a political environment. A civil servant, a bureaucrat, would come up here and throw up his hands in dismay at the disorder, the lack of coherence, and the inability to function and produce an action program that really was meaningful. [But] congressmen, senators, and representatives would see it in a very different way; they would go to work and they would be out there logrolling and buttonholing, happy as clams, and doing it much better than any bureaucrat you could imagine. And much of what goes on in the GA is analogous to what they're used to in the so-called sense of the Senate, or sense of the House resolutions which have no binding effect on the executive, but which simply issue a warning: here is how representatives who were in touch with the grass roots feel about this particular issue.

That to me is politics. I think it's not only diplomacy but it's modern diplomacy. It is much more interesting and much more the wave of the future, if you like, than bilateral diplomacy, which amounts to a large degree today to merely reporting—so much of our apparatus abroad is just devoted to keeping people in Washington well informed about attitudes in another country, starting with the prime minister of that country and going down through the political structure. And when it comes to really doing business, that tends to be done by an envoy sent from Washington, who arrives informed by what he has learned from the administration. Most of my colleagues in the Foreign Service like bilateral diplomacy. They think that's really what they came to the Foreign Service to do. I think [multilateral diplomacy] is far more interesting and challenging—complicated and maybe unsatisfactory, but it's clearly the way governments have to interact with each other in the future.

There are UN agencies set up to deal with a specific problem, like the agencies that exist for telecommunication, air safety, and a whole range of questions of that sort—here, it seems to me, is the character of international interaction between nations in the modern age. And the questions that are dealt with bilaterally very often are simply a part of that. They are one strand in a fabric that's all woven together in the international agency. In many cases, because of the importance of a dozen or so major countries, bilateral relations can be decisive, and these multiple bilaterals can amount to an effective multilateral.

But multilateral diplomacy doesn't have the clear career ladder that the bilateral path has. There is such an established pattern [in the State Department] of moving from one position to another. The general public and Congress look down on multilateral agencies like the UN, the exception being something that is clearly military, like NATO. But even there, I think most diplomats would rather work on bilateral political-military issues than multilateral business. For example, even though NATO clearly has a very special importance, the decisions that are made at the council table in NATO by the NATO ambassadors are not the key defense decisions. Those tend to be done between defense ministers, or defense ministries, working with each other and gradually developing a consensus, which then is eventually reflected in formal decisions taken at the table in Brussels—that leads people who want to work on the substance of it to think they can do better if they stay on the bilateral channel.

Respecting the United Nations

I think our approach to the UN was about right in the Carter administration. That was: to take it seriously and treat it accordingly.

You know, it's not the only forum in which you get things done. But it is one that is capable of assisting and dealing with a number of problems from economics to human rights. It's a powerful piece of machinery. My complaint is [aimed] not at the United States but at the inability of the United States to get others to take the UN equally seriously, because almost no one except the British and the Scandinavians approach it in the principled fashion that we do. The rule of law really means something to them, and they do take it seriously.

I am sympathetic with people who criticize our allies for acting one way at the UN, expressing themselves in public in a fashion that is very troublesome to us, and then going down to Washington and having their ambassador come in and explain, "We didn't really mean it, you know, that's just the UN. Never mind." I don't think we ought to allow that. There ought to be more talk between us and the allies. The problem becomes one of how much energy the people in Washington can put into remonstrating and scolding. Moynihan wanted to do much more of that. I was generally sympathetic, but I felt he picked bad cases and handled them not very well at his end. It wasn't the general doctrine that I was hostile to; it was the specifics of the particular issues.

I think the Third World will see that they'll get farther if the machine works better. They have had more than ten years now of total dominance of the [General Assembly] voting machinery and it hasn't produced a thing. That's not lost on them. I do think that the international economic crisis, and the disastrous impact it has had on a lot of developing countries, has had a sobering effect. I think their leaders have been trying to think harder about economic problems and development, and it certainly has been brought home to them that developed countries are not going to allow their unemployed to starve in order to assist developing countries who have badly managed the enormous loans that they were getting during the boom period.

Moving to the domestic leadership, I'm very critical of a number of things that have been done under the present administration. But I must say I think that in some ways it will perhaps have the effect of leading to the correction of some of the complaints that I've voiced here. I've said to several people who were grumbling about this administration, "Well, maybe the next time you get an administration like the Carter administration, you'll be nicer to them." And they said, "Boy, we sure will!"

It's not that they think the Carter administration was perfect; it's just that they recognize what the range of possibilities is a good deal more clearly. Maybe our best legacy, if we did anything good back in those Carter years, will be five or ten years from now.

CHARLES WILLIAM MAYNES: Assistant Secretary of State for International Organization Affairs, 1977-79.

> *It is not possible to be an effective ambassador to the UN if you don't have a positive attitude toward the Third World. You can be an effective political figure in the United States and be hostile to the Third World; you cannot be an effective ambassador. That doesn't mean that you have to be soft publicly. But if you believe the Third World is the enemy, then the only thing you can do at the UN is make a commotion.*

Charles W. Maynes began his State Department career in the late 1960s, serving as chief monetary economist for the Agency for International Development (1965-67), and as economic officer in the American embassy in Moscow from 1968 to 1970. In 1972 he was an assistant to Senator Fred Harris of Oklahoma, and a member of the issues staff of Sargent Shriver during Shriver's campaign for vice president on the Democratic ticket. After serving as secretary of the Carnegie Endowment for International Peace (1972-77), Maynes became assistant secretary of state for international-organization affairs, a post which he held until 1979. In 1980 he became editor of *Foreign Policy.*

I had been the director of international organizations for the Carnegie Endowment for International Peace in New York. As a result of that, particularly during the Moynihan period, I wrote a number of articles on the UN which got quite a bit of attention. Those articles, and, I suppose, also my own activities in the foreign-policy community, led to my being asked to join the Carter transition team. I was told frankly that the chances of my being appointed assistant secretary [at IO] were one in a thousand. But I was appointed, and I presume the reason is that I was asked to brief Andy Young before he was appointed [to the U.S. Mission] and he obviously must have liked me. Also I had Vance's support.

I don't think there's any mystery to what IO does. Most of the time it's simply getting a cable from the U.S. Mission, digesting the issues, coming up with a U.S. position, trying to clear it in time to send out a cable which will reach the delegation before the vote takes place.

IO works just like any other bureau, with one exception: There is a tremendous amount of reporting [involved], with action requests from our mission. And the bureau spends most of its day, particularly during the General Assembly, digesting these cables when they arrive in the morning, and writing up the U.S. position, and then trying to clear it with the other elements of the State Department. The problem for IO obviously is that a number of the issues that come up in the UN affect directly the interests of several other and often very powerful, more powerful, bureaus. These bureaus, which know nothing about the UN, nothing about the issue in the UN context, are irritated that the UN is even discussing the damn question. They try to dominate the substance completely and often without taking into account anything other than the narrow interests of the bureau in question. The coordination responsibilities of IO at times are quite difficult.

"Chemistry" is particularly important in this job because you have to satisfy two cabinet officers (the perm rep and the secretary of state). That is a difficult job because they often disagree just by the nature of their responsibilities. The person up at [the] U.S. [Mission] wants somebody in IO that he or she thinks they'll be comfortable with. Elliot Abrams had to leave because Mrs. Kirkpatrick didn't like him. If the perm rep doesn't like the IO assistant secretary, there's no way that he or she can do his job.

I was very fortunate, I must say, while I was assistant secretary in that even though our ambassador at the UN [Andrew Young] was very controversial and said some things that Vance strongly disagreed with, neither Andy nor Vance ever took out on me any personal problems they had between themselves. That was not always the case in earlier administrations. The assistant secretary was often blamed for what the ambassador at the UN regarded as a bad decision. The [ambassador] felt that if the assistant secretary had pushed harder, the decision would have gone the other way; or the secretary of state felt that the assistant secretary was not adequately explaining the department's views to the ambassador and [that], therefore, the ambassador was acting in a way that the secretary didn't approve of.

The "Ideal" Permanent Rep

I think there are two legitimate views on the best type of permanent representative. One would be that it's important to appoint somebody with real public stature because that person can then force the government to take more seriously long-range concerns in the articulation of U.S. foreign policies—such concerns as international law, international institutions, Third World issues, economic development, a whole variety of so-called soft issues which, in the long run, are the hard issues, but in the short run are not. There aren't many people who speak for that constituency in the U.S. government. That's the role of the secretary of state, but he has got a lot of concerns that are very short-run [ones], and so there's an argument that can be made that it's very useful to have an Adlai Stevenson or a Cabot Lodge or an Andy Young kind of person, or an Arthur Goldberg at the UN and in the cabinet.

The other view is that to do that means to bring incoherence into the policy-making process because you are making it difficult for the secretary of state to run a unified crew, a unified command. It is true that as long as you have somebody like Moynihan, or Lodge—people who are national figures or who are almost quasi-cult figures—it's going to be very difficult for any secretary of state to treat that person as though he were an ordinary ambassador. The person is going to be special. Once he's special or she's special, then they're going to want all of the policy privileges that go with being special, and that makes things difficult.

So the other argument is that you should never appoint someone like that, and that Charles Yost is the ideal ambassador to the UN. He was a super ambassador from a professional point of view, articulate and dedicated. However, Yost concluded at the end of his career that the appointment of someone like himself was a mistake. But many people believe that it would be desirable to downgrade that office from cabinet status, not to appoint someone with an outside reputation, but to professionalize it.

I don't think this second course will ever happen. This is not because presidential candidates love the UN. Increasingly, they don't. But they love having another important position [with which] to pay off political debts. When you run for president of the United States, a number of very powerful people and powerful groups help you get there. And when you finally get there, you look around and you see there are very few things you can do for them in the short run, and there are very few cabinet slots to go around. Once you have given one to all the key constituencies—once you're through with all that and after you've put in the people you want, your close confidants—you don't have much left. So every senior job, I think, will be protected, and it's very difficult to change that. The Reagan administration, before it came into office, promised that it was going to downgrade the job [of permanent rep]. It didn't, because it desperately needed to appoint a prominent woman to a senior post, and that was one position they could give.

For all of the bad-mouthing of the UN by many people, a lot of people want the job, because it provides instantaneous prominence nationwide and makes the person who knows how to exploit the job into a national figure, if not international. Andy Young received thousands of speaking requests. Nobody else in the government, except the secretary of state and the president, is such a focus of popular attention. That is a big attraction to someone like George Bush, who has national ambitions and [in 1971] lost his race for Congress, yet doesn't want to get out of politics. The UN post got him into the big time. People remember that.

The United States and the Third World

I think the case can be made, and Moynihan at times makes it, that he was doing something constructive: that if he had not conducted a diplomatic temper tantrum [against the Third World], the reaction to the UN in the United States would have been permanent rather than emotional and rhetorical. The country would have lashed out and gotten out of the UN and closed off our contributions. Also, I will acknowledge that I don't think any representative of the United States has ever been provoked as much as Moynihan. He was ambassador at a time when the hubris of the Third World delegates moved to levels of high irresponsibility on some issues. He exaggerated it and made a political case out of it. But I think it was a very difficult period to be ambassador at the UN; the revolution had come with oil prices, and other nations had the whip hand. Even so, I think Moynihan went too far.

I have no problems with taking a tough line. As a matter of fact, when I was assistant secretary, we told the Arabs we would walk out of the World Health Organization—I wrote the speech for Califano—if they punished Israel or Egypt for signing [the] Camp David [accords]. I don't have any problems with that. What I do have a problem with is professional anti-Third Worldism—emotional, reactionary, hateful, bigoted, knee-jerk hostility to the Third World. There are some Third World countries that I think are absolutely reprehensible and I have no problem with taking a tough line against them. But, I don't think that all developed countries are good and all developing countries are bad, as one sometimes begins to conclude from some of the statements of the right wing or [in] *Commentary* magazine. My experience is that some support us and some don't, depending on the issue.

There is toward the Third World a residual racist attitude on the part of some Americans, even some very well-placed, well-educated Americans who should know better. I don't know why they have these attitudes, which are so destructive of our national interest, but they do. It may have something to do with the fact that this country was created by destroying one Third World culture, the Indian nations, and enslaving blacks from another continent. Maybe there's a psychic transferal that goes on here and that explains it. There's a fear of the Third World that's irrational, because the Third World is not that strong and not that unified and not that powerful and not that threatening. But it's seen that way; the perception is that way, and I think it must come from almost an atavistic, visceral feeling on the part of people who remember almost from the subconscious the history of this country. I can't explain it any other way.

Human Rights

I think it's important for the United States to defend itself and its ideals. The trouble is that the people who take that position often have in mind an ideological crusade against the USSR, which I think is counterproductive. Crusading is not always my idea of what this country ought to stand for. [If we do], we then may end up either remaining silent about, or covering up for, countries that I don't think we should be covering up for, like Chile, El Salvador, and Guatemala. I think the only really honest discussion of this was William Buckley's piece in *Foreign Affairs* [Spring 1980] on human rights, where he argued that we ought to free the human-rights representative from instructions and let him or her speak openly. I had a very similar idea when I was in the State Department, namely, that we shouldn't instruct our representative to the Human Rights Commission; this person would have high standards and would apply them regardless of where the chips may fall. That is unacceptable both to the left and to the right in this country, but I think it's an honorable position and the one we ought to take. I don't like the

Kirkpatrick position; nor, for that matter [did] I like the Carter position, for one ends up with a double standard: There is a double standard that both the left and the right follow on human rights. The only way to avoid it is to depoliticize human rights and make it a more judicial type of exercise. There are ways to do it, but administrations are always against it because it has political consequences.

U.S. Attitude Toward the United Nations

When you ask what our position should be regarding the UN, I have to say that a lot depends on what you mean by the UN. If you mean how much attention should the United States pay to whatever happens to be the majority view in New York, my answer is that, on a lot of issues, not much. If you define the UN in a different way, to say how much attention should the United States give to world-order values and the creation of norms and institutional restraints and precepts, international law, I would say a great deal. Unfortunately, people confuse those two. You might argue that we spend too much attention on the UN as a body that produces all these resolutions, and too little on the UN as a motivating ideal or rationale for policy. The two are linked: If we did more of the second, we might have a better record in the first.

The United States has lost some of its earlier interest in and enthusiasm for world-order values, and that's a tragic change. It probably got lost on some hillside in Vietnam, along with 50,000 troops. We're a very nationalistic country. We've never been terribly enthusiastic about listening to the advice of others. We were enthusiastic about the UN as long as others agreed with us, but not very enthusiastic about making compromises in order to get their support. I think that Andy Young and Cyrus Vance are people of unusually high integrity and solid character, and I liked working for them. I think that their basic priorities for American life, as they would see it projected abroad, are good priorities, and that was inspiring. But I can't contend that I was inspired by the overall attitude of the majority of people in the Congress, or in the executive branch, toward the UN; because I wasn't inspired. I was distressed at how hostile they were, at how difficult they were.

There is a policy fatigue regarding the UN. People just don't want to stand up and fight for it. There is just no desire on the part of any government, with the exception of a very few, to make sacrifices for the UN. In order to accomplish something in almost any walk of life, you've got to be willing to make sacrifices for it to work. In marriage, you've got to make a sacrifice; if it gets to be too big a one, you get a divorce. And I would use almost the same metaphor with an international organization. If you want it to be vibrant, strong, and relevant, you've got to be willing to make some sacrifices in your own outlook, in your own position, in order to accommodate the position of others. We don't have that attitude now. We go up there and just say yes or no, that's the U.S. position. And more and more countries are doing that. Like the Soviets. They made zero concessions on the disaster [involving] Korean Air Lines. They just said, "We had a right to shoot it down, we shot it down. We're right. You're wrong."

Well, if that's the attitude that people are going to take, then the organization can't do anything, because it has no powers of its own. The organization cannot be strong and vibrant except in a period of détente—East-West and North-South [détente]. We're not in a period of détente; we're in a period of conflict. And as long as that's the case, the UN is going to be weak, very weak.

I think the heyday of the UN, the high period of the UN, was 1960 to about 1973. I think more was accomplished then—this is my revisionist view of UN history. We launched many of the development programs during that period, many of the functional programs that benefit the membership: the World Food Programme, World Weather Watch, campaign against smallpox, Environmental Protection Agency. You set up a number of peacekeeping operations: ONUC, UNEF II, UNDOF; that was the best period of the UN. Hammarskjöld was, I think, an unusual man. But Trygve Lie's period was a disaster; the UN was totally stalemated; it couldn't do anything except collect Soviet vetoes and American propaganda victories.

Everybody looks for some fix that's going to improve the situation. Only one thing can improve it, and that is a commitment by the [U.S.] secretary of state to the importance of the role of the UN, of the multilateral ideal, and of international law as a strong component of our foreign policy. If you have that, then you can do quite a bit, particularly if you've got a secretary who stays in office for four years. I think that has to be combined, however, not with a benign attitude toward the UN, which allows the UN to get whatever it wants except that which Congress won't endorse; it has to be combined with a U.S. attitude of being a sympathetic but tough parent, or brother, toward the UN. You don't give this dependent child everything it wants, because it will abuse the affection and the attention. It needs to be both disciplined and supported.

Unfortunately, we get tied in knots for two reasons. The first is that we can't get our allies to support us, and of course one of the reasons is that we so often come up with an unrealistic agenda for change. The other is that, at least formally, trying to exert discipline on the UN is difficult because it seems to be illegal. Withholding your contribution is illegal. For that reason, we've always been reluctant to do it. But the law—I think it was [Samuel] Johnson who said the law is an ass, or can be an ass. It's a knee-jerk concern that is destroying the UN because we can't bring it to heel in time to strengthen it. We're making a big mistake. The problem is, though, to get a consensus in this country for a constructive program of reform, because in the end that would cost us more money. People don't want to do that.

Another point, and one that isn't always realized, is how much U.S. diplomacy suffers from the blight of poor appointments. I think IO suffers even more than other bureaus. That may be too harsh. But we've had a number of really bad appointments throughout the system, as ambassadors, primarily; but also some deputy assistant secretaries have been really disgraceful appointments. I would advise the assistant secretary of state to fight very, very hard for the right to appoint really competent people within IO and, one hopes, within [the U.S. Mission] as well, and to resist efforts from the White House and the Congress to turn IO and [the U.S. Mission] into a coop, where various breeds of turkeys are placed. I think actually I was quite lucky there. Vance did not impose candidates on me, and it wasn't until the very end that I started having imposed on me, by the White House, candidates I would regard as turkeys—staff people. We had a couple of appointments in the specialized agencies that fall into the turkey-coop category.

The other thing that I would advise the assistant secretary [to do is] to see if he or she could find some way to persuade the ambassador at the UN and the secretary of state to sit down once every ten days for a philosophical discussion. And it really could be philosophical, about the underlying direction of American foreign policy, or the underlying goals of American foreign policy. That would very quickly become practical and concrete, to see if there couldn't be a greater meeting of the minds than we've had in the past. I think the only way something is really going to be accomplished is if you have some kind of consensus at the top, and a first-class staff underneath that can push for it.

I resigned as secretary a couple of months before Andy Young [resigned]. I just was increasingly unhappy in the Carter administration because it had run out of steam, politically, and a job was offered to me that seemed to follow my interest in the field of foreign policy, and it seemed to me that I would be better placed running a magazine than heading IO—that was a better point from which to push for the kinds of things that I was interested in. Carter was in full retreat across the board in the field of foreign policy, and even if he wanted to continue with his earlier agenda, he would never [have been] able to carry it out. The country wasn't behind him. They might have elected him narrowly, but they would not support him. So it seemed to me that the main problem in the field of foreign policy was not reelecting Carter, but changing some of the basic approaches to some of the problems that we face.

I think that the basic goal today is to try to reestablish a liberal-internationalist coalition in the country that can reflect American strength and concern toward other parts of the world. A strong but benign American face to the rest of the world is what I think needs to be shown. And it's very hard—sometimes we have a strong face; it's not always benign. Or at other times we have a weak face, or an uninvolved face, or an indifferent face. I think that changing the cast of that face is the key priority in American foreign policy.

ELLIOT L. RICHARDSON: Ambassador at Large, and Special Representative of the President for the Law of the Sea Conference, 1977–80.

The biggest stake the United States has is in leadership approaches to dealing with the pressing realities of global interdependence. We can't put ourselves on the sidelines and expect to exert effective leadership. We can't suffer the consequence of being discovered to be irrelevant.

After service in the army during World War II, Elliot Lee Richardson served as a law clerk at a U.S. circuit court and later at the U.S. Supreme Court. In 1957 President Eisenhower named Richardson assistant secretary of state for legislation in the Department of Health, Education, and Welfare (HEW). In that post, he helped draft the National Defense Education Act, as well as social-security, public-health, and juvenile-delinquency legislation. Under the Nixon administration, he held many high positions in quick succession, including undersecretary of state, secretary of HEW, secretary of defense, and, finally, attorney general. By this time the Watergate crisis was unfolding. When President Nixon refused to surrender to Congress the famous White House tapes in their entirety, Richardson declared that the "very integrity of the governmental process" was at stake and resigned in protest.

He returned to government service under the Ford administration, as, first, ambassador to Great Britain and, later, secretary of commerce. In 1977 he became U.S. ambassador at large and the president's special representative to the Law of the Sea Conference.

Currently Elliot Richardson practices law. He chairs the Public Advisory Committee on the Law of the Sea, and heads the UN Association of the United States of America.

I think there is no prospect that the Reagan administration will sign the Law of the Sea Treaty. On the other hand, I think that it is virtually certain that the United States *will* sign the treaty in due course. I think we'll be unable to get the other industrial countries to go along with the minitreaty [which would rest on a formal treaty among deep seabed mining states in lieu of the UN Law of the Sea Treaty]. And I think we'll have problems with securing adequate recognition of our navigational interests and our interests in scientific research.

The first thing that has to be really understood about the Law of the Sea negotiations, and their behind-the-scenes aspects, is that there are so many negotiations going at once. The head of the U.S. delegation is responsible, in the first place, for negotiating with the U.S. government. How do you develop a position? What degree of latitude to you have [for committing] the United States?

The most extreme example of the problems of stretching every limit was the negotiations [regarding] the so-called financial arrangements: that is, the provisions for payments by companies to the International Seabed Authority. This had been the subject of negotiations going on for a long time, beginning in 1978 under the leadership of Tommy Koh [of Singapore]. There had meanwhile been developed a computer model, at MIT, showing the financial impact on the mining companies' rate of return that would result from variations in the amount and types of taxes; for instance, [impact of] initial fees, royalties, and profit sharing.

A number of people on the U.S. delegation worked exclusively on this subject for the whole time between 1978 and meetings in New York at the Spring session of 1980. By that time the key issues had been narrowed down to what you might call the tax rates; that is, what would be the initial amount of the royalties? Would the amount be changed when a company had recovered its initial investment? What would be the triggering mechanisms for the change? What would be the percentages of profits paid by a company and, again, would these percentages be affected by recovery of its initial investment? How do you measure investment in any case? Did you take the whole investment by the company in a single, integrated seabed-mining project, or limit the recognition of investment involved only to the area beyond the limits of national jurisdiction subject to the control of the international seabed authority? This raised the question, as it was technically expressed, of earnings attributable to the area.

Group of Five vs. Group of 77

I became involved in the negotiations when all these numbers and definitions were still unresolved, but after there had emerged general agreement on the approach. We had regular meetings from then until the final negotiations last spring [1982] in New York of a group that I originally called the Coordinating Group of Five, or CG5. This was a group including the United Kingdom, France, the Federal

Republic of Germany, Japan, and the United States. Its membership was the same as [that of] the so-called Group of Five that had been meeting from the beginning of the [Law of the Sea] Conference, except that it had the Federal Republic of Germany as a member instead of the Soviet Union. The Soviet Union was never willing to allow the West Germans to belong to the Group of Five (which would have made it the Group of Six), without also including East Germany. The Federal Republic of Germany, on the other hand, had, and has, major interests in deep seabed mining, so the GC5 was created as a means of coordinating deep seabed-mining strategies among the major Western industrial countries.

I informed the CG5 generally of what was going on in the final negotiations on financial arrangements and kept myself alerted to what I thought they would go along with and what they wouldn't. But in the actual negotiations, I represented all the Western industrial countries, including the United States, without any explicit authority from anyone. The other participants were the representatives of Pakistan, Mauritius, Argentina, and Singapore for the Group of 77.

We concluded agreements on all tax rates and [on] the definition of attributable proceeds, and they have stuck ever since. Even the Reagan administration has not raised any serious question about them. This is significant, I think, partly because it illustrates the need to know what the maximum limits of your authority are and what you may be able to achieve without straining those limits to the breaking point. It illustrates the impossibility of concluding any deal like this except in a small group, and it illustrates the necessity for knowing exactly with whom you can make such a deal. The representatives of the Group of 77 had to believe that I could deliver the other Western industrial countries as well as the United States. I had to know that Pakistan, Mauritius, Argentina, and Singapore could deliver the 77. Why those four? The answer of course is: because of the individuals representing these countries—their knowledge of the issues, their standing with the rest of the 77 and, particularly, their own geographic groups. These are things one could not possibly know at the outset of a negotiation like this. The initial tendency is to suppose that the significance or influence of a country is dependent upon its size and the scale of its economic or national-security interests. In fact, its size and presumed stature or economic significance have virtually no correlation with its influence in a negotiation like this. The role of individuals is far more significant.

The conference has always operated through an effort to achieve a consensus on issues that often are complicated and involve intensely held national interests. There is also the problem of numbers, and so you need, first of all, a fundamental commitment to the effort to produce a consensus. The people who have made the greatest contributions have been people who have seen the objectives of the conference as affording an opportunity to achieve a major milestone in the strengthening of the rule of law. They have been inspired by this vision. That's a first requirement. You have to be intelligent, resourceful, flexible in trying out various possible ways of producing consensus under these circumstances. You have to deal with such a large variety of people, in so many circumstances, that it's essential that they be able to trust you, that they have confidence in your integrity. If, in addition to this, you have charm, patience, humor, courage where necessary, you have a combination of qualities that can make an immense difference, without regard to the size or the importance of the country you represent. Tommy Koh, perhaps more nearly than any single human being in the conference, combines these characteristics. He's made an immense contribution himself to the achievement of consensus on some of the most complex issues in the conference. Of course, that's how he got to be chosen president to succeed Ameresinghe, when Ameresinghe died.

Ideology had very little to do with any issue in the conference except insofar as the attitude of the 77 was colored by the ideology associated with the concept of the so-called new international economic order. But one of the achievements of the four years in which I was involved was that we were gradually able to develop, with encouragement both from our side and from intelligent and realistic people within the 77, a process of increasing willingness to deal with the realities and to minimize ideological factors. In the case of the United States and the USSR, there was no room for the intrusion of extraneous considerations to get in the way and so we continued to deal with each other, after Afghanistan, exactly as we had done before.

We dealt, for example, with Cuba as we would with anybody else. The Cuban representatives to the Law of the Sea Conference were intelligent and realistic people. They included two senior diplomats, one of whom had been a diplomat in the Cuban Foreign Service before Castro's takeover. The other was a senior vice minister, and the third, the one with whom we had the most dealings, was a mining engineer who got his degree from Indiana University and was a very sensible man.

Washington and the United Nations

I had no direct contact with President Carter at all. My relations with the U.S. Mission at the UN involved occasional conversations with the head of the delegation, just to fill him in on what was going on. We took advantage of the help of the political officers at [the U.S. Mission] in contacting members of the delegations when we wanted to get word around quickly on something. But my principal contacts were with Cyrus Vance and the deputy secretary, Warren Christopher. I viewed my role primarily as one of keeping them informed and generally seeking their concurrence in what I was doing. I reported to the president through the National Security Council [NSC] rather than through the secretary of state. I chaired the Group on the Law of the Sea, which was an interdepartmental unit under the NSC; the Law of the Sea staff was created by an NSC memorandum. I viewed the staff as responsible to the whole interdepartmental group and not simply as a State Department staff.

I thought that I could gain concurrence of the interdepartmental group for 95 percent of all the issues we dealt with, and get it to go along with what I wanted to do. In the remaining 5 percent we would occasionally have to take the issue to the next higher echelon in the NSC, which was called the Policy Review Committee, chaired by Vance. He never came to any of the meetings where an issue on the Law of the Sea was involved. Christopher generally chaired those meetings. There weren't many in four years, maybe one or two a year when we had issues that couldn't be resolved in the interdepartmental group.

My position always prevailed in the Policy Review Committee. I knew from the beginning that I could win any bureaucratic battle, so that I was responsible for my own instructions. It was one of the reasons why it was such a tough job. It was, substantively, extremely complex, to begin with. It was made more complex by the difficulties of trying to negotiate with so many people at once. In the example I gave earlier of the financial arrangements, if I had been wrong in believing that those other four representatives could deliver the 77, I would have showed my whole hand, I would have exposed, in effect, my bottom line and I couldn't retrieve that.

Of course they were in the same position. If I couldn't deliver my own government or the other four, they would have exposed their bottom line. The problem of negotiating in a very large forum like this is always, therefore, one of trying to figure out, for the given issue (and it varies with the issue), who are the key people with whom you can make a deal that will stick. A large amount of pressure derived also from my own perception that the role of the United States was important to the outcome and that I really controlled the role of the United States. So it gave me a sense of pressure greater than any of my cabinet jobs ever did. A cabinet officer is really a portfolio manager. On a given day, you may have a lot of things you're concerned with—let's say maybe 17 different problems. Some of your accounts will do well, more or less whatever you do; some may do poorly no matter what you do; and your main effort is concentrated on the margins in between. Your overall sense of satisfaction in your performance is a function of how the account, as a whole, performs. But in this case, I was like the manager of a single account on which everything depended.

Another factor was that we were negotiating, on any given day, simultaneously in perhaps a dozen different, separate groups. Simply to keep track of these and figure out what to do next and how to get the best possible deal in all 12, day after day, was a considerable strain in itself.

Departure

I resigned in October 1980 for several reasons. I don't think I would have resigned for any one of these reasons alone, but they added up to what I thought was a pretty clear decision.

One, I thought that as far as anything I could do was concerned, the treaty was substantially finished. The remaining issues were the so-called three P's (participation, the Preparatory Commission, and preparatory investment protection) and a couple of other little things.

Second, I thought that Reagan might win and that if he won and wanted to change the negotiating instructions of the delegation, I would have to get out anyway because I couldn't be head of the delegation and also try to renegotiate deals for which I had a share of responsibility. I would therefore be likely to have more influence in trying to help salvage the treaty from outside than I would trying to hang onto my job, which I probably couldn't do anyway.

Third, I had been an active Republican for a long time. I have been involved in every Republican presidential campaign since 1952, and I wanted to get out in time to play some part in the campaign.

A fourth factor was that I had the opportunity to join this law firm [Milbank, Tweed, Hadley & McCloy] and I couldn't expect them to stay around forever with an opportunity that appealed to me in many ways. For that matter, I was finding the financial pinch of continued government service increasingly difficult. Then I had the chance to become the chairman of the United Nations Association in succession to Scranton. I had already deferred this from earlier in the year 1980, and [it] seemed to me an organization whose aims were consistent with my principal interests. Adding it all up, I finally decided that was a good time to get out.

WILLIAM J. VANDEN HEUVEL: Deputy Representative to the United Nations, 1979–81.

Nothing prepares you better for the United Nations than to have been active in the Democratic Party over a period of time. There are no conflicts in the United Nations more intense than the conflicts within New York City democracy. If you have survived all of the battles of New York's Democrats, you are sufficiently battlescarred to endure the international conflict of the United Nations.

William J. vanden Heuvel served as executive assistant to the U.S. ambassador to Thailand in 1953–54 and as special counsel to the governor of New York in 1958. After working as a special assistant to the U.S. attorney general (1963–64) and as acting regional director of the Office of Economic Opportunity (1964–65), he became a partner in the firm of Stroock, Stroock & Lavan in 1965. Vanden Heuvel has also been chairman of the New York City Board of Corrections, vice president of the International Rescue Committee, and vice chairman of the International League for Human Rights.

After leaving Stroock in 1977 to become U.S. ambassador to the European Office of the United Nations, in Geneva, he became deputy U.S. representative to the United Nations (1979). He returned to private practice in 1981.

He is chairman of International Relations Consultants, Inc., in Washington, D.C., co-chairman of the Council of American Ambassadors, and President of the Four Freedoms Foundation.

I had the experience of being the [U.S.U.N.] ambassador in Geneva, seeing the specialized agencies at work, and dealing with the United Nations in its more substantive aspect. New York is much more political—the Security Council, the General Assembly, the various political confrontations that go on. Geneva is oriented much more to programs and substantive work. That gave me a view of the UN, and its meaning and impact, that I think enhanced my sense of its possibilities when I came back to New York. If you see the World Health Organization and the International Labor Organization, the Office of the High Commissioner of Refugees, and a variety of other major specialized agencies at work, you get a sense of the interdependence of the world, for one thing, and of how crucially important the leadership and support of the United States is in making many of these international programs work.

I think, for example, of the World Health Organization. I was ambassador in Geneva when WHO announced in November 1978 that it had succeeded in eradicating smallpox, an achievement of extraordinary importance in the history of the world. Millions and millions of people in the recorded history of mankind had died of smallpox. The eradication of smallpox could never have been done unless all of the nations of the world had worked together, and unless the financial support and the intellectual leadership of the American medical community had been given in support of that objective. But all of those things did happen, and this monumental achievement resulted.

I like to remind audiences, when I speak about the UN, that those people who complain about the cost of the UN to the United States really have very little basis for their complaint. The assessed contribution of the United States, on an annual basis, to the UN is not much more than $200 million. We save, as a nation, much more than that each year by not having to give smallpox vaccinations. That simple arithmetic shows you how important, in terms of the well-being of the world, an agency of the UN can be.

International Organization Bureau

When you consider the United States and the UN, and their relationship to each other, one of the most important persons is the assistant secretary of state for international organizations [IO]. Just recently I met with the designee for that post in the Reagan administration, Gregory Newell, who is 32. He's had no international experience, except being a Mormon missionary in Luxembourg and France. He knows nothing about the UN. He was an advance man in the presidential campaign. I'm sure he is a person of exemplary moral qualities and undoubted intellectual vigor, but the sadness about the appointment, in my judgment, is that what you need in the department in that position is someone who is knowledgeable in the conduct of foreign policy. If you have someone in the post who is a substantive cipher or who is being trained on the job, he has essentially left a vacancy at a very crucial point in the process of decision making relating to the UN.

That post is crucial because it is the backup for [the U.S. Mission]. A strong assistant secretary, such as Bill Maynes, doesn't dominate the mission in New York by any means, because the ambassador in New York is a member of the cabinet, but he carries your message to the secretary of state and argues the point of view of the United Nations and [the U.S. Mission] and the specialized agencies throughout the department. It is also crucial to argue these views before the Congress. Certainly from the outlying posts of the United Nations—Geneva, Rome, Nairobi, and wherever else the UN is located—the office of IO and of the assistant secretary is a crucial post.

I think of it particularly in the context of the Falklands crisis. I doubt that there was anyone in the immediate circle of the secretary, certainly not at the assistant-secretary level, who was capable of arguing with him on the strategy of how to use the UN in resolving the conflict between Argentina and the United Kingdom. The failure to use the UN in the beginning and the intrusion of the United States as a mediating force, to the exclusion of the UN, cost very valuable weeks that might have prevented the violent confrontation that occurred.

Jeane Kirkpatrick may not want a strong assistant secretary of state because she wants her line to the secretary and the president to be direct. But, generally speaking, I found it very healthy to have a strong office in the State Department so that it can both support and challenge. The Reagan administration's disdain for multilateral diplomacy, and for the UN in particular, is so destructive of what bipartisan efforts have tried to achieve in the last 30 years that to speak about background and experience for those who hold the present offices is almost irrelevant.

The U.S. ambassador has to have a profound feeling for his own country and for a world in which the United Nations represents an affirmative instrument for international order and justice. You have to have a person who has a sense of history and a sense especially of the history of the last 35 years, or [of] the history of the efforts of this century to create international institutions.

Negotiating skill is crucial because you have to have the ability to define a disagreement, dissect its elements, and candidly assess what are the available options for the resolution of a conflict. Then you need the personal means of keeping your own government in line while you are negotiating with a lot of other governments. Some people have a knack for bringing diverse forces together and [for causing] them to see a common interest. But the ambassador of the

United States at the UN has to represent the UN to the United States, as well as the United States to the UN, and that is what makes it such an enormous job. It is so time-consuming, so pressurized. A political background is also a helpful background. To be described as an astute politician is an accolade as far as I'm concerned. The skill of the politician is being able to communicate; being able to relate to many different points of view; finding a compromise, middle ground, or consensus; and enjoying contact with people and establishing personal relationships of trust.

Third World

One of the problems that has perhaps diminished the UN in some ways, and maybe enhanced it in others, is the so-called Group of 77. The developing countries were faced with the permanent members on the Security Council, [who have] veto power, and with the colossal political and economic power of the developed countries generally. It was only in their union that they could find the strength to make viewpoints to be taken seriously in the international community. Nehru, Tito, and Nasser saw that in 1953-54, when they created the nonaligned movement. The Group of 77 was, in a sense, an extension of the nonaligned movement in the UN, but including a larger number of states.

Creation of that bloc, although it gave political power to the developing countries, also served to stifle honest debate and limit honest disagreement. The debates then took place within the blocs, and they were frequently polarized at their most radical end because everything operated by consensus. Once you operate by consensus, you essentially give a single country a veto power. If a country has an extreme point of view about a question, they can force a political posture that may not reflect what is truly the majority view of the group. In the General Assembly, I believe that is particularly true. The votes there frequently reflect the split of the developed and the developing countries and the Communist bloc. So if you have 22 countries in the Soviet orbit, and you have the Western countries and the industrial countries together—the Organization of Economic Cooperation and Development [OECD] countries, so to speak—and then you have the developing countries in the Group of 77 bloc, you have blocs coming at each other, rather than [having] individuals, and sometimes nations, rising above their historical past, or their own self-interest, to try to find a larger framework for the resolution of conflict.

That has in a sense diminished the effectiveness of the UN and certainly the General Assembly. It made impossible the attempt to have global negotiations, because in the global-negotiations discussion, there really is very little difference between a Carter and a Reagan administration's viewpoint. I think if you could get countries to deal with it realistically and individually in terms of their interests, you could find a solution by which important, significant, substantive discussions could take place in a New York-United Nations environment. Decision making would be left to the relevant agencies that had the substantive responsibility. But the Group of 77 countries were absolutely adamant. They forced the issue in a way that permitted no one to find a solution. That is what frequently happens. With these discussions and negotiations, it's not a matter of everybody giving until you reach a center point. The developed countries have certain interests that they are not going to give up no matter who shouts at them. They are not going to permit the decision-making process, especially in relationship to important economic factors that are significant to them, to be made by countries and individuals who have no material concern for those problems.

Also, the people who come to the New York conferences at the UN are frequently much more political than the bankers who would go to the World Bank conferences, or the food specialists who would go to FAO, or the health specialists who go to WHO. Why politicize every issue? I suggest the only way to depoliticize these conferences is [by having] most countries come to realize that an enormous amount of time is spent in endless and meaningless debate. They must understand that they either are going to avoid a large number of issues in the UN or they are going to have to find an accommodation that permits the discussions or the negotiations to go forward. In the kind of impasse that now exists with global negotiations, probably the better thing is to just drop it and wait for the day when the spokesmen for the developing countries are prepared to accept the idea of discussion in one area and decision making in another.

The Group of 77 rotates its leadership. Cuba was head of the nonaligned movement during 1979–80. It was ridiculous, first of all, to think of Cuba as a nonaligned country. The members of the nonaligned movement felt they could not avoid choosing Cuba because their rules worked out that way. But it was very destructive for the nonaligned movement because we weren't going to listen to anything that Cuba was telling us as a spokesman for their interests. That's too bad because the nonaligned deserve an important voice and should play a critical role in the world.

The Reagan administration takes the point of view, through its intellectual spokesmen, that the Third World wouldn't exist but for the United Nations, because it's the United Nations that gives it a forum and gives it an existence. Let's assume that is the case—which it isn't, but let's assume that it is. What's wrong with that? Wouldn't we want these countries to have a sense of pride in their own sovereignty and to have a sense of responsibility in the world, where you are trying to create order and justice? Just because you have something that's called the Third World doesn't necessarily mean that it's a hostile force. It isn't. As we saw frequently in the UN, the overwhelming majority of the developing countries voted to condemn the [Vietnamese] occupation and invasion of Cambodia.

The Hostage Crisis

I always thought that Iran, caught up in its fanatical revolution, was as violent to the UN as it was to the United States. Iran's attitude hurt the United Nations badly, I think. Had the Third World countries been able to force a resolution of the hostage crisis through the UN, that would have enhanced [their] prestige. I spoke to that point often in the UN.

In the hostage situation, we were able to get the Security Council, unanimously on two different occasions before the end of 1979, to call upon Iran to release the hostages. Even countries that are veteran enemies of the United States recognized that this basic violation of the code of diplomatic conduct was a threat to the very structure of international communications.

The problem, of course, was that the opinion of the world was totally irrelevant to Iran and Khomeini, and the more that people pressed upon him to do something, the more the Iranians turned their backs on it. There was a crucial moment in late November 1979 when Bani Sadr, then foreign minister, was scheduled to come to the United States to make the Iranian case. Interestingly, the U.S. government at first did not want to bring the subject to the UN. We expected to resolve the problem on a bilateral basis, between Iran and the United States. By the time we were agreed on a strategy of bringing it to the UN and internationalizing it, Khomeini withdrew from contact in the UN. He forbade Bani Sadr to come into the United States and he withdrew the Iranian ambassador. For a while, it was just a matter of talking to the wind because Iran wasn't there except in the presence of some nominal charges, who obviously had no real contact or political power in Teheran.

We decided to press for sanctions against Iran in January, and we prevailed on Secretary General Waldheim to go to Teheran in an effort to convince the Iranians to release the hostages, which we hoped would make it unnecessary to compel the vote on the sanction question, because obviously many countries didn't want to vote sanctions, especially our allies in Europe. The secretary general began the discussions that ultimately led to the only possible option that could have led to the release of the hostages at that time—namely, a UN commission and a very intricate charade that involved a UN investigation of Iranian charges against the United States, in return for the release of the hostages in a specified way. That fell apart through no fault of the secretary general. It was just the nature of Iranian politics not to settle the question.

The Security Council voted and, even though the Soviets vetoed it, we had a charter majority voting for that resolution on sanctions, which gave the nations of Europe and Japan a legal basis for imposing sanctions in their own parliaments.

In terms of American interests, the UN did everything we asked of it. The president spoke to heads of state in many countries to make sure we had their vote. We had ten affirmative votes for the sanctions resolution; you need nine for a majority. That was vetoed by the Soviets but, as I say, the fact that we had ten votes enabled us to go to countries in the world and say, "The constitutional majority of the United Nations is behind you." So that worked out very well.

Algeria, which had maintained a line of communication to the Khomeini government, and which was a Muslim as well as politically revolutionary [land], was able to mediate between Teheran and Washington more effectively than any other [country]. And when Rajai, the prime minister of Iran who was later killed in an explosion in Teheran, came to the UN, Ambassador Bedjaoui of Algeria and Ambassador Kaiser of Bangladesh, who was another very helpful person on the Security Council and in the General Assembly, went to see him and helped convince him of how destructive it was to the presumed objective of Iran's revolution to have the whole world against it because of the hostage question. I think that led to Rajai's going to Algeria and then going back to Teheran and beginning the negotiations that ultimately led to the release of the hostages.

I hope to be supportive of the United Nations, critical of it when necessary, but involved with the UN for the rest of my life. I think it's an absolutely essential instrument for humanity to avoid the terrible possibilities of war and to enjoy the great possibilities of peace. If you didn't have a United Nations, you would have to create one if you wanted to live in the complicated world we live in. You must have some means by which all the nations of the world come together and are allowed to agree and disagree. It's much better to have the fireworks in the Security Council than the shooting in the Falkland Islands. The UN is a reflection of the world, and the mirror is often distorted. So it's a wonderful challenge to try to create some sense and order out of all of that.

My experience has been that no country [is] more respected generally in the United Nations than the United States. Americans have such a different viewpoint because our media play up all of the criticism there. That's not the way it is. Our political system, our economic achievements, our goodwill internationally have been greatly admired and appreciated by most of the countries of the United Nations. It's too bad to see the positive, affirmative aspects of that lost on the American people, who should be made aware that their contributions to the UN and to the world generally have been greatly appreciated.

PART V:
THE REAGAN YEARS,
1981–

OVERVIEW

The opening years of the 1980s saw the appearance of new chief executives for the two governments that most impinge on world relations: Ronald Reagan in the United States and Yuri Andropov in the Soviet Union. The United Nations also elected a new executive, Javier Pérez de Cuéllar of Peru. All three men began their tenure in office with candid re-appraisals of the events of the past decade, and with calls for unity and rededication in the face of deepening problems that threatened to undermine the health of their respective states and organization. Reagan, denouncing the excesses of socialism, social decay, and rampant godlessness, called for a return to the days of a purer form of capitalism, a greater role for local governments, and a closer relationship between morality and government. Pérez de Cuéllar, who succeeded Kurt Waldheim as United Nations Secretary General in 1981, bemoaned the declining influence of the United Nations in the attainment of its major goal—world peace. He promised to make more use of his own power under Article 99 of the charter, in bringing threatening situations to the Security Council, and sought to improve the working relationship among the big powers.

Andropov, like Reagan, criticized the moral laxity of his age and the waning of commitment to the official national ideal—in his case, communism. He attempted to remedy the situation through a program of hard work and honesty in the workplace and government, but his efforts, which began vigorously, waned under the pressure of a serious illness which claimed his life in February 1984. Andropov's successor, Konstantin Chernenko, died about a year after taking office and was succeeded by Mikhail Gorbachev in March 1985.

The Western media hailed Gorbachev's elevation as a turning point in recent Soviet history and perhaps in Soviet-American relations as well. The new man was young—only 54—and sufficiently vigorous and intellectually sophisticated to bring some hope that he might ease the chronic economic problems facing the U.S.S.R. Many observers, hoping that he might also be more flexible on major foreign-policy issues, like arms control and Afghanistan, urged the White House to extend a conciliatory hand. (A few years before, President Reagan had described the Soviet Union as an "evil empire.") In fact, the White House made a guardedly optimistic assessment of chances for a summit meeting and for real progress at the Vienna arms-control talks that opened shortly after Gorbachev came into office. Observers in Europe, the U.S., and the Eastern Bloc expressed the hope that Gorbachev and Reagan might reverse the downward trend in U.S.-Soviet relations that had begun at the end of Jimmy's Carter's presidency with the Soviet intervention in Afghanistan. Complicating factors were the Reagan administration's announcement of the so-called Star Wars space-defense system and the willingness of the Soviets to support the left-wing Sandinista government in Nicaragua.

The American president began his first term with a foreign-policy victory—the release of the hostages from the American embassy in Teheran. Almost simultaneously, the administration moved to put its stamp on U.S. relations with the United Nations. Declaring the need for a new look in American foreign policy, Reagan appointed Jeane Kirkpatrick the permanent representative to the United Nations. To her job Kirkpatrick brought impeccable scholarly credentials and a reputation as one of the more creative minds among neoconservatives. She had been one of the earliest to stress that American foreign policy, in its assessment of human-rights violations under repressive regimes around the world, should distinguish between non-Communist authoritarian and Communist totalitarian ones. She argued that the United States had sometimes tried to impose or encourage the creation of democratic regimes in nations that lacked the necessary democratic substructures, thereby producing not true democracy, but the undermining of legitimate authority. Her conclusion was that sometimes the United States must acquiesce in the existence of human-rights violations in friendly countries.

In the United Nations, Kirkpatrick quickly assumed a combative stance when responding to criticisms both of the United States and of its friends and allies. She evinced a greater interest in questions of anticommunism than in issues of human rights, and tended to regard the United Nations principally as an instrument of U.S. foreign policy. She took on the Third World in a series of rhetorical confrontations—for example, in 1981, after nonaligned nations issued a communique bitterly attacking American foreign policy while only obliquely chiding that of the Soviet Union. Again, after the Soviet Union shot down a Korean civilian jetliner near Kamchatka, in 1983, and Zimbabwe, then a member of the Security Council, abstained on a vote to condemn the Soviets for their action, Kirkpatrick criticized the abstention and advocated a substantial cut in American assistance to the African country.

Early in 1985, Kirkpatrick resigned—out of frustration, it was rumored, over not being appointed to a more influential position in the making of foreign policy. A *New York Times* story about her in 1985 declared that she had "reasserted American authority" in the UN. The White House announced that her successor as permanent representative would be Vernon Walters, a retired army general, confidant to presidents, ambassador-at-large, and former deputy director of the Central Intelligence Agency.

Middle East

The Arab-Israeli conflict remained a major factor in UN affairs. In 1981 the UN condemned an Israeli bombing raid on an Iraqi nuclear reactor. In 1982 additional condemnation came after the Israeli invasion of southern and central Lebanon. The invasion, following years of hostilities between the Israelis and PLO fighters in southern Lebanon, reached as far as Beirut and was an attempt by Israel to root out the PLO from its Lebanese bases and destroy it as an effective military force. The PLO, surrounded by Israeli forces encircling Beirut, was forced to negotiate a humiliating evacuation of its main forces to various Muslim countries, including Syria.

In an effort to assure the peaceful and orderly withdrawal of the PLO units, four Western countries—France, Italy, Great Britain, and the United States—agreed to send troops temporarily to occupy certain parts of Beirut.

In the summer of 1983, Prime Minister Menachem Begin, feeling the pressure of continued losses in fighting between Israelis and Muslim militia units, ordered a partial withdrawal of troops, taking them out of the Shouf mountains near Beirut. With the Israeli units gone, the pro-Western Gemayel government and the multinational force became more vulnerable to attacks from the anti-government militias.

Late in 1984 the international forces were withdrawn from Beirut after suffering a series of guerilla attacks. In 1984, the Israelis, also suffering high casualities, announced a pullout from most of occupied Lebanon. By the middle of 1985 the Islamic forces, especially the Shiites, had become the dominant force in Lebanon outside the areas occupied by Syria.

In all this the UN peacekeeping force in Lebanon, UNIFIL, played no meaningful role, having been brushed aside by the Israelis when they entered Lebanon in 1982. However, the United Nations force in the Golan Heights remained in place as a buffer between Syria and Israel, and the Security Council repeatedly extended its mandate for six-month periods.

The Issue of the UN's Effectiveness

As in the past, events during the Reagan years often pointed up the inability of the United Nations to shape world affairs, and this again raised questions about the future of the world organization. The issue had come up repeatedly, for example, regarding the Soviet occupation of Afghanistan and the Libyan incursion into Chad. The most striking instance, however, involved the surprise American invasion of the Caribbean island of Grenada. Made ostensibly to rescue U.S. nationals from potentially dangerous civil strife that had broken out on the island, the operation also involved the overthrow of a Marxist-oriented government that had been friendly to Cuba.

In the United Nations the invasion drew harsh criticism, especially from Third World nations and the Soviet bloc, but also from traditional friends of the United States. The United States was forced to use its veto against a Security Council resolution deploring the invasion; a similar resolution in the General Assembly was opposed only by the United States, Israel, El Salvador, and the half-dozen Caribbean island-states that had joined in the military operation. Despite the overwhelming majority voting in favor of the resolution, and the great weight of world opinion that seemed to be behind it, however, it had little real impact.

In the United States a different reaction occurred, as popular opinion focused less on the ineffectiveness of the United Nations than on its perceived bias against the interests of the United States. One American representative to the United Nations, in a remarkable statement, suggested that the United Nations might "go elsewhere" if it was not pleased with the United States. "We will put no impediment in your way," noted Charles M. Lichenstein, one of Ambassador's Kirkpatrick's deputies, "and we will be at dockside bidding you a fond farewell as you set off into the sunset." President Reagan seemed to support these sentiments, and the U.S. Senate, in an apparently unrelated move, voted to reduce the American financial contribution to the United Nations. Additional U.S. displeasure with the world body developed over the policies of UNESCO, which was accused of being heavily politicized (against American interests) and wasteful in its spending habits. In December 1984 the Reagan administration announced U.S. withdrawal from UNESCO until the problems were remedied. The U.S. was not alone in its criticism of this particular agency; several other Western nations are poised to follow the U.S. withdrawal.

This was not all. In November 1983 Congress passed Public Law 98-164, which set several conditions upon American participation in the United Nations. Two of the provisions are particularly important. The first (115) directs that if Israel is illegally denied its "credentials" at the United Nations, the United States will "suspend its participation in the General Assembly or such specialized agency until the illegal action is reversed." The second section (117) enjoins the Secretary of State to report to Congress each year regarding "the policies which each member country of the United Nations pursues in international organizations of which the United States is a member." The two sections, when read in the context of other parts of the law, clearly arose from a desire to make American participation in the United Nations conditional upon the "good behavior" of the UN as a whole and of its individual member states. This was a striking reversal of the historic U.S. position on the United Nations. No longer was it assumed by Congress that the United Nations—which was created largely with U.S. initiative and money—is an indispensable component of American foreign relations. Rather, it was viewed as one of many international organizations to which the United States belongs, and the assumption seemed to be that under certain circumstances the United States might find it beneficial to withdraw.

Fortieth Anniversary

A major concern of the world body was preparing for celebrations of its fortieth anniversary in 1985. The slogan for the celebration was "United Nations for a Better World," not, as one spokesman noted, "*The* United Nations..." The slogan was intended to reflect the "commitment of Member States for a better world, and not only that of the Organization." As its birthday drew near, the UN faced a major test of its effectiveness with the drought crisis in Africa. To help coordinate international relief efforts, in 1984 the UN established the Office for Emergency Operations in Africa (OEOA), headed by American Bradford Morse, who is credited with rebuilding the United Nations Development Program during his tenure there from 1976 to 1984. Against the somber background of famine in Africa, the UN presented other, more hopeful programs, including the 25th anniversary of the beginning of decolonization, the International Youth Year, the International Year of Peace, and the World Conference to Review and Appraise the Achievements of the United Nations Decade for Women.

The U.S. Mission

When the Reagan team assumed office at the United Nations, it was criticized for being short on experience. During the first Reagan term, however, the team was remarkably stable in its personnel, and the charge of inexperience faded away. The only major change involved deputy representative Kenneth Adelman, who resigned in April 1983 to become head of the Arms Control and Disarmament Agency. His successor, Jose Sorzano, had been serving as Representative on ECOSOC. In a recent interview with the author, Sorzano commented on the relatively long tenure of Jeane Kirkpatrick as perm rep: "You have to go back to Arthur Goldberg to find another ambassador here for three years: the average tenure of an American ambassador here has been 1.89 years—less than two years!" With Sorzano's move to the number-two spot on the delegation, Alan L. Keyes became the representative on ECOSOC. William C. Sherman, a career diplomat, occupied the number-three spot as Deputy Representative on the Security Council, until the end of 1983 when he returned to Washington, D.C., as deputy assistant secretary of state for East Asian and Pacific affairs. Charles Lichenstein continued in the number-five position, Alternate Representative for Special Political Affairs, but resigned in March 1984 to join the Heritage Foundation. He was the person who most often occupied the U.S. seat in the Security Council and General Assembly during Ambassador Kirkpatrick's absences.

The congressional delegates to the General Assembly during this period included Senators J. Bennett Johnston of Louisiana and Robert W. Kasten of Wisconsin, and Congressmen Steven Solarz of Brooklyn and Joel Pritchard of Washington. Other delegates included such former government figures as Congressman Bruce Caputo, Senator John Sherman Cooper, Ambassador John D. Lodge (brother of Henry Cabot Lodge), and Ambassador John L. Loeb, Jr.

SOURCES

General information about the United Nations and the U.S. Mission during this period may be found in *U.N. Annual Yearbook* (New York: United Nations, 1981-82); *Issued before the General Assembly of the United Nations* (New York: United Nations Association of the U.S., 1981-85); *U.S. Participation in the U.N.* (Washington, D.C.: Department of State, 1981-82); *New York Times* 1981-84.

Vernon A. Walters
George Gedda, "Larger Than Life: Peripatetic Ambassador-at-Large Vernon Walters—the Country's Premier Portable Diplomat—Brings New Meaning to an Old Title," *Foreign Service Journal* (Dec. 1984): 28-31; "Vernon Walters: America's New Trouble-shooter at U.N.," *U.S. News & World Report* (June 3, 1985): 13; press release, U.S. Mission to the UN (June 1985).

JEANE J. KIRKPATRICK: Permanent Representative and Chief of the U.S. Mission to the United Nations, 1981-1985.

Pat Moynihan and I are the first tenured professors, I think, to serve as U.S. permanent representatives. It is said that Henry Kissinger brought Moynihan to Nixon's attention basically because of his article in Commentary *magazine on "The U.S. in Opposition" (1975). It was in a similar kind of way that I was brought to Reagan's attention. You could say accurately that we were the two permanent reps that, at least individually, were appointed because of our ideas.*

A prolific author, Jeane Jordan Kirkpatrick has contributed to a number of journals and publications. She also edited *The Strategy of Deception: A Study in World-Wide Communist Tactics* (1963) and has written monographs on foreign students in the United States, on mass behavior in wartime, and on Peronist Argentina. Her 1974 book, *Political Women*, was an in-depth study of the political careers and personal characteristics of 50 women state legislators.

Kirkpatrick took an active interest in politics in response to what she saw as the unrealistic and misguided antiwar and counterculture movements of the 1960s. She supported Hubert Humphrey's 1972 presidential-primary bid against George McGovern. After McGovern's nomination, she helped form the Coalition for a Democratic Majority, a group of neoconservative intellectuals who were liberal on domestic issues but favored a conservative, anti-Soviet foreign policy. She supported Sen. Henry Jackson's unsuccessful run for the 1976 presidential nomination, and later switched to the victorious Carter bandwagon.

In 1977 she became a resident scholar at the conservative American Enterprise Institute. Increasingly disillusioned with President Carter's foreign policy, she wrote the now-famous *Commentary* article, "Dictatorships and Double Standards" (1979) in which she argued that the Carter administration had set a double standard by criticizing the flaws of right-wing but pro-American governments, while rarely doing the same against more repressive and pro-Soviet regimes. In addition to being contrary to American strategic and economic interests, the Carter foreign policy, she claimed, was counterproductive because the authoritarian regimes were more easily reformed and made more democratic than left-wing ones, which sought to control all aspects of society. The *Commentary* article impressed Republican presidential candidate Ronald Reagan. Kirkpatrick met with Reagan and became his supporter and, later, foreign-policy adviser.

After Reagan's 1980 election victory, Kirkpatrick became U.S. representative to the United Nations. At first, she seemed to spend more time in National Security Council and cabinet meetings in Washington than in New York. "I'd rather be in Philadelphia" than at a UN debate, she once said. Indeed, the sharp tongued professor was criticized for her inflexibility during negotiations. "She hasn't accepted the notion that the U.S. needs allies to do what it wants in the world," one diplomat has said. Her tendency to lecture, rather than discuss, upset many fellow delegates. "I am a professor," she responds to her detractors. "I don't mean to lecture my colleagues. It may be that I sound like a professor. So be it."

The reality of U.S. impotence at the United Nations is stunning. The decline of U.S. influence had proceeded to a much greater extent than I had realized before I got here. I guess I spent the first few months I was here trying very hard just to understand this process. What is it that goes on here? What's the structure of influence? What are the levers of influence? Why is it that some countries are so much more influential and successful than others? How did it happen that the United States declined in influence to such a nadir? Then, finally, what could we do about it?

The first step, for me, anyway, is what, as a social scientist, I would call "to map the phenomenology," or simply to understand what is going on. That's the preface to understanding why, which is a preface also to understanding what we might do about it. Of course, as in life generally, it's necessary to act while you're learning what is going on. My mandate was to go forth and represent the policies of the Reagan administration, and certainly those involve a restoration of American influence and an end of the period of American retreat and apology.

I think that the State Department deliberately minimized the importance of what went on at the UN. This is reflected in Moynihan's book (*A Dangerous Place*) when he quotes Kissinger as saying, "Don't bother me with that stuff." Now that attitude has been quite pervasive with regard to the State Department and the UN system. It coexists with another attitude, which is that we ought to support the UN. Nobody in the State Department ever thinks about not supporting the UN. Nobody ever thinks about withdrawing from the United

Nations. That would be a dramatic political decision, and I think in the State Department there would be no support for that at all. But, on the other hand, nobody wants to put really good heads to thinking about it, and to make policies which would result in preserving or restoring U.S. strength here.

I believe that U.S. influence at the United Nations has been frittered away. It wasn't inevitable that the United States should lose its influence at the UN; it wasn't a necessary concomitant of the proliferation of members, the rise of the Third World, or other changes in the UN. I don't believe it at all. It is true that the number of nations has increased very dramatically: [from] 51 to 157. It is true that most of the nations that became members are so-called Third World nations and Fourth World [ones] —unrich, undeveloped, and unhappy. It is true that those nations, for the most part, are not democracies, that they lack experience in the ways of democratic Western liberal values.

However, two other things are also true. Their two overriding concerns are and have been decolonization and development. Now, both of those issues, as I think I have argued with historical accuracy, are subjects where the United States is on exactly the same side as the less-developed countries. We were the first new nation. We came into being out of the first anticolonial war, virtually, in the modern epoch. We have never been a colonial nation; we have consistently opposed colonialism and supported national independence movements. There is no reason [why] anybody interested in national independence should have found themselves on the opposite side of these issues with the United States.

Development? We almost invented development assistance: [the] Point Four [Program], Harry Truman, and all that. UNDP [United Nations Development Program] is an American agency. If there is an American agency here, it is UNDP. There is no reason why anybody interested in economic development should find themselves at loggerheads with the United States. I do not believe that the rise of the Third World had, as a necessary concomitant, the rise of Soviet influence. The Soviets, after all, are the principal contemporary colonial power, who do not respect national independence and territorial integrity. They are a failure at economic development themselves and disinclined to help anybody else achieve it. It is simply not so that the current structure of influence of the Soviet Union in the UN reflects any sort of necessary historical evolution. It reflects, in my view, U.S. incompetence in multilateral politics.

I believe that incompetence has been consistent, persistent, from sometime after Adlai Stevenson; from the early days, anyway. Something interesting happened in the spirit of U.S. representation here after the period of Henry Cabot Lodge and Adlai Stevenson. Both of them were men with very large, national political reputations, independent constituencies—which is to say, some clout. They effectively represented the United States at the UN. Sometime after that point, not long after, but by the time Goldberg was here, the problem arose.

I haven't studied the history of the U.S. role at the UN in as much detail as I want to. I don't know exactly what the point was or what happened. I only know that we went from a condition of high influence, under a couple of people who also had long tenure and large personal reputations and national standing, to a period of very low influence and rapid turnover.

I believe that in the relationship between [the U.S. Mission] and the U.S. permanent representative to the UN, the bureaucratic situation is an impossible one. It is structured for disaster. There is a division of what may be called experience and responsibility. On the one hand, you have the U.S. permanent representative, appointed by the president, who is responsible for the representation of the United States at the U.N. All U.S. perm reps have been members of the cabinet [since Henry Cabot Lodge], by the way; all are appointed by the president. But the State Department has developed an ever-larger bureaucracy, which came into being at the time the UN was established and which claims an ever-larger share in managing U.S. representation in the United Nations system. This bureaucracy is IO, basically. There is a miserable relationship between the perm rep and the assistant secretary, which, I repeat, is simply structured for disaster. What each is capable of doing is preventing the other from doing their job. And they're quite capable of doing that.

I deal with the president in the first instance, the secretary of state in the second instance, and Larry Eagleburger, because I like him, about matters of policy. I deal with [Secretary of State] Schultz and Lawrence Eagleburger on policy on a regular basis. On questions of administration, I deal with IO, and Greg Newell, whom I like. By administration, I mean personnel, budget, and coordination. There are a lot of coordination questions. The UN system is a huge, far-flung system, and it's a very big job to coordinate policies between New York and Geneva, and make sure that they're doing in Geneva what we're doing here so that we are consistent and speaking with the same voice.

There is a legitimate kind of distinction between policy functions and a lot of administrative-support functions, which, I think, can be perfectly well handled someplace besides here. But I think that policy and tactics, above all, cannot really be handled except by people in a higher-level bureau than the IO bureau of the State Department. My view about the State Department is that they developed some very odd habits and orientations concerning the use of power. They have an aversion to use of power. I don't mean force, I mean power. There is also an aversion to the participation of Congress in the foreign-policy process.

I think congressional delegates are marvelous, just marvelous. I wish I had some congressional delegates here the year around. I believe in close collaboration between Congress and the State Department. I do not believe that the State Department is the keeper of some sort of esoteric knowledge to which the Congress is not privy. I think that there are experts on foreign policy in the State Department, in Congress, and in the White House. But there's a very important, legitimate role for Congress.

Politics First and Above All

We [at the United Nations] spend a lot of time engaged in what may be called lobbying activities in the most classical sense. I think that it's very useful, conceptually, not to think of what we do here as multilateral diplomacy. It's no kind of diplomacy; it's politics. There is a multilateral political arena and it functions very much like any other political arena, especially like a legislature. I spent about the first six months here figuring that out.

One thing that became clear to me quite early on is that, obviously, U.S. success in this arena depends directly on cutting through bloc-voting patterns, because bloc-voting patterns simply guarantee U.S. isolation and failure. I was very interested in the voting patterns during the Falklands dispute when I watched our good friend Tony Parsons, the British permanent representative, cut through the normal bloc-voting patterns with the Commonwealth alliance.

Now we, of course, cut through bloc voting with the Puerto Rico issue. Cuba has repeatedly sought to embarrass the United States in the General Assembly by trying to treat Puerto Rico as a colonial issue. It was our first clear voting victory, the first vote that the United States has won in the General Assembly for more than a decade. But to do it, we had to cut through the floss, the bloc-voting patterns. It proves that under certain circumstances on certain kinds of issues, it is possible to defeat Cuban-Soviet initiatives against us and win. But it was a defensive vote; let's be fair about that. It was defending ourselves against the Soviet-Cuban initiative. Nobody's interests were involved but ours. It was neither historically, politically, legally, nor morally ambiguous. We worked very hard on it for literally months down to the wire, and we produced a stunning victory—stunning in the sense that nobody expected it, least of all the Cubans. It means that they are no longer able to simply do anything they choose to us in this arena.

Our policy is out of kilter with the rest of the world on a number of issues, as I just had occasion to remind some of my friends. One [issue] is the Arab-Israeli conflict. I wouldn't call it the Middle East. We are squarely inside the consensus on the Iran-Iraq war. It's the Arab-Israeli conflict we're talking about here, and it's true we are in a relatively isolated position.

Second, we are in a relatively isolated position on what I would call protection of the rule of law in South Africa. Actually, we're even prepared to protect South Africans under the basis of the rule of law. Third, we're out of kilter or out of step on questions like the infant-formula issues. Fourth, we are out of step on questions like the Law of the Sea. Fifth, we are really out of step with the majority on global negotiations. Sixth, we're out of step on the UN international information order. So there is a range of issues on which there is an uncomfortable kind of UN consensus which the United States alone regularly opposes.

Now, could we alter or affect our isolation by switching sides on any of these? Sure. All we would have had to do, to break out of isolation on the Law of the Sea, is to sign the treaty. Never mind that we failed to sign that treaty because we thought there were very important principles and interests at stake there that were worth defending even at the cost of isolation. We never, repeat, never take a position which isolates us in the UN without seriously considering all alternatives and broadly consulting other nations to try to work out some kind of consensus that will be acceptable to us. And our isolation, I would like to emphasize, is not new.

Again, take Pat Moynihan. Talking about 1973 and 1974, he asserts that very frequently the United States was reduced to voting in a bloc of three, along with Chile and the Dominican Republic. I am wont to say that since then we have lost Chile and the Dominican Republic, but we are working hard to get them back here. The fact is that, as in many groups, there is a powerful kind of a group dynamic, and a good many of our group friends whom I think share our values have adopted what might be called different strategies of accommodation. You know, cynicism is the most pervasive mode at the UN; there's a very great deal of cynicism here. We [Americans] are not a cynical people. The most hardheaded of us is an idealist. Sometimes I think people like Pat and I are the most idealistic of all about the UN. We're unwilling to weaken.

Now whether our policy in any one of those cases is right or wrong is, in my opinion, a very different question. I don't think our Middle Eastern policy is wrong; I think it's right. I think that there are a lot of complicated reasons [why] larger numbers of nations here have been progressively unwilling to stand against the Arab bloc. Most of those complicated reasons begin and end with oil, however, and our isolation on the Middle East begins with OPEC; in fact, that cartel is the cause of our real isolation. We were in a minority before that, but it was after that that we became truly isolated, in addition to which we don't really believe in simply getting along by going along. (I'm talking now about Americans in general.) It's not our style, and fortunately we have until now been large enough and powerful enough that we don't find the pressures to conform overwhelming. When we do, why, that would be different.

Through a Looking Glass Darkly

The UN is a reality. But it is no more accurate a reflection [of the real world] than a football game is a reflection of the drama of life. I think what happens here matters, but I do not believe that what happens here is an accurate reflection of the real world—the world outside. It bears the same kind of a relationship to relations outside that mirrors in a spookhouse bear to some kind of a more accurate reflection.

There is a difference between alliances, for example, inside the UN and outside the UN. I always remember, in this regard, a day when the Jordanian permanent representative in the Security Council was avidly, ardently stating the case of the Syrians; he was acting like an agent for Syria. It was the same day that King Hussein was cutting short a trip, to rush home because he thought that the Syrians had a plot against him which made his absence dangerous for his throne.

If nations could be brought to express here at the UN the rational, enlightened interests, as it were, of their own countries, rather than some sort of bloc consensus, then I think it would be a much more effective institution. The United States, by the way, would be a good deal better off because we have a great deal more influence in the outside world than we do in this inside world. There's no doubt about that—this [UN] world does not reflect U.S. influence in the outside world, thank God.

KENNETH L. ADELMAN: Deputy Permanent Representative to the
United Nations, 1981–83.

> *What have we been trying to do here?—fundamentally, to convey the
> idea that the UN is a serious place that is taken very seriously by the
> U.S. government. When the United States is being attacked, we respond
> quite vigorously in various forums and on various levels throughout the
> system. We consider it part of the war of ideas that is raging around the
> world, so we have spent an enormous amount of time and effort trying
> to hold countries and delegates accountable for what they say and for
> the actions they take at the UN.*

Kenneth Adelman served with domestic-poverty agencies, such as the Office of
Economic Opportunity and VISTA, during the early 1970s. After receiving his
doctorate from Georgetown University in 1975, he joined AID, the international-
development organization. One year later he became an assistant to Secretary of
Defense Donald Rumsfeld. When the Ford administration left office, Adelman
joined the Strategic Studies Center of the Stanford Research Institute (now SRI
International).

Adelman was appointed deputy permanent representative to the United
Nations, with the rank of ambassador, by President Reagan in 1981. In 1983 he
became director of the Arms Control and Disarmament Agency.

The political culture at the UN has been that statements and votes
against the United States, and against democratic values and interests
around the world, go cost free; and that the statements and votes
against others, Soviets or Africans or Arabs, do not go cost free. The
United States is a happy hunting ground for attacks. What we're
trying to do is turn that political culture around. But this is not
something that happens quickly or easily. In my opinion, over the
last decade or so, the United States has not been very vigorous within
the UN about meeting or answering irresponsible attacks. So I think
there was a tendency for delegates to be shocked during the last General Assembly, and it takes time for such shocks to sink in and
change behavior.

Our right of reply is what we are best known for. During the
1981 General Assembly, it became characteristic of the U.S. delegation to be exercising rights of reply fairly constantly. That was, again,
intentional, designed to put people on notice that we were listening

to what they said, that we took them seriously, and we weren't going to take lying down any irresponsible statements attacking the United States and our interests or values.

We would respond to an attack and then counterattack. We would tell them what we thought about how Libya was conducting itself, or Nicaragua, or Cuba. In the plenary session, when debating Afghanistan, our rights of reply answering Libya, Ethiopia, Nicaragua and Cuba were, in my mind, outstanding.

We are now trying to hold countries accountable for the way they vote at the UN and to let them know that in their capitals. We want their ambassadors in Washington and at various levels to understand that we care a great deal about the actions they take in the UN. We don't consider their words and actions excusable because of a mob psychology, but, rather, we hold them individually responsible for what they're doing.

We try to work with other Western nations and with Third World nations. To give one illustration, before the vote of the Special Session on the Golan Heights, I had a meeting with about 15 ambassadors from Africa, explaining how seriously we took a certain vote; and how negative the repercussions of a "yes" vote to an irresponsible resolution like that would be in future [U.S.] relations with those countries, not only [involving] the State Department but on Capitol Hill and elsewhere.

They began to take things a little more seriously. I think that if people are infused with a sense of responsibility, a sense that words matter and ideas matter and facts matter, they will be more responsible. I think that the UN then will be elevated in terms of its prestige and its usefulness, too.

Whether we succeed or not is [in doubt], but I think it's worth a try. The approach is a hopeful one: that the UN can become more responsible over the next ten years than it has been over the last ten years, if the adverse trends of the UN in recent years could be reversed. Otherwise, there is just going to be declining support from the American people for the UN.

To our national interest, NATO may be more important than the UN. The OAS [Organization of American States] may be more important to us as an institution—to our national interest—than the UN. The legacy of the past has been, of course, to consider the UN as more important.

We have five ambassadors here. We have a cabinet member who heads the delegation here; we treat it as a more important organization. If the kind of infusion of responsibility that we are talking about does not take place, then I would expect that the UN will be downplayed in the years to come.

The UN is not a place for many tangible kinds of things. It is, above all, an arena for public diplomacy. That's not to discount its importance, because public diplomacy is very important and the war of ideas raging in the world is a very fundamental one. Ideas do have consequences and they do, over time, influence behavior.

WILLIAM C. SHERMAN: Deputy Representative on the Security Council, 1981–1983.

There's a great deal of difference between what goes on in the United Nations and what goes on in the real world of international power politics. The United Nations has a role, but it is primarily a role of whipping up public opinion or public sentiment or providing a forum for someone to speak. Nobody seems to pay a great deal of attention to what is going on there. Yet it's worth all that, as long as the organization continues to do other things effectively.

I think U.S. policy should basically be to strengthen the things that the United Nations does well, support them, enhance them, and concentrate on them, and try and diminish and attenuate the things that it does very badly—and it does a lot of things rather badly.

William C. Sherman served in the U.S. Navy from 1943 to 1946, and then worked for two American agencies in Korea, before joining the Foreign Service in 1951. His State Department assignments have included posts in Italy and Japan; in Washington, D.C., he was an intelligence-research specialist, Belgian desk officer, special assistant to the deputy undersecretary of state for administration, and country director for Japanese affairs. In 1981 President Reagan nominated him deputy representative to the Security Council with the rank of ambassador.

Although my job title is deputy representative on the Security Council, by and large I haven't been involving myself with the Security Council. Ambassador Lichenstein is doing that. When Jeane [Kirkpatrick] asked me to come, she said, "I need somebody to run the mission, somebody who'd do what a DCM [deputy chief of the mission] does overseas, somebody who knows the system and how to make it produce, and that kind of thing." So I've concerned myself in the first instance with the management of the mission—trying to make the interface between the mission and the State Department work, which, depending upon circumstances, can be easy and can be very difficult.

I also supervise and monitor the work of the political section of the mission; the administrative section of the mission; and the resource-management section, which serves as a general accounting office for the U.S., making sure that its budget doesn't grow too rapidly, that our contribution [to the United Nations] is going to the right places, that new projects are examined for their fiscal soundness, etc. It deals with U.S. citizens who are working for the United Nations—recommending people, supporting people, or opposing people, and making sure that we are adequately represented within the UN system. I also handle the Trusteeship Council when it's in session, and the Fourth Committee, which is the Decolonization Committee of the General Assembly. I handle all the Far Eastern matters that come up and am ready to do anything else that anybody asks me to do. We are rather loosely organized. We are the only mission in the world that has five ambassadors, and sometimes I think that the biggest contribution to effective mission management would be to get rid of three of those, at least—just have two, the boss and the deputy. But it still is necessary, I think, and useful to have somebody from the career side of the service to rely on to do a managerial job, and that's the way Jeane has used me.

The big thing that has happened is the proliferation of mini-states—157 members now, with places like Vanuatu, which used to be the New Hebrides. They hire a lawyer here in New York, to represent them. He is not a Vanuatu citizen. Obviously they can't participate in the full range of activities, but they have a vote and it's the same weight in the General Assembly as the vote of the United States. A lot of the decision making is done by the so-called consensus process, where no vote is taken but nobody voices any opposition and you get a compromise text; and that's consensus.

It's basically a good way of addressing some issues, because in essence, that gives everybody a veto. If someone doesn't join the consensus, there is no consensus, and they have to take a vote. You might get voted down. I think as long as we have the system, people should vote their conscience. They shouldn't be constrained by the fact that they're the only one voting against it. They should explain their vote. Many times we have stood alone on issues which we have made a matter of principle. It's just the fact that it's so unbalanced—all of the condemnations of the Latin American countries for violations of human rights, with no reference made whatsoever to the countries in Eastern Europe, and no reference whatsoever made to Afghanistan. What can I tell you? The UN tends to use itself, in the General Assembly particularly, as a forum in which to wallop South Africa and Israel at every opportunity but not to deal with an even hand. That is not to say that the UN doesn't do some things very well. The UN Development Program is extremely well run and it provides development funds for lots of the Third World, and it's organized in a competent way. The UNICEF (children's emergency fund), is a good, useful, and well-managed organization. The UN peacekeeping activities in Cyprus and Lebanon and other peacekeeping activities have been extremely helpful as buffers to keep people from killing each other. I think actually [the United Nations] has probably been more helpful in the crisis in the Falklands than it has been on anything for a long time. One of the reasons, of course, has been that most of the action until very recently has been taking place quietly and not in public sessions. The secretary general has been operating and consulting with the Security Council in informal sessions and with individual Security Council members. The whole argument has been kept out of the limelight, and away from the posturing that takes place when you are on camera and talking for the record. That's good, and it's a tribute to the way this current secretary general [Perez de Cuellar] is operating. He's a creature of the system, he's been with it for a long time, he knows its weaknesses as well as its strong points. He's a bona fide Third World figure himself. He's a very skillful diplomat, and he is an activist. His predecessor [Waldheim] was much less eager to be engaged and came under criticism from people for not doing more and not endeavoring to assert himself more. The Secretariat does what the member states ask it to do. On the other hand, there are always ways for the Secretariat to operate to insure that the member states ask it do the right things.

Multilateral Diplomacy

Multilateral diplomacy is a totally new world for me. It's not that you don't engage in multilateral diplomacy in the embassies. You are constantly talking with the country where you are about how we can concert with others to achieve objectives. You are aware of what is going on in the world. But over here it is a lot of just horse trading back and forth between delegations—trying to whip up support; trying to find ways of accurately analyzing just how helpful or unhelpful a given country has been to the things that you have wanted to achieve. During this last session, we kept a list of all the votes which were taken—and we had them prioritized into issues that were very important to U.S. interests or less important, on a scale of one to three. We weighted the various issues and then made computer print-outs of the actual voting. Needless to say, you can't use this kind of record as an absolute measure that country x is very much for you or very much against you, because many times there are individual circumstances affecting an individual country. Its vote might seem negative by your lights but it wouldn't be as serious a breach as it might for some other country. Sri Lanka might have to vote some way because of its proximity to India or because of its longstanding position on the Indian Ocean "zone of peace." Sri Lanka's negative vote on some resolution might not be as significant as a negative vote of France or some other country.

What we tried to do is to make the necessary corrections and come up with a score at the end of the session, and then provide that information to our embassy in the host country. We'd say, "This is what happened in the United Nations with your country." Our people in the host country might know that Pakistan, say, voted this way or that way on one issue or another in the UN, but they don't put it together in one conceptual package. We put it together in one package and provide embassies with ammunition so they can approach the host country and say, "If you want our help to support your candidate for the International Court of Justice," or "If you want $100 million in U.S. aid," then "we'd be much more sympathetic if we had had some unswerving support during the last session of the United Nations." It's not a big thing but it's one way of looking at across-the-board performance. And that's the kind of thing that multilateral diplomacy can do. The embassies in the field, on a bilateral basis, are now prepared to say, "Swaziland, you haven't been doing anything for us lately, so why do you expect us to do something for you?"

During the 1982 session, the nonaligned movement issued a communiqué that was markedly hostile to the United States. It singled out the United States by name at least nine or ten times. The resolution, which was mostly produced by Cuba, was rammed through the conference in the middle of the night when a lot of people were not there. They deplored the situation in Afghanistan and in Cambodia but they didn't name any country that might be connected with those two operations. Anyway, Jeane wrote letters to each of the nonaligned signatories who professed to be friends of the United States or who considered themselves as allies. She just said, "I'd like to know why you lent your name to a document which so impugns the good name of the United States and which is totally unbalanced. I'd be interested to hear from you." Then, there was a brouhaha over this being an undiplomatic way of dealing with the situation. She could have ignored it, of course. There have been delegates here whose attitude toward the Third World was: encourage them, be nice to them, don't get upset when they run off the reservation, because they don't really understand what they are doing, or they have other factors that condition this action. The best way to get them on the democratic side is to be friendly and provide aid, and to ignore their peccadilloes, as we'd do with a child. Jeane has not taken that approach at all. She has asked people, required people, to say why they do what they do. It produced some interesting results. Some people were outraged by it, but not many. Other people were quick to disassociate themselves from the communiqué, saying formally, "That resolution was not signed by us, nor did we agree with it."

Our aim has been to make people understand that they are accountable for the kinds of things that they do. And some ghastly things are done. I mean, some lousy resolutions get through, and by a large majority. We want them to know we take them seriously.

Most of the complaints about U.N. irrelevancy have very little justification to them. It's not the fault of the UN, but of the member states. The UN is not, never has been, and probably never is going to be a world government which has any authority or responsibility or opportunity for action that is not given to it by the member states. Starting with the early concept of the veto in the Security Council, the great powers have the authority to stop action before it ever gets started. The only time really there has been any massive action by the UN was under the Uniting for Peace Resolution on Korea.

In recent years, that [Korean] situation has never repeated itself. As far as Lebanon is concerned we had worked within the United Nations but we also have worked independently, with the multinational force, with the Marines, with our own special negotiators out there trying to do things. Meanwhile the UN has continued to extend or reconfirm the mandate of the UNIFIL forces out there. But we have never sought a new mandate. The resolutions brought to the Security Council dealing with Lebanon over the roughly two years [1981–83] that I have been here dealt mainly with extending the UNIFIL mandate, keeping things going, and trying not to interfere with the negotiating process.

Another issue in which the UN obviously has some involvement is Namibia. The negotiations, the actual front-line work has been done through the contact group, the five major powers—the United States, France, Canada, Germany, and England—and those negotiations continue. We have independent contacts with the Angolans and directly with the South Africans in attempting to bring to fruition a process which will eventually be ratified or sanctified by the United Nations but where the United Nations ipso facto has not itself played a direct role. They were very much involved with special representatives of the secretary general and others working in this area with whom we are very closely in touch. But institutionally the United Nations has not been so much involved. I think this is good in many respects, because it is a realistic acceptance of where power is. There's no point in having a world situation that requires application of power be handled by some organization that is impotent. You have to be able to put your money where your mouth is. You can go back to Carlos Romulo [former president of the Philippines], who has always said there are two UNs. There is the UN of the specialized agencies and institutions—the UN of UNDP, the UN high commissioner for refugees, UNICEF, WHO, ITO, and all those—and there is the UN of the Security Council and the General Assembly. The Security Council is the only place where resolutions are fewer and further between than they have been in a long, long time. There is a continuing politicization in the Security Council. The General Assembly is irretrievably politicized. I'm fond of saying it's a valid world and an important world, but it's not the real world. People go to the United Nations to make a public statement within a world forum. It provides that forum, and it provides instant headlines for anybody who speaks there, but I don't think that people tend to speak there with much more than the public relations aspect in mind. In other words, you don't go to the UN to ask it to find solutions, because it's unwieldy for doing—it's not an easy forum in which to get a solution.

The Security Council has turned, unfortunately, into a mini-General Assembly. We have had virtually 40 speakers speaking in the Security Council. It's very discouraging, and depressing. Time and again in recent months, issues that are brought up in the Security Council are not even brought with a resolution, or a request for a statement by the Security Council president. They are simply brought up and everybody comes and speaks and then it all stops. There's no resolution, the Security Council remains seized with the matter, or they call on the secretary general to report, but there's no resolution.

Any member of the Security Council can request the Council to hear somebody from outside. If it's an Arab who is not on the Security Council and wants to talk on the Palestinian question, he works through the Arab representative on the Security Council. With respect to the Libyan complaint against Sudan, for example, the Soviet Union and Poland and other surrogates on the Security Council would produce the people to speak. Of course the Korean Air Lines issue was one in which we were very much engaged and in which the Security Council provided to us a forum that attracted world attention. We pursued a resolution, we got a resolution that was in the end vetoed by the Soviet Union, as one would have certainly anticipated. However, the Soviets had only two votes, theirs and Poland's—even Nicaragua abstained; China abstained, to my surprise.

China tries to maintain as independent a position as it possibly can, and to take the philosophical position that all the troubles of the world come from great-power confrontation, and that China allies itself with the aspirations and expectations of the Third World, and takes no sides in the great-power confrontations, that it opposes hegemony by whatever name it is called, etc. Their role has been rather low profile.

Some people say that by our confrontational attitude we've succeeded less than we should have. But I don't believe that's the case. I think that our policy of standing up and exercising the right of reply, of stating our position, stating those things in which we feel our basic principles are engaged, has caused a lot of the nonaligned Group of 77 to think more deeply about their position, their own relations with the United States. This in the end is constructive for us. We don't have to accept so-called built-in majorities. We don't have to just sit there and take it. We are very active here in New York and also in capitals on issues of concern. We've certainly lobbied heavily on Puerto Rico, we did a lot of talking around on the Korean Air Lines issue, not that we had to do a great deal, but we did it. This mission has very good personal relationships with almost every other delegation, and that's not to say just with our friends. We aren't talking to the Libyans every day, or the Iranians, or people like that, but we have elsewhere—we're open and candid with the Soviets, and certainly with all of our principal allies, all the members of the Security Council, with the major people on committees, and with the Secretariat.

It's hard to say what kind of a backdrop the Korean Air Line incident will continue to provide. Those things don't live in public-consciousness very long, but certainly the worldwide revulsion against the overall brutality of the incident will stick around for awhile, and it may make less attractive or less reasonable sounding some of the proposals, initiatives or rhetoric of the Soviet Union. Not just with us, but with people in the Third World who found that incident so repellent.

Taking the UN Seriously

As long as there are these vast majorities and bloc voting, and people do not seriously deal with issues, the UN can't be taken too terribly seriously. Virtually 80 percent of the resolutions that come to the General Assembly have to do with condemning Israel or South Africa. They all pass by vast majorities. Since they don't have any effect, nobody feels terribly strongly about them, and rather than disturb their relations with people who aren't directly engaged feel compelled to vote, and to cultivate votes against. So time and again the United States and Israel have stood alone against 155 votes over there on one issue or another. South Africa also has a built-in absolute majority—it may not be 157 to 2, but it could be 123 to something.

The UN's resolutions don't have any particular force if no one chooses to abide by them. Hundreds of resolutions are passed every year by the G.A. that just lie fallow; nothing happens, except that they are publicized and the formal debate is published. There is a moral force implied but the moral force doesn't require a follow-up course of action. Sanctions are limited at best and the UN is always very reluctant to vote to impose sanctions, which require, of course, Security Council action. Reluctantly I would have to say that there isn't much being accomplished over there except that, by its presence in some situations, the United Nations is able to defer or put off war.

To be taken more seriously, the UN should be encouraged to do the things it does well, and to stop doing the things it doesn't do well. And the only way to do that is by voting against, or withholding funds as we are required to do by Congress. The UN should not be in the business of provided training for the PLO, or SWAPO. Those are not organizations recognized by the charter, and are in essence terrorist groups.

I would be hard-pressed to say that I thought the future of the organization was terribly bright. I hope it gets better, and it does some things very well indeed. Nobody else could do it. My experience here has made me a good deal more realistic about the possibilities of achieving anything in a multilateral forum. We can do a lot of things bilaterally, and we continue to do a lot of things bilaterally, and based on those bilaterally achieved alliances or concurrences of view we were occasionally able to do things in a multilateral forum too. But the forum itself is not all that relevant to the *Realpolitik* of the world. Decisions that are being made are not being made in the UN. And I don't think anybody, even the most idealistic, ever suspected that they would be.

At certain heavily trafficked street intersections in Japan, they have traffic lights that play a little tune for the blind, to let them know when to walk. I keep wanting to get one installed here at First Avenue and UN Plaza—one that plays the theme from "Twilight Zone."

VERNON A. WALTERS: Permanent Representative and Chief of the U.S. Mission to the United Nations, 1985—

I am no stranger to multilateralism and internationalism—to neither its goals and aspirations, nor to its peculiar problems. As the aide to U.S. Secretary of State George C. Marshall, I was present at the Rio Conference in September 1947 and at the Seventh Pan American Conference held under the aegis of the Organization of American States in Bogota, Colombia, in April 1948. I was fortunate to have the opportunity to serve with Ambassador Averell Harriman in implementing the Marshall Plan, which restored the economic well-being of a war-ravaged Europe, and with General Eisenhower as his aide at NATO in the early 1950's. During this period, I was exposed as well to United Nations sessions in Paris. So over the years, I have had an opportunity to be involved in and to reflect on multilateralism and internationalism and their potential contribution to world peace.

General Vernon A. Walters has had such a distinguished and varied career that he eludes easy classification or characterization. The lead paragraph in one recent magazine story described him as "tough as a general, smooth as a diplomat, alert as a spy—and little wonder. He has been all three." Walters entered the Army in 1941 as a private and retired in 1976 as a lieutenant general. From 1972 to 1976 he was deputy, and briefly acting, director of the Central Intelligence Agency (CIA), and during and after his military and intelligence careers he was variously interpreter (fluent in seven languages) and special aide to presidents Truman, Eisenhower, and Nixon.

So well did Walters perform his duties, earning the praise of Henry Kissinger, among others, that he was recalled to service by the Reagan administration, which appointed him ambassador-at-large. In that capacity Walters traveled as much as 10,000 miles a week on special missions for the President and the State Department. It was Walters who received the task of explaining to Argentina that the United States was going to support the British in the Falklands dispute; he also went to Cuba at then Secretary of State Alexander Haig's request to explore a possible lessening of tensions between Washington and Havana.

Until recently, Walter's low profile had kept him a shadowy figure in the public mind, but this will change as he speaks out in his UN post. Journalists and others who follow international affairs have long known of the general's important role in American diplomacy and his fervent anti-communism. He is known as a hardliner on East-West issues, a deeply patriotic man who is impatient with both domestic and foreign critics of the United States. In a recent formal reply in a Security Council debate about Namibia, the general commented that countries "which crush opposition in their own country are scarcely qualified to judge the functioning of democracy....it was curious for me to hear one representative attack my country in this respect." In a San Francisco speech at the UN's fortieth-anniversary celebrations in June 1985, Walters reiterated the commitment of the United States to pursue successful multilateral relations among nations. Such relations, he observed, imply "a single standard,...an international environment based on reciprocal rights and obligations." Unfortunately, he continued, in the aftermath of World War II "two orders emerged," one engaged in "a process of continuing expansion through the use of violence," and the second a "Western democratic order committed to democratic values." This divergence of views is, in Walter's view, the major disruptive element in the world order, whose presence makes the proper working of the UN much more difficult than its founders expected.

In previous missions and duties, Walters demonstrated a remarkable ability to communicate effectively with an extraordinary diverse range of personalities and ideologies, a skill that will help him greatly at the UN.

Walters has written his memoirs, *Silent Missions* (1978), and two other books: *Sunset at Saigon* and *The Mighty and the Meek.*

I am very happy to be appointed to this position, not only because it's a prestigious one but because the United Nations can serve a very useful purpose in the world. The UN has a great role to play, if we can only get it to play that role instead of becoming a propaganda forum. It can be the conscience of mankind. But to be the conscience of mankind, it must have some semblance of impartiality and not be organized into voting blocs where 122, or 77 percent, of the people vote the same way all the time. I have nothing against nonalignment which is genuine, but I do with nonalignment which is permanent against the United States. It is just as hard for the United States to be wrong all the time as it is to be right all the time. Some countries vote against their own national interest because of this imagined solidarity with some bloc.

Public Disenchantment

That disturbs me because opinion polls indicate that a large segment of the American public is very disenchanted with the UN, and questions the usefullness of the United States belonging to the UN. For those of us who believe in the UN, it is quite disturbing when the UN continues to pass resolutions that essentially accuse the United States of helping South Africa's nuclear effort or of selling weapons to South Africa—although in fact the United States in 1977 instituted an embargo on arms sales to South Africa much more comprehensive than that of the UN (and many of the members who condemn us sell arms to South Africa). When they pass resolutions on human rights violations in South Africa, in both resolutions the United States is specifically named, but when they pass resolutions on the violation of human rights in Afghanistan, you can read the resolution from beginning to end and you'll never find the Soviet Union mentioned. Now, that is a patent degree of unfairness that offends Americans' sense of fair play. If I am unable to persuade the delegates not to continue this kind of thing, then the number of Americans who are disenchanted with the UN will grow.

This has been going on because there is no cost with the United States. We have just got to establish a much better correlation between the way the people vote in the UN and our bilateral relationship with them. Until now you can vote against the United States: nothing happens. When you vote against the Soviet Union, something unpleasant happens, various unpleasant things happen. We haven't got the ability in our society to make unpleasant things happen.

There is some fault on the part of the United States that we have made nonalignment a sort of noble and virtuous thing, which lets down our allies a little bit, the people who have the courage to take a stand alongside of us, who are let down when we give warm blessings to nonalignment. I think there is a basic issue in the world, of freedom and slavery, and nonalignment between freedom and slavery is not a noble cause. In future times, nations are going to have to understand that if they have these unilateral, not-really-nonaligned, genuinely hostile resolutions against the United States there is going to be some cost in their relationship with us.

A New but Familiar Challenge

I look forward to this general assembly (1985) as a tremendously challenging, tremendously difficult task, but then I like difficult tasks. I've had them most of my life. It's not like coming to a strange place. I know a large number of the delegates—I couldn't venture a figure, but I would say 40 or 50 at least, that I've met in various incarnations before.

I am already being subjected to a torrent of abuse from the Soviet world, accusing me of plots and killings and all sorts of things because of my affiliation with the military and the CIA. And this is almost before I've done anything here (at the UN) that this barrage of abuse has descended upon me. Kurt Waldheim was a captain in the German army in the tank company that came closest to Moscow, but who spoke about that? But they emphasize my military background. You see, I've committed a very grievous sin. I fought Fascism in all its colors—black in Italy, brown in Germany, red in Vietnam and Korea—and that's pretty unforgiveable. It hasn't manifested itself so far in my personal relations here with the Soviet and Ukrainian delegates. I don't carry the burden of heavy ideological dogma on my shoulders that they do; I don't have a lot of that kind of baggage. In our society there is flexibility, in theirs there is not.

The UNESCO Decision

I think the United States action on UNESCO was highly justified; it was based on bookkeeping, not racism as some allege. Racism is a very convenient excuse when you do not like something. Everyone forgets that the United States is the fifth largest black power in the world; only Nigeria, Ethiopia and Zaire have more black people than the United States. In the case of UNESCO, a large percentage of the expenditures intended to help the third world are actually being effected in Paris—something like 75 to 80 percent of the expenditures. The third world is not getting its fair share.

I would hope that the UN would express its abhorrence for terrorism—and the killing of bystanders and innocent people who have nothing to do with the quarrel at hand—but terrorism touches so closely to the sovereignty of nations, and nations are so jealous of their sovereignty, that the UN may act in the future. But I am not sure of the immediate future. The whole problem is you have a large number of people who have no concept of democracy; who terrorize their own citizens, so terrorizing is not particularly offensive to them.

Immediate Goals

It's too early for me to tell what my chances of achieving any real results are. Ask me in six months again and I'll be able to tell you. I'm at a peak of ignorance about the UN which I expect to reach never again, but I'm sliding off it fast. (Regarding UN affairs to date) I have had nothing particularly newsworthy, except how much time can be spent arguing about a comma. I was present at a meeting where they argued for four hours about having the word "the" included or not. I thought it excessive to tie down the services of the many high-ranking, highly paid people for four hours. I would like to see us working on things related more directly to the well-being of the people of the world—improving their living conditions, conditions of health, opportunities for development, for work, for creating new jobs. Those are the things we should be working on. At least that is my understanding of the Charter of the UN and the purposes of the organization.

I don't think there will be that many differences (between Kirkpatrick and me). There will be differences in style, but not in substance. I believe more in personal diplomacy, in meeting people and talking to them, trying to persuade them or at least planting a seed that may at some future time grow. Fundamentally, I work for the same country, the same president, the same secretary of state, the same administration as Jeane Kirkpatrick. I certainly intend to work closely with the State Department; I believe the United States can only have one foreign policy. And if I have any problems, I'll take them directly to the secretary of state, privately—or the president.

Afterword

The recurrent theme in this book is dissatisfaction with the current state of U.S.–UN relations. The dissatisfaction concentrates primarily on how the UN's political organs function and how the United States has operated within the UN framework. The exact nature of the problems and the solutions proposed to resolve them vary from person to person. A common complaint is that the non-aligned nations, the Group of 77, in their practice of bloc voting, and because of their preoccupation with such issues as condemnation of Israeli policies, have exercised an irresponsible majority control over the General Assembly. In particular, it is argued, this majority has shown a bias against the West, especially the United States.

Another complaint is that many member nations do not act consistently in their United Nations affairs versus their non-UN affairs. In other words, a nation may speak disparagingly about the United States in the General Assembly, while it lobbies for additional American aid in Washington—a practice that would diminish the utility of the United Nations as a forum for serious discussion of national interests and problems. Other critics focus more on the American end of the problem, observing that the United States has not really appreciated the implications of the great changes in the world during the past thirty years, such as the evolution of the nonaligned movement, and the transformation of the world economy. The United States, by this argument, continues to behave as if it is living in the old world of bilateral diplomacy, when in fact the world has become multilateral. Power, in its social, economic, and military aspects, has become much more diffused among nations and can no longer be regarded as the monopoly of a few. Until the United States understands this fact, it will suffer failure in the United Nations.

Still other criticisms are directed at the internal organization of the United Nations: the rules that allow seemingly endless debates on relatively minor issues; that give voting power to nations which in reality have little real power in the outside world; and the unenforceable nature of UN resolutions, which threatens to make them as irrelevant as anything except debating chips.

Finally, the issue has been raised here of whether the United Nations really is worth preserving. Is it a useful part of America's foreign policy, or is it an expensive luxury? In a sense, this is the most basic question of all, because to answer it is to decide on a fundamental course of action. If the United Nations is not worth saving, from the American viewpoint, then the most sensible course is to let it die or encourage it to move its headquarters to another country. In this scenario the United Nations would, like the League of Nations before it, not have the benefit of U.S. participation. If history is any guide, the United Nations, like the League, would not survive the lack of U.S. participation. The League of Nations failed at a time of growing international tension and rearmament, and the final result was war. If the United Nations were to fail, also at a time of growing international tension and world rearmament, would there also be war?

There is another factor to ponder. Is the United Nations as unpopular in the United States as many would have us believe? It is a curious fact that in its history no nation has ever voluntarily given up its seat at the United Nations, not even Israel, which has been the target of countless UN resolutions of disapproval or censure. Evidently membership in the United Nations is highly regarded by these nations. That it is also highly regarded by the American public is evident from Gallup Polls conducted throughout the years. Furthermore, a *New York Times*/CBS News Poll taken during September 24–28, 1983, at the height of vocal domestic hostility towards the United Nations, revealed that Americans overwhelmingly favored retaining membership. According to this poll, 89 percent of Americans believed that the United States should remain in the world organization; 65 percent believed that the United Nations should remain in the United States; and only 20 percent believed the United Nations should leave the United States. Another interesting fact is that other opinion polls have seen the United Nations ranked consistently higher in public esteem than the U.S. Congress. Unless we are prepared to scrap our own legislative bodies and start over, or ask Congress to take up residence elsewhere, we can hardly use public opinion as a justification for asking the United Nations to leave the United States, or the United States to leave the United Nations.

But if the United Nations is here to stay, can something be done to make it work better, and to make the United States more comfortable in it?

First, we must reassess the role that we expect the United Nations to play in today's world, both in the short term and the long term. Perhaps the United Nations has been oversold as a panacea for the world's problems. Certainly this is one conclusion drawn by many of the persons who have spoken in this book. We need to decide just what the United Nations can and cannot do. Everyone agrees it is a useful forum for debate, a place where even the very small or very poor nations can be seen and heard. And everyone agrees that in certain instances the United Nations remains a functional keeper of the peace. Moreover, there is general agreement that the various UN agencies—for example, the WHO and FAO—perform many important functions that cannot be replaced easily through bilateral arrangements. But what else? How far should we go as a nation, for example, in entrusting our sovereignty to a world body; how far should any nation? At a pragmatic level, we make this decision at the beginning of each new presidential administration, when the new permanent rep takes office and the mission staff is reorganized. Is it possible to make this decision at a more theoretical level, freed from some of the internal rhetoric that characterizes domestic politics? Can this be done in other nations? Can we and they reach some agreement on how far the United Nation's powers and moral influence can be pressed to make it more useful? In other words, can we generate an international debate on the role the United Nations should and can play in today's world, given the fact that the world into which the United Nations was born has changed almost beyond recognition. Surely such a debate, with its potential for constructive reform, is a more intelligent approach than simply abandoning the United Nations, and trying to start over on another site. At the very least, it would be the most inexpensive way to make the United Nations better.

Second, we must decide how the United Nations relates to U.S. foreign policy. This is separate from, but related to the issue of how the world body does, or might, affect issues of national sovereignty. Here, whatever the degree to which we think our sovereignty must suffer some infringement by the needs of the world body, we must address the question of how we maneuver in the actual political process that is the United Nations. We must begin with the observation that no worldwide organization such as the United Nations, with its

40-year history, its pedigree of being created by the United States, and its far-reaching programs in every nation on earth, can be ignored by the United States as it conducts its foreign policy. Indeed, it can be argued that to the extent that the United States has chosen to circumvent the United Nations, or prevent issues from being brought up there, the United States has been the cause of its own problems there. The United Nations, we might argue, is not a broken tool, but a slightly rusty and dulled one that only needs constant use to make it effective again. Perhaps we have been engaged in a game of self-fulfilling prophecy: the less we value the organization, the less we use it; the less effective it becomes, the less we value it.

If we are to use the United Nations more effectively, however, we must alter our patterns of behavior. We must, first of all, give UN affairs a higher priority in the government, especially the State Department. A constant theme in this book has been the frustration experienced by those powerful political figures (Stevenson is a classic example) who were permanent representatives. Today that frustration still exists—although the permanent representatives lately have not been as politically prominent—because foreign policy is not made in consultation with the American staff at the United Nations; it is made in Washington.

Somehow, we must bring the mission closer into the decision-making process if we are to make our presence in the United Nations more effective.

We must also provide more continuity in staff at the mission. During the past 15 years, we have had 11 permanent representatives, serving under five presidents and nine secretaries of state, and with nine assistant secretaries of state for international-organization affairs. This rapid turnover, itself symptomatic of a lack of consensus regarding U.S. foreign policy, reduces our impact at the United Nations and adds to the difficulties of our friends and allies in the United Nations, who must contend with a new face and a new approach at frequent intervals.

Perhaps we should return to the policy of appointing prominent political figures as permanent representatives. This is one immediate way of indicating that we take the world body seriously. On the other hand, since the U.S. delegation is an instructed one, which lacks the authority to make policy on its own, the post of perm rep might not appeal to established figures, who might feel constrained by the limits of their authority. A politically prominent perm rep would only work, therefore, if, as suggested above, the UN delegation had more impact on formulation of U.S. foreign policy.

There are some other things we can do, as well. We should pay more attention to multilateral diplomacy when we train our future diplomats. Bilateral diplomacy will always be the mainstay of our foreign policy, but at least, our people should understand the potentials of multilateral relations and be able to use them effectively when the opportunity arises. There is much to be said for heightening our awareness about multilateral relations—even if we do not always employ them—simply to give us a second approach as a possibility when we contemplate various courses of action.

In addition to these various governmental efforts, there must be a greater input from the American public. It does no good for the public, in opinion polls, to express strong support for the United Nations if the perception in the media is that the public does not support the United Nations. We need a national debate, of the sort that has developed over the issue of nuclear weapons. The debate should not be an attempt to propagandize for the United Nations, or to whitewash its record, but to make explicit in the public mind what has been implicit for the past 40 years: that in the final analysis, people agree we must have some kind of world body as a means of preserving peace and order. Partly, the debate would be designed simply to provide information. As with any major issue, misinformation abounds. Votes in the United Nations invariably go against the United States, it is argued; yet this has been true only sometimes, and for many years the United States enjoyed an automatic majority, as the persons interviewed for this book often note. There is room, accordingly, for some public reeducation about the longterm history of the United Nations.

One organ to lead such a debate would be the United Nations Association of the United States, which does indeed try to keep the United Nations before the public eye. But one organization by itself is not enough. At the very least there must be public outreach programs in the schools, in libraries, on TV, and on radio. We need a public information forum about the United Nations that will stimulate a new interest and generate new excitement over the possibilities of making the United Nations more effective both as an element of American foreign policy and as a real force for peace and development in the world.

List of
Biographical Sources

p. 21　**W. Averell Harriman**
Current Biography (New York: H. W. Wilson, 1941), pp. 244-45; *Political Profiles* – Kennedy Volume (New York: Facts on File Inc., 1976), pp. 208-10; *Who's Who in America* (Chicago: Marquis, 1982), p. 1408.

p. 26　**Philip C. Jessup**
Current Biography (New York: H. W. Wilson, 1948), pp. 313-16. Interview with Jessup (1981).

p. 34　**Ernest A. Gross**
Current Biography (New York: H. W. Wilson, 1951), pp. 248-50; *Who's Who in America* (Chicago: Marquis, 1982), p. 1321.

p. 46　**Francis O. Wilcox**
Who's Who in America (Chicago: Marquis, 1982), p. 3564. Interview with Wilcox (1983).

p. 55　**Phillip M. Klutznick**
Who's Who in America (Chicago: Marquis, 1982), p. 1838. Interview with Klutznick (1982).

p. 62　**Seymour Maxwell Finger**
Who's Who in America (Chicago: Marquis, 1982), p. 1039. Biographical notes.

p. 79　**Francis T. P. Plimpton**
"Bar Association Chief: Francis T. P. Plimpton," *New York Times Biographical Edition* (February 11, 1970), p. 379; *Who's Who in America* (Chicago: Marquis, 1982), p. 2672.

p. 83　**Marietta Tree**
Current Biography (New York: H. W. Wilson, 1961), pp. 459-61; *Who's Who in America* (Chicago: Marquis, 1982), p. 3362. Interview with Tree (1982).

p. 91   **Franklin H. Williams**
        Who's Who in America (Chicago: Marquis, 1982), p. 3530. Interview
        with Williams (1982).

p. 98   **Arthur J. Goldberg**
        Current Biography (New York: H. W. Wilson, 1961), pp. 178–80;
        Who's Who in America (Chicago: Marquis, 1982), p. 1235. Political
        Profiles – Johnson Volume (New York: Facts on File Inc., 1976),
        pp. 217–220.

p. 106 **Joseph J. Sisco**
        Current Biography (New York: H. W. Wilson, 1972), pp. 393–95;
        Who's Who in America (Chicago: Marquis, 1982), p. 3094.

p. 112 **Frank Church**
        Current Biography (New York: H. W. Wilson, 1978), pp. 75–79;
        Who's Who in America (Chicago: Marquis, 1982), p. 582.

p. 116 **William B. Buffum**
        U.N. "Biographical Notes"; *Who's Who in America* (Chicago: Mar-
        quis, 1982), p. 445.

p. 121 **George Ball**
        Current Biography (New York: H. W. Wilson, 1962), pp. 23–25;
        Political Profiles – Johnson Volume (New York: Facts on File Inc.,
        1976), p. 32; *Political Profiles* – Nixon-Ford Volume (New York:
        Facts on File Inc., 1979), pp. 33–34; *Who's Who in America* (Chica-
        go: Marquis, 1982), p. 150.

p. 147 **Christopher H. Phillips**
        Who's Who in America (Chicago: Marquis, 1982), p. 2647. Interview
        with Phillips (1982).

p. 153 **Shirley Temple Black**
        Current Biography (New York: H. W. Wilson, 1970), pp. 36–39;
        Who's Who in America (Chicago: Marquis, 1982), p. 287. Interview
        with Black (1982).

p. 163 **Rita A. Hauser**
        Who's Who in America (Chicago: Marquis, 1982), p. 1438. Interview
        with Hauser (1982).

p. 169 **George Bush**
Current Biography (New York: H. W. Wilson), pp. 63-65; *Political Profiles* – Nixon-Ford Volume (New York: Facts on File Inc., 1979), p. 101-102; *Who's Who in America* (Chicago: Marquis, 1982), p. 467.

p. 172 **W. Tapley Bennett**
Who's Who in America (Chicago: Marquis, 1982), p. 236; *New York Times* (June 11, 1983), p. 8.

p. 177 **William E. Schaufele, Jr.**
Political Profiles – Nixon-Ford Volume (New York: Facts on File Inc., 1979), p. 571-572; *Who's Who in America* (Chicago: Marquis, 1982), p. 2949.

p. 193 **John A. Scali**
Political Profiles – Nixon-Ford Volume (New York: Facts on File Inc., 1979), p. 571; *Who's Who in America* (Chicago: Marquis, 1982), p. 2942. Interview with Scali (1982).

p. 203 **Daniel Patrick Moynihan**
Political Profiles – Nixon-Ford Volume (New York: Facts on File Inc., 1979), p. 457; *Who's Who in America* (Chicago: Marquis, 1982), p. 2396; *New York Times* Biographical Service.

p. 210 **William W. Scranton**
Current Biography (New York: H. W. Wilson, 1964), pp. 398-400; *Political Profiles* – Nixon-Ford Volume (New York: Facts on File Inc., 1979), pp. 583-584; *Who's Who in America* (Chicago: Marquis, 1982), p. 2996.

p. 219 **George McGovern**
Current Biography (New York: H. W. Wilson, 1967), pp. 205-208; *Political Profiles* – Nixon-Ford Volume (New York: Facts on File Inc., 1979), pp. 404-408; *Who's Who in America* (Chicago: Marquis, 1982), p. 2230.

p. 231 **Andrew Young**
Current Biography (New York: H. W. Wilson, 1977), pp. 449-452; *Who's Who in America* (Chicago: Marquis, 1982), p. 3662; *New York Times* Biographical Service (February 5, 1977), p. 315-319.

p. 237   **James F. Leonard**
Who's Who in America (Chicago: Marquis, 1982), p. 1978. Interview
with Leonard (1983).

p. 252   **Charles William Maynes**
Who's Who in America (Chicago: Marquis, 1982), p. 2186. Interview
with Maynes (1983).

p. 261   **Elliot L. Richardson**
Political Profiles — Nixon-Ford Volume (New York: Facts on File
Inc., 1979), p. 524-28; Who's Who in America (Chicago: Marquis,
1982), p. 2797.

p. 268   **William J. vanden Heuvel**
Who's Who in America (Chicago: Marquis, 1982), p. 3406. Interview
with vanden Heuvel (1982).

p. 283   **Jeane J. Kirkpatrick**
Current Biography (New York: H. W. Wilson, 1981), pp. 255-59;
Who's Who in America (Chicago: Marquis, 1982), p. 1823; New
York Times Biographical Service (December 23, 1980), pp. 1744-45.

p. 291   **Kenneth L. Adelman**
Press releases, U.S. Mission to the United Nations (1981).

p. 294   **William C. Sherman**
Who's Who in America (Chicago: Marquis, 1982), p. 3049. Press
releases, U.S. Mission to the UN (September, 1981).

Index

Reagan and, 283
UN, criticism of, 65
  debates and resolutions, 65
  globalized dispute participation, 65
  issue brought to UN, as hostile act, 66
USUN
  IO communications, 48–49, 270, 286–87
  permanent representative and, problems,
    286–87, 294
  State Department and, 284–85
  view of Kirkpatrick
    Ball's, 123
    Finger's, 64–65
    vanden Heuvel's, 270
  views on
    Congressional delegates, 287
    State Dept. and use of power, 287
    Third World rise and USSR influence, 285
    UN concern for decolonization and devel-
      opment, 285
    U.S. impotence at UN, 284, 285
    U.S. policy, effect, 288
Kissinger, Henry A., 65, 135
  détente policy, 139–40
  Hauser's pressure on, genocide, 165
  Middle East negotiations, effect on UN, 65–
    66, 180
  Peking trip, 140
    effect on PRC seating, 149, 177–78
  relationship with
    Moynihan, 204
    Scali, 198
  Resolution 338, Yom Kippur War, 194–97
Klutznick, Philip, 55–61
  government service, 55
  UN Development Decade, 58–59, 90
  UN
    accomplishments, 60
    bond issue, Congo operation, 81
    fiscal problems, 59
    in 1957, appraisal, 55–56
  UN service
    delegate, General Assembly, 55
    Economic and Social Council representa-
      tive, 55, 76
  view of Klutznick
    Plimpton's, 81
    Williams', 91
  views on
    diplomacy, 55
    Kennedy, 58
    Lodge, 56
    Stevenson, 56–57
    UN operation in New York, 59–60
  World Jewish Congress, 55
Koh, Tommy, 262, 264
Korea
  North Korea, U.S.S. *Pueblo* incident, 102
  reunification, 211, 213–15

rounding up votes, 214
Scranton's work for, 213–15
UN Commission for the Unification and Rehabilitation of Korea (UNCURK),
  13
Korean Air Lines episode, 258, 278, 300
Korean War
  armistice negotiations, 44
  border incidents, 40
  cover plan, 40
  Gross's observations, 40–44
    U.S. response, 40–44
  invasion by North Korea, 13, 40
    USUN anticipation, 40
  side effects, 43
  Sino-Soviet conversations before, 40, 43
  UN
    Commission on Korea, 40
    intervention, 13–14, 41–42
    Uniting-for-Peace Resolution, 13, 32, 41–43
      language of discussed, 42
      USSR absence, effect, 42–43
    U.S. briefing other nations on, 43
    USUN view, 40
Kotschnick, Walter, 91–92
Krushchev, Nikita
  Cuban Missile Crisis, 70
  Hammarskjöld replacement demand, 16
  Hungarian revolt response, 12
  UN visit 1960, 16
Kuznetsov, Vasily
  1967 War negotiations, 103–04
  replacement for Malik, 217

LDC's *See* Less Developed Countries
Lake Success, Long Island, 5
  communication to State Dept., 31
Laos, 140
Latin America
  Economic Commission for, 92
  1967 Middle East War negotiations, 103
Latin American countries
  PRC seating and, 149
  women delegates, 160
Law of the Sea
  attributable proceeds, 263
  "common-heritage-of-mankind", 150
  consensus problems, 264
  financial arrangements, 262–63
  Group of 5 v. Group of 77, 262–63
  Group of 77 representatives, 263
  Koh, work of, 262, 264
  Phillips work for, 150–51
  Richardson work for, 150, 261–65
  Seabed Authority, 151, 262
  Seabed Committee issues, 150
  tax rates, 262–63
  Third Conference òn (UNCLOS III), 227
    Treaty signed, 227

About
the Author

LINDA M. FASULO, a fellow at The Institute for Research in History, is a freelance writer and a student of international affairs. She has participated in UN internship programs in New York and Geneva, Switzerland, and founded and co-directed an alumni association of former UN interns and fellows. She served on the board of directors of the New York Chapter of UNA–USA from 1978–1984 and is a board member of the Metropolitan Committee for UNICEF.

Linda Fasulo holds an AB from Rutgers College, a Masters from Bernard Baruch School of Business and Public Administration, and has done graduate study in international affairs at Columbia University. She is host and co-producer of *Speaking of History*, a public affairs television series produced by The Institute for Research in History and is co-editor of its forthcoming occasional paper "Eleanor Roosevelt: Her Leadership and Legacy."

Ms. Fasulo is a consultant to several institutions, including the New York Public Library, and has chaired and moderated many educational forums in foreign affairs, such as the Great Decisions Series of the Foreign Policy Association. She is the 1984–85 editor of the *Womens' Caucus for Political Science Quarterly*.